Music in the Chautauqua Movement

Music in the Chautauqua Movement

From 1874 to the 1930s

PAIGE LUSH

McFarland & Company, Inc., Publishers
Jefferson, North Carolina, and London

LIBRARY OF CONGRESS CATALOGUING-IN-PUBLICATION DATA

Lush, Paige, 1980–
    Music in the Chautauqua movement : from 1874 to the 1930s / Paige Lush.
        p.   cm.
    Includes bibliographical references and index.

    ISBN 978-0-7864-7315-1
    softcover : acid free paper ∞

    1. Chautauqua Institution — History.   2. Music — Instruction and study — New York (State) — Chautauqua — History.   3. Chautauquas. I. Title.
    ML27.U5C544 2013
    780.9747'95 — dc23   2013020811

BRITISH LIBRARY CATALOGUING DATA ARE AVAILABLE

© 2013 Paige Lush. All rights reserved

No part of this book may be reproduced or transmitted in any form or by any means, electronic or mechanical, including photocopying or recording, or by any information storage and retrieval system, without permission in writing from the publisher.

On the cover: The Weatherwax Brothers Quartet (author's collection, gift of Fred Crane); Antique photo frame and background pattern (iStockphoto/Thinkstock)

Manufactured in the United States of America

McFarland & Company, Inc., Publishers
   Box 611, Jefferson, North Carolina 28640
   www.mcfarlandpub.com

To Chunk and Jean

Table of Contents

Preface	1
Introduction	5
I. The Chautauqua Movement: An Overview	9
II. Chautauqua Musicians	25
III. Musical Selection in Chautauqua	60
IV. Musical Programming in Chautauqua	93
V. Music Defines Chautauqua as an Educational and Cultural Institution	123
VI. Music Defines Chautauqua as American	141
VII. Music in Chautauqua's Decline	174
Epilogue	193
Appendices:	
A. Itinerary: Standard Chautauqua Bureau, 1904	195
B. Redpath–New York–New England Itinerary, 1925	195
C. List of Known Chautauqua Musical Acts	196
Chapter Notes	209
Bibliography	219
Index	227

Preface

Four young musicians stand on a small, temporary platform facing a crowd of hundreds in a massive tent on a humid July evening. They will play or sing (often both) and then hurry to catch an overnight train to the next town on their circuit where an identical tent awaits them. Their program, which might comprise their entire repertoire, is a mix of heavily altered art music, a few select (inoffensive and suitably out of date) popular numbers, novelties, hymns, and marches. Following one day behind on the same circuit is an aging opera star, and a day behind her is a group of bell ringers. All of them share the stage with lecturers, debaters, and dramatic companies. The audience may have their favorites among the lineup, but most will watch every performance, having bought season tickets supporting the chautauqua.

While rural Americans may have had limited cultural and educational opportunities relative to their urban counterparts, the chautauqua was not their only option. From the 1880s through the 1920s, however, chautauqua was clearly favored by civic leaders throughout rural America, especially in the Midwest. The chautauqua industry (and by the turn of the century, it certainly was an industry) reciprocated by policing its own content so that communities would have no reason to distrust or waver in their support of the annual chautauqua. Music was critical in the establishment and maintenance of chautauqua's image as a positive, edifying, educational, and thus essential facet of a community's life.

This book grew out of my interest in rural America's experience of art music. For my master's thesis I examined band transcriptions of opera, and it was through that research that I first encountered chautauqua. I chose to survey the music of circuit chautauqua for my doctoral dissertation, avoiding discussion of independent chautauquas, lyceums, and the Chautauqua Institution for brevity's sake. But even during my early research I felt I was telling an incomplete story and should I ever write a book on the subject, I would address music across all facets of the chautauqua movement.

During my initial research for my dissertation, I discovered one article about music in the chautauqua movement. While that article mentioned an upcoming monograph on the subject, no such book had ever been published. On my first research trip to Iowa, I learned that the author of that article, Fred Crane, lived in Mt. Pleasant, Iowa, and had amassed a considerable collection of chautauqua materials. Fred had donated much of his chautauqua collection to the University of Iowa and the State Historical Society of Iowa; most of the remainder he gave to me. He had conducted his research — including several interviews — decades before, at a time when many former chautauqua musicians were still alive. These interviews, as well as scores of photographs, programs, and other ephemera, were invaluable in linking my research work to the chautauqua era.

It seems odd to write a book about music in chautauqua and spend so little time discussing the Chautauqua Institution. The importance of the "Mother Chautauqua," both to the chautauqua movement and to American culture, is undeniable. But the Chautauqua Institution outgrew and outlived the chautauqua movement, and is thus largely beyond the scope of this book. Furthermore, most of the previous scholarship of music in chautauqua has focused on the Institution, which drew high-profile performers throughout the twentieth century, or to the chautauqua ventures of musical celebrities such as Sousa or Schumann-Heink. But to focus on celebrities is to ignore the vast majority of chautauqua musicians, and in fact betrays the democratic spirit of chautauqua. Chautauqua communities expected — and welcomed — a variety of musical styles and ability levels. Many great musicians graced the chautauqua platform, as did many inferior acts. I have tried to present the reader with a panoramic view of chautauqua's musical landscape, encompassing the profound, the banal, and the hundreds of performers who fell somewhere in between. Fighting my own initial urge to focus on art music and the few chautauqua acts with name recognition beyond the chautauqua circuits, I endeavored to study a cross section of musicians that would accurately reflect the experience of an average chautauqua patron.

The lyceum movement was so enmeshed — ideologically, financially, and in terms of personnel — with chautauqua that no discussion of chautauqua can ignore the lyceum. Similarly, lines between the independent assemblies and the commercial circuit chautauqua movement are not as clear as some recent literature seems to suggest. I have tried to delineate, whenever possible, between chautauquas that were planned and produced by a committee of community members and those that were booked through commercial agencies; but even with the benefit of technology and access to the records of most major bureaus, it is not always possible to discern whether a chautauqua was truly independent.

Preface

The chautauqua movement is a fascinating example of the collision between idealism and reality. I have no reason to doubt that most of the decision-makers within the movement believed their own rhetoric regarding chautauqua's emphasis on culture and uplift. At times, however, it is difficult to reconcile chautauqua's lofty rhetoric with the final product on the platform. It is my hope that this study will shed light on the ideological underpinnings of chautauqua's musical programming.

The chautauqua movement had a lexicon all its own. *Prelude* was a verb, the plural of *lyceum* was *lyceums*, and no one could agree on whether to capitalize the word *chautauqua*. (Following the convention of recent scholarship, I capitalize only when referring to the Chautauqua Institution.) Chautauqua performers and managers had their own trade magazines and a professional organization. Several schools existed for the sole purpose of training chautauqua performers.

The extant chautauqua ephemera is in some ways maddeningly incomplete. For instance, the tens of thousands of documents in the files of the Redpath Lyceum Bureau contain only a few dozen pieces of sheet music, a fraction of which seem to have actually been used in chautauqua. Conversely, the breadth and depth of extant performer and bureau correspondence, business records, trade publications and promotional materials related to the chautauqua movement is overwhelming. In researching this book, I became engrossed in heated telegram exchanges between angry stars and skittish managers, diatribes in the *Lyceumite* against this new style of music or that scandalous stage costume, and the inner workings of the early twentieth-century culture industry. It is my hope that by introducing the principal players and themes in chautauqua's musical story this book can help the reader reconnect with this fascinating, but largely forgotten, aspect of America's musical history.

Fred Crane passed away before I finished this book, but he was unquestionably the driving force behind its creation and completion. Not only did he provide most of the images I would eventually use, but he also did much of the "leg work" of interviews and data collection over several decades. Fred was adamant that this was a book worth writing, and it was his enthusiasm that spurred me to complete the book even after my career path no longer dictated that I had to.

I am also grateful to the University of Iowa libraries, especially the staff in special collections, and the State Historical Society of Iowa in Iowa City. The enthusiasm for chautauqua and Midwestern history shown by the Midwest Old Threshers was instrumental in the early phases of this project, as was their opening the archives of the Theatre Museum of Repertoire Americana to me. The University of Kentucky supported my first two trips to Iowa and the digitization of many of the images obtained on those trips. My dissertation advisor, Ronald Pen, was immensely supportive of my research.

Early versions of sections of this book appeared in my doctoral dissertation, as an article in *Americana: The Journal of American Popular Culture* and in papers given at meetings of the Society for American Music and the North American Conference on Nineteenth-Century Music. I am greatly indebted to Elizabeth Barnes, who helped weave a narrative out of those disparate works. Finally I would like to thank my incredibly patient and long-suffering family, who know far more about chautauqua than they ever wanted to, yet have never wavered in their support of my work.

Introduction

The program for the 1912 chautauqua at Elmwood, Nebraska, described the chautauqua as "the acme of the best cultural instincts in the human thought. It is the stage improved and purified.... It is classic music popularized, popular music dignified.... It is entertainment having educational value." The program concluded by imploring citizens to support the chautauqua "if you believe in making better homes, better churches and schools, better character, better civilization, in making life brighter and happier and in making young men and women less anxious to go to the big city to live but satisfied to stay in the home community."[1] While promoters were rarely this explicit about chautauqua's philosophical underpinnings, ideas of cultural elevation, progressivism, and the desire to disburse urban cultural opportunities while reinforcing rural value systems were integral to the movement.

While chautauqua events were certainly entertaining, entertainment was not the primary objective of the movement, nor did the industry view itself as an entertainment outlet. In fact, many in chautauqua management expressed open scorn for vaudeville, which made no claim to edification or education and directly competed with chautauqua in many communities. And while it might come into town on a train, be welcomed by a parade, and make its temporary home in a tent outside town, the chautauqua was not a circus. Chautauqua's self-identity was inextricably linked to its educational value. Music would strengthen chautauqua's image as an educational and cultural institution, and deliberate musical choices were made by promoters, managers, and performers throughout the early twentieth century that would define chautauqua's place in American society.

The heyday of the chautauqua movement occurred during a time of considerable interaction between, and discussion of, entertainment and education in the United States. Notably, radio and motion pictures were establishing themselves as fixtures of American popular culture. Both the radio and motion picture industries were aware of the role music played in their perceived cultural value. Early radio producers struggled to strike a balance between music, which was popular, and spoken word, which was perceived as inherently educational and thus valuable.[2] Conversely, the motion picture industry used art music to elevate public perception of the industry, staging live art music performances immediately prior to motion picture screenings and creating film roles for prominent art music performers.[3]

Music was important to the public perception of these early twentieth-century phenomena, although it meant strikingly different things in different contexts. It was also important to the self-image of those involved in the entertainment and education industries, and especially to those who could not easily be labeled as either entertainers or educators. Chautauqua performers, and the movement itself, held an uneasy position on the continuum between education and entertainment. Music helped to define chautauqua, both as an edifying factor and as an empty diversion. Popular music attracted crowds, while art music enhanced chautauqua's image as a valid educational outlet. Music's role in defining chautauqua's identity was often more complex, however, as the lines between art and popular music, and thus between education and entertainment, were rarely clearly defined. Much of the programming billed as cultural outreach would have been more accurately labeled as novelty, while the popular music often espoused patriotism, loyalty, piety, and other sentiments that would cause audiences and critics to deem such music edifying, if not purely educational.

This situation calls into question the core mission of chautauqua. What type (and quality) of education did an audience have the right to expect from a one-hour lecture or performance? Eckman argues that chautauqua educated by exposure to better things, by planting a seed of curiosity rather than by traditional instruction.[4] If this is the case, then chautauqua's propensity for presenting art music in highly altered formats is perhaps understandable. This idea also lends credence to the validity of the various exotic musical acts which, like their oratorical counterparts, were far more capable of piquing interest in other cultures than providing useful cultural information. Of course, this theory does not take into account the large number of popular and novelty acts programmed at the height of the movement's popularity. However, if chautauqua saw itself as a form of "distance education" (and this is certainly how it was often billed), then the validity of presenting truncated operas, dance-band transcriptions of symphonic music, and a myriad of novelty musical acts is suspect.

In this book, I address the place of music in chautauqua, the place of chautauqua on the spectrum between education and entertainment, and the role of music in defining that place. I take into account the perception of chautauqua as a conduit by which higher culture and urban intellectual discourse could reach rural Americans, as well as the implications of this perception on musical programming. Finally, I address the place of chautauqua in early twentieth-century American culture, its relationship with other entertainment and educational phenomena, and the role of music in setting circuit chautauqua apart from vaudeville and similar entertainments. The book focuses on the years between the founding of the Chautauqua Institution and the collapse of the circuit chautauqua industry, during which various assemblies bearing the chautauqua name, most of which had no official relationship with the Chautauqua Institution, dotted the American landscape. It will profile chautauqua musicians, analyze their programming choices, and examine the ways in which musical acts were used to craft an image of the chautauqua movement that would ensure community support. Chautauqua performers needed their audience, of course, but many audiences needed the chautauqua, as hosting an assembly signaled that a community was hungry for, if not yet in possession of, better things. This interdependence between the platform and the public and the role of music in chautauqua's formation and maintenance are central to this work.

I
The Chautauqua Movement: An Overview

The chautauqua movement sprang from two primary antecedents: the Chautauqua Institution and the American lyceum. Elements from each of these were appropriated and adapted through the late nineteenth and early twentieth centuries to create several phenomena, collectively known as the chautauqua movement. Of these, the Chautauqua Institution is the longest-lived, while the circuit chautauqua was arguably the more influential in shaping American (particularly Midwestern) culture. Independent chautauqua assemblies also flourished during this time, as did reading circles bearing the chautauqua name. The oldest phenomenon rightly considered part of the chautauqua movement is the American lyceum.

In 1826, Josiah Holbrook published a letter in the *American Journal of Education* presenting guidelines for organizations he deemed "societies for mutual education." Holbrook outlined the aims of such a society, inspired by the mechanics' institutes forming in England, and suggested an organizational hierarchy stretching from local boards to a unified national organization.[1] This organization met for the first time in May 1831 in New York City and was called the National American Lyceum (NAL). It involved delegates from roughly one thousand local lyceum societies, and addressed issues such as government involvement in education, women's education, and the validity of manual labor colleges.[2] While the National American Lyceum was not terribly successful, the lyceum movement flourished on the local level. The one thousand local lyceum delegates present at the inaugural meeting of the NAL represented a fraction of lyceum committees in existence (Noffsinger cites 3,000 local lyceum bureaus operating in the eastern U.S. alone in 1834). There were eight annual meetings of the National American Lyceum, which ceased to exist in 1840. The annual meetings were perpetually poorly attended, in part due to an inability of the national organization to address issues relevant to the local committees.[3]

The failure of the National American Lyceum should not be taken as an indication of the health of the movement as a whole. In fact, the lyceum continued to be a driving force behind adult education in the United States until the Civil War. Local lyceums often began by using local lecturers, who generally offered their services at no charge. As a local lyceum became more financially secure, the committee would often seek outstanding lecturers from neighboring areas, and would offer small compensation — often travel expenses or less — to these individuals. By the 1850s it was not uncommon for the more successful lyceums (nearly all of these were in urban areas) to pay a fee above and beyond expenses for a particularly desirable lecturer.[4]

The use of the term lecturer rather than performer or act is intentional; antebellum lyceums rarely involved anything other than lectures and scientific demonstrations. Holbrook had believed the purpose of the lyceum was to "diffuse rational and useful information throughout the community," and "to apply the sciences and the various branches of education to the domestic and useful arts."[5] In his writings, Holbrook most often refers to chemistry, biology, and geology as "sciences," though he does not specifically exclude other fields as "scientific" lecture subjects. While he made allowances for non-lecture formats when a lecture was not practical, it is clear from early documents that Holbrook did not, in the early years of the movement, consider the performing arts to be appropriate for the lyceum stage.

Before the Civil War, a typical local lyceum committee would schedule a series of lectures throughout the winter and spring. Patrons could purchase tickets to the entire course, as the series was generally known, or to a single event for a substantially higher rate. Until 1850, the standard ticket price was twenty-five cents for a single event, while a lyceum membership granting admission to every event cost, on average, $1.50.[6] During the early years of the American lyceum, when lecturer compensation was minimal, these ticket sales adequately covered the operating costs of the local lyceum. Because local lyceums did not intend to make a profit, and were relatively content to employ local lecturers for little or no compensation, the economic situation of the American lyceum movement would remain relatively unchanged until the 1850s.

As previously noted, the early lyceum committees were not interested in profit and saw the lyceum as a purely educational movement. By the middle of the nineteenth century, lyceum committees found themselves in competition for popular lecturers, who used a greatly expanded railroad system to broaden their areas of engagement. Having multiple possible venues in which to present their material, lecturers by the 1850s would regularly demand compensation beyond expenses. This increase in operating costs necessitated higher ticket sales, and the need to sell more (or more expensive) tickets drove lyceum committees to attach an unprecedented importance to the popular appeal of prospective lyceum events. This shift in economic and programming strategies would drastically alter the American lyceum movement through the end of the nineteenth century.

Early lyceums focused on "practical" topics such as science and agriculture. Many local lyceums avoided politics and religion, a practice seemingly retained from the English system on which they were modeled. Moses Coit Tyler, observing the English system, quipped that everything was allowed, except "those things in which men are most interested: politics and religion." The arts were similarly avoided. A study of the Chicago Lyceum between 1855 and 1870 found that only 2 out of 52 lectures involved the arts. It is also important to note that these were most likely lectures about the arts and not performances. Performances (musical or otherwise) were exceedingly rare in the lyceum movement prior to its commercialization in the 1870s.[7]

Lyceum activity declined sharply around 1857 due to an economic depression. With the onset of the Civil War, lyceum lectures became politically polarized. Combined with the drastic diversion of resources, manpower, and audience interest caused by the war, the transformation of the lyceum stage from an educational outlet to a political stump would threaten the continued existence of the lyceum movement by the war's end.[8]

In the years immediately following the war, the American lyceum underwent drastic changes in programming and philosophy. Local lyceum committees began forming regional associations, and by doing so they were able to attract more popular lecturers through guarantees of multiple bookings in each region. Entrepreneurs took notice of these associations, and by the end of the 1860s commercial lyceum bureaus had formed to intercede between lyceum talent and local committees. Several scholars, most notably Noffsinger and Knowles, point to this development as the death knell of the true American lyceum, arguing that the for-profit nature of the postwar commercial bureaus meant an emphasis on popularity and entertainment over educational value as well as an abandonment of Holbrook's original concept of the lyceum as "meetings for reading, conversation, discussion, [or] illustrating the sciences."[9]

The desire of the commercial bureaus to increase audience size in their search for greater profits may have been a departure from earlier lyceum philosophy, but the postwar American lyceum could offer a broader array of experiences to its audience than could its predecessor. Dramatic reading, introduced to the lyceum in the 1850s, became a popular feature of the lyceum season after the war. The late 1860s also saw the gradual introduction of drama to the lyceum stage, although it generally was presented as one-man shows without staging or costumes. Perhaps the most dramatic departure from Holbrook's concept of the lyceum was the establishment of the musical act as a staple of the lyceum, beginning in the late 1860s.[10]

The first commercial lyceum bureau was founded by James Redpath, a journalist and activist, in the fall of 1868. Known as the Boston Lyceum Bureau, and later as the Redpath Lyceum Bureau, it was the first commercial organization to act primarily on behalf of lyceum talent, whereas the existing regional lyceum association had represented the interests of local lyceum committees.[11] Redpath soon realized that the demand for lyceum programs in the Midwest was so great that management from Boston was not feasible, and in 1871 he opened a regional office in Chicago. Although his name would become synonymous with the lyceum business, James Redpath's career as a lyceum booking agent was brief. In 1875, Redpath resumed his journalism career, becoming managing editor of the *North American Review*, and sold the Redpath Lyceum Bureau to George Hathaway and Major J.B. Pond.[12]

Hathaway had been an administrator in the bureau for several years at the time of the purchase; he had initially been hired as an administrative assistant, was for a time in charge of the Chicago office, and at the time of Redpath's retirement had complete control of the bureau's business correspondence. Pond, however, was only tenuously associated with the bureau prior to 1875. He was an independent booking agent focused on celebrities whose fame was likely to be brilliant but short-lived. For instance, at the time of his initial interaction with Redpath, Pond was managing the lecture tour of Eliza Young. Young was recently divorced from Brigham Young; her fame stemmed from the sensation caused by the divorce and her subsequent campaigns against polygamy and Mormonism.[13] Pond focused on markets that could bring large audiences for his performers, and he handled most of the publicity personally. His portfolio of talent was hardly diversified and relied on the popularity of a few celebrity clients. Pond's business model was far riskier than the Redpath model followed by Hathaway, which incorporated both celebrities and unknown talent and supplied lyceum acts to established urban markets as well as struggling rural communities.

Although their partnership would dissolve after five years, the business strategies of Hathaway and Pond would shape the course of the Redpath Lyceum Bureau and set a precedent for the circuit chautauqua movement of the next century. In the late 1870s, the Redpath Bureau began offering "star courses," prescribed lyceum courses built around popular and expensive lecturers such as Mark Twain and Henry Ward Beecher.[14] The introduction of star courses created within the Redpath Bureau a two-tiered system of lyceums. Smaller, less affluent communities could book any number of solid, but not famous, lyceum attractions through the Redpath Bureau, while urban and wealthy areas often opted for a fixed slate of well-known lecturers and performers through a star course. Circuit chautauquas, also booked through the Redpath Bureau, would eventually take the place of these star courses, leaving the lyceums to provide attractions to smaller and less affluent communities.

While the Redpath Bureau was laying the foundation for the postwar lyceum movement, the "Mother Chautauqua" was taking shape at Chautauqua Lake in New York. The first meeting, dubbed the "Chautauqua Assembly," was held between August 4 and August 18, 1874, and was essentially a training seminar for Sunday school teachers. The Chautauqua Assembly was established by John Heyl Vincent, a minister and later bishop in the Methodist Episcopal Church, and Lewis Miller, a wealthy Methodist layman. Both men shared interest in Sunday school; Vincent had created the curriculum for the Methodist Episcopal Sunday School, and Miller had been a Sunday school superintendent. Miller was also an official in the group that held evangelical camp meetings on Chautauqua Lake in the 1860s.[15]

The first Chautauqua Assembly lasted two weeks and consisted of lectures, sermons, and church services, as well as pedagogical exercises for Sunday school teachers.[16] There is no record of the precise musical works performed at that first meeting, but records indicate it most likely consisted of group singing of hymns. The 1875 Chautauqua Assembly included two full concerts and five praise services with music.[17] Later, the Chautauqua Assembly became known as the Chautauqua Institution, and it expanded to offer a variety of educational, cultural, and religious activities throughout the summer.

As early as 1876, communities began to host summer events modeled on the activities at Chautauqua Lake.[18] In the eastern United States these events, generally called "chautauquas," were usually sponsored by specific religious denominations, primarily Methodists and Baptists. In western communities, however, sponsorship tended to be more ecumenical and community-based.[19] These local chautauquas focused on literature, elocution, and Bible study. Like the Chautauqua Institution, community chautauquas presented programs intended to instruct individuals so that they might in turn instruct others. The influence on (informal) teacher training set the community, or independent, assemblies apart from the local lyceums, and later from the circuit chautauqua of the twentieth century. Like the Chautauqua Institution, independent chautauquas were normally held on chautauqua grounds, in permanent structures erected by the community. The independent chautauquas also emulated the Chautauqua Institution in scheduling, preferring summer for the vast majority of meetings, and concentrating instruction into an event of several consecutive days, rather than the sporadic lectures of a lyceum course lasting several weeks.

Although they emulated the Chautauqua Institution in many respects, none of the independent assemblies could claim an official relationship with the "Mother Chautauqua." John Vincent wrote of the independents: "Many of them are closely modeled after the parent assembly; others have simply taken the name and adopted a part of the plan, usually the so called 'popular feature' [sic] which are chiefly important as a source of revenue. For any shortcomings of these independent assemblies Chautauqua should not be held responsible."[20] Years later, leaders of the commercial chautauqua bureaus would express similar concerns about the independent assemblies, fearing that the perceived amateurism of the independent chautauquas would ruin the movement's reputation.[21] The independent chautauquas leveled similar charges at the commercial bureaus, arguing that they had cheapened the movement by commercializing it.

Independent chautauqua committees faced many of the same challenges encountered by the local lyceums decades before. In order to secure popular attractions, they needed to form regional associations and guarantee multiple bookings to star performers. While they did allow communities access to more popular attractions, these associations also restricted the ability of individual committees to set their own programs.

Many independent chautauqua committees, rather than join associations, turned to the commercial lyceum bureaus to provide talent for their events. By the 1900s, it was not uncommon for a lyceum bureau to provide a complete chautauqua, consisting of several days of attractions, to an independent chautauqua committee. A 1909 advertisement for the Redpath Bureau stated that Redpath would "sell talent to independent assemblies" and would "consider operating chautauquas for local committees or managers."[22] By 1919, the majority of independent assemblies were in fact run by commercial agencies. The agency's name would not appear on the program or any promotional material, however, with credit for operation of the chautauqua still being given to the local committee.[23] Often the only evidence today of production by a commercial bureau is a program consisting of the same acts as nearby chautauquas that readily admitted to commercial affiliation. A prime example of this phenomenon is the Waterloo, Iowa, "independent" chautauqua, which was produced by Midland Chautauquas, a commercial bureau. The independent chautauqua at Ames, Iowa, had no connections to commercial booking agencies, and advertised this fact in its 1915 program:

> There are a large number of so-called chautauquas being run by the bureaus, and we submit to you the fact that they care nothing for the town or community where they show, nor do they care for their patrons, except for the profit they can make out of them, as you will readily see if you take the time to investigate their programs and prices. The Ames Chautauqua Association runs its chautauqua for

I. The Chautauqua Movement

an altogether different purpose. It is an unincorporated body, organized for the purpose of running the Chautauqua only, and all revenue derived from the assemblies can be used for the purpose of perpetuating the Ames Chautauqua and for nothing else, so you can readily see that all money paid in by you will be RETURNED TO YOU IN ENTERTAINMENT, and will not go to make up a profit for some bureau.[24]

The Ames program is interesting not only in its opposition to the commercialization of the booking process, but also for its emphasis on the entertainment facet of the chautauqua. The program does not assure patrons that their money will be returned in education, enlightenment, culture, or any of the high-minded terms found so often in earlier chautauqua literature. An analysis of programs from the Ames Chautauqua Association supports the assertion that entertainment had become increasingly important in independent chautauquas as the twentieth century progressed. The same analysis shows a significant decline in popularity of the Ames chautauqua, indicated by a markedly shortened schedule, as well as a dramatic shift in programming, leading to the cancellation of the chautauqua program at Ames in 1927. This pattern was repeated throughout the United States and Canada during the 1920s, affecting the independent and commercial circuit chautauquas.

The sixth annual Ames chautauqua took place from August 11 until August 20, 1909. It began on Wednesday evening, with a concert by the Cleveland (Ohio) Ladies' Orchestra, and ran through the next Friday, closing with a "concert extraordinary" by the Ernest Gamble Concert Party. The event was, at ten days, exceptionally long and involved sixty-one distinct events. Every full day (the opening Wednesday was a half day, as was Sunday) began with a morning Bible hour at nine o'clock, followed by either an educational hour or children's hour. The afternoons began with a concert and included one more musical act as either the final or penultimate event of the evening. Evenings also included one or two lectures or demonstrations of new technology. Of the sixty-one scheduled events, twenty were musical, six were dramatic readings (called "recitals" in the program), nine were events specifically for children and mothers, two could be considered strictly entertainment (performances by Pamahasika and his Performing Pets) and the rest would be classified as lectures. Musical acts of note included the Cleveland Ladies' Orchestra, the Royal Hungarian Orchestra, the Dunbars, and the Ernest Gamble Concert Party.[25] These groups were well known in chautauqua and lyceum circles and traveled throughout North America. The only clearly local musical group listed in the program was the Norwegian Choral Union of Story County (Iowa), although the program also includes a group that was likely local, the Choral Union of One Hundred Voices, and two listings for nonspecific musical performances that might have included local musicians.

The 1915 chautauqua at Ames followed roughly the same format and involved a similar array of events in similar proportion. It was eight days long and consisted of forty-five listed events. This figure may be misleading, as no mention of events for children and mothers is made in the program. These almost certainly took place, and would have added eight or more events to the program had they been listed. The most obvious difference between this program and that of 1909 is the inclusion of five motion pictures, four of which are listed as "educational." The films are not named in the program, they were used as postludes to conclude the evening. The 1915 program includes popular professional musical acts as before, but it also featured the Ames Band, which opened the chautauqua on Thursday afternoon, played a concert Thursday evening, and also played two concerts on closing day.[26]

The final Ames program to be discussed in this study is that of the last Ames chautauqua, which took place August 2 through 6, 1926. The assembly lasted five days, but began at three o' clock on each of those days. The program lists thirteen events. Of these thirteen, ten are musical, one is a magician, and two are lectures. The opening concert was not performed by a famous professional orchestra, or even the town band, but by Emory Parnell, "The One Man Band." The headlining musical act of the 1926 chautauqua was Goforth's Black and Gold Band, a nine-member dance band led by percussionist George Goforth. These inclusions represent a monumental departure, in both scale and programming, from the previous decade and show the final struggle of the independent chautauqua movement against not only motion pictures, radio, and other changing cultural factors, but also against the commercial circuit chautauquas that will be discussed in greater detail later in this study. On March 9, 1927, the Ames Chautauqua Committee announced that the chautauqua was no longer viable and would be discontinued effective immediately. The committee cited several factors responsible for the declining interest in the chautauqua, including an increase in summer travel among local residents, summer programs offered by the college, and apathy among the younger residents of Ames. The committee concluded by stating that "there will be something to take its place."[27]

The independent chautauquas were not alone in drawing inspiration from, and co-opting the name of, the Chautauqua Institution. There were "chautauqua reading circles," traveling carnivals calling themselves "amusement chautauquas," and even a circuit of "Klantauqua" meetings operated by the Ku Klux Klan.[28] Although a variety of activities were called "chautauquas," the early twentieth-century circuit chautauqua would become the most popular and influential incarnation of the chautauqua idea.

The development of the circuit chautauqua in many ways mirrors the shift from local lyceum committees to commercial bureaus forty years earlier.

I. The Chautauqua Movement

The 1925 Redpath–New York–New England circuit, derived from a schedule housed at the Pelletier Library, Allegheny College, Meadville, Pennsylvania. The first community on the circuit, Niagara Falls, New York, is denoted by the white pennant at the far left. For a list of communities on this circuit, see Appendix A.

The circuit chautauqua system was a streamlined, standardized, commercial alternative to the independent chautauqua, just as the commercial lyceum bureaus offered an efficient, if restrictive, alternative to the struggling independent lyceums. Ultimately, the impetus behind the creation of circuit chautauqua would come from within the leader of the commercial lyceum movement, the Redpath Bureau.

Keith Vawter, a manager for the Redpath Lyceum Bureau responsible for the territory west of Pittsburgh, had become familiar with the independent chautauquas through the local committees' frequent use of the Redpath Bureau to book talent for their chautauquas. Vawter realized that the inefficiency of the booking methods employed by the independents caused operating costs, and thus ticket prices, to be unnecessarily high, and performers were spending excessive amounts of time in transit between far-flung independent chautauquas. After several years of observing the independent assemblies, Vawter devised a plan to offer a standardized chautauqua program, similar to the star courses pioneered by Redpath in the nineteenth century, to several preexisting chautauqua committees in a given geographic area. Vawter would manage all logistics, and the communities could count on a complete chautauqua at a substantially reduced cost.

Vawter's self-contained traveling chautauqua, henceforth referred to as a circuit chautauqua, involved complex travel, business, and programming logistics. While circuit chautauqua was advertised and delivered to communities as a complete, multiday event, much like a circus, circuit chautauqua presented logistical challenges beyond those of a circus or other traveling show. Most important among these was the speed of the chautauqua circuit. Chautauquas, as a rule, did not involve repetition. A lecturer who appeared twice at a given chautauqua presented two unique lectures. Similarly, a musical group booked for multiple performances at a single chautauqua (a phenomenon considerably more common than multiple appearances by one lecturer) would be expected to offer an entirely new program for each performance. This reluctance to repeat programs was primarily because chautauqua patrons, unlike patrons of other traveling shows, were expected to attend multiple performances throughout the course of the event.

Because chautauquas consisted of a string of distinct performances presented over the course of several days, rather than one day of programming repeated for several consecutive days, circuit chautauqua performers did not travel as a complete unit, but rather traveled the circuit according to their place in the program, moving only with those slated to perform on the same day. For instance, a lecturer booked to speak on the first day of the chautauqua would lecture in the first community on the circuit and then immediately proceed, along with the other first-day performers, to the second community, where another tent and crew were waiting, arriving in time to perform on the first day of that community's chautauqua. Second-day performers would follow the same circuit, one day behind the first-day acts. This pattern would continue for three to seven (rarely eight or nine) days, depending on the length of the chautauqua. At the close of the first chautauqua on the circuit, the tent and crew from the first community would "leap frog" the performers, traveling to the eighth community on the circuit (assuming a seven-day chautauqua), arriving a day before the first-day performers arrived. This description assumes an ideal situation. Long distances between chautauqua communities often necessitated an extra tent and crew, as it might be impossible for the first-community tent crew to cover the distance between the first and eighth communities in time to set up for the eighth chautauqua. In addi-

I. The Chautauqua Movement

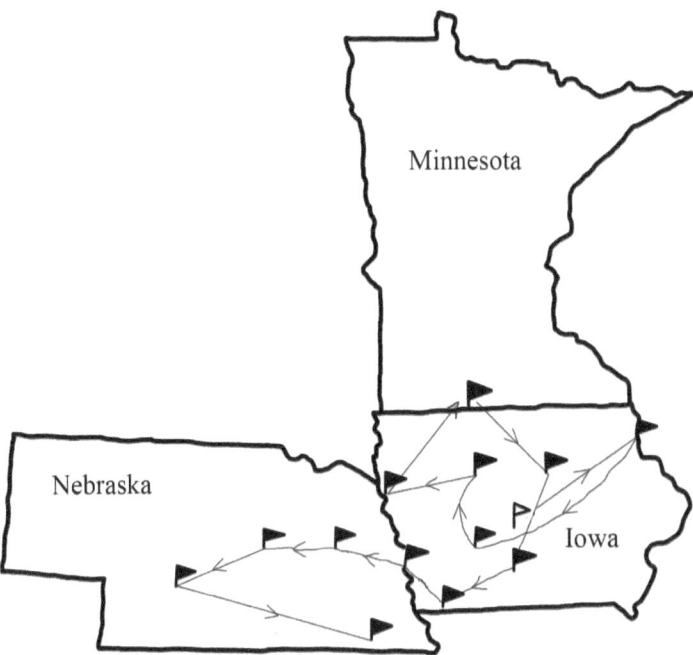

The 1904 Standard Chautauqua circuit, derived from Harry Harrison's description in *Culture Under Canvas*. For a list of communities on this circuit, see Appendix A.

tion to this extra tent, many bureaus stored a spare tent within reasonable distance of the communities on a circuit, in case a tent became delayed in transit or was damaged during the season.

Vawter was reluctant to use the Redpath name for his new venture for fear that it might fail and damage the reputation of the Redpath Lyceum Bureau. Instead, Vawter chose to call his circuit operation the Standard Chautauqua Bureau of Chicago.[29] In 1904 Vawter and partner Roy Ellison proposed their circuit chautauqua to thirty independent chautauqua committees in Iowa. Of these thirty, only nine signed on with the newly formed Standard Chautauqua.

The small number of bookings was insufficient to be fiscally viable, and the distance between locations was too great. In order to salvage the inaugural season of the Standard (Redpath) Chautauqua, Vawter and Ellison contacted leaders of communities without established independent chautauquas that could bridge the gaps between contracted communities. Six more communities signed on in this manner, creating a circuit that, while feasible, was smaller than Vawter had imagined. Since these new communities had no pre-existing chautauqua grounds and lacked public meeting places suitable for a chautauqua, Vawter provided circus tents in which the events could be held.[30] These tents would soon be standard for circuit chautauquas and would become an icon of the movement. In addition to the standardized program, Vawter offered local committees the option of booking any of twenty-five additional acts from his Redpath Lyceum roster. This supplementary list consisted primarily of lecturers, most of whom were religious leaders or prominent figures within the Democratic Party.[31]

The inaugural program of Vawter's new circuit lasted nine days and included thirty-five events. Eighteen of these events were primarily musical in nature and were performed by four different musical acts. Three of these were vocal quartets, the fourth a one-man band. In a pattern that would become standard for circuit chautauquas, the 1904 program began with a concert. Throughout the chautauqua, quartets performed their own concerts as well as shorter preludes before featured lectures. For the 1904 circuit, each quartet spent three days in a town before moving to the next town on the circuit, while the lecture and novelty acts appeared only once in a given location. The practice of engaging musical acts for several consecutive days originated in the independent chautauquas and became less common as the commercial circuit chautauqua evolved.

The one-man band, George W. Garretson, was also a juggler and was billed as both for the 1904 season. He gave two short performances on consecutive afternoons, one billed as "musical novelties" and the other as "musical novelties and juggling." The vocal quartets on the program included the Chicago Lady Entertainers, the Giant Colored Quartette, and the Temple Male Quartette. The Chicago Lady Entertainers performed popular numbers such as "Grandfather's Clock"[32] and "The Old Oaken Bucket,"[33] as well as hymns, ballads, and songs from the Civil War. The Giant Colored Quartette performed primarily Stephen Foster songs. It is unclear why the group was given this name, and no ephemeral evidence of the Giant Colored Quartet aside from the 1904 program has been found. It is possible that the members of the quartet were simply large men of color. Similarly, another early chautauqua group was named "The Auburns" and consisted entirely of singers with red hair. The oldest and most famous of the quartets on the 1904 program, the Temple Male Quartette, performed music from the standard art music repertory of the day. A profile of the group in *Talent* stated, "Their standard for songs is probably higher than any other quartet in the country. Their idea is, that if they commence with humorous songs, the audience will soon fail to enjoy the productions of the best composers. So the entire program is made up of comparatively heavy music, and they trust to the encores to lighten it up."[34]

While innovative, Vawter's initial attempt at a chautauqua circuit was a logistical failure. The distance between communities was too great and the discrepancy in size and quality of chautauqua facilities among the towns severely complicated Vawter's travel logistics. The ability of communities to book supplemental talent and otherwise alter the standard program negated many of the benefits gained from Vawter's efforts to streamline the chautauqua process. Finally, and most important, communities that had hosted independent chautauquas in years past were reluctant to move the date of their chautauqua to accommodate Vawter's schedule. Thus, the initial circuit chautauqua was hardly a circuit; performers, equipment, and crews backtracked across the Midwest incurring significant unnecessary rail fare and other travel expenses.

The 1904 season was also a financial failure: Vawter lost $7,000 on the venture. Despite the staggering financial loss, Vawter resolved to attempt another circuit. He had come to the realization that the failure of the 1904 season was not due to flaws in the circuit chautauqua idea, but rather was caused by multiple departures from that idea, including allowing local committees to alter programs and dictate chautauqua dates.[35] Vawter's second attempt at a circuit chautauqua, launched in 1907, was a truly standardized operation. Local committees could not alter the standard program. They were required to guarantee $2,000 in pre-sold season tickets and to give the first $2,500 in gate receipts and half of anything beyond that to the bureau. Of most significance, local committees could not dictate the date of a Vawter chautauqua. Vawter set the dates according to the needs of the bureau, and once set, the dates could not be changed. This new strategy, which Redpath manager Harry Harrison called "program as whole, take it or leave it," proved successful. The 1907 Standard Chautauqua traveled to thirty-three communities in three states.

The success of the Standard Chautauqua encouraged other entrepreneurs, especially lyceum managers, to establish chautauqua bureaus across the United States. No longer afraid to use the Redpath name, Vawter called his circuit Redpath-Vawter. Eventually, there would be five bureaus operating as Redpath Chautauquas, including Redpath-Vawter, Redpath-Chicago, Redpath-Horner, Redpath-Columbus, and Redpath-New York–New England. These chautauqua bureaus operated independently, with no direct connection to the Redpath Lyceum Bureau. The Redpath Bureaus were managed by regional Redpath Lyceum managers, who paid a 3 percent fee to use the Redpath name for their chautauqua organizations. Several other prominent chautauqua bureaus formed during the 1910s, including Ellison-White Chautauquas, Swarthmore Chautauqua, and Alkahest Chautauqua. To curb disputes over territory and talent, the managers of the major bureaus formed the International Lyceum and Chautauqua Managers Association in 1914.[36]

Circuit chautauquas were promoted as wholesome, educational, and entertaining. Emphasis was placed on the circuit chautauqua's role as a stabilizing force in a rapidly changing society. Promotional materials stressed that circuit chautauqua enforced rural values and preserved accepted societal norms while providing access to educational and cultural outlets previously limited to urban areas. The 1920 Redpath-Horner circuit program brochure described the Chautauqua: "For American Ideals. In support of Honor, Law and Order: Against Idleness, Waste, Anarchy, Lawlessness. A Happy, Purposeful Week."[37] Furthermore, circuit chautauqua promoters welcomed — and often created — the public perception that circuit chautauqua was linked to the Chautauqua Institution or to the established independent assemblies.[38]

The commercial bureaus grew in part by selling their chautauqua programs to communities that had not previously held chautauquas. By the 1920s, however, the commercial bureaus had taken over chautauqua production in many communities in which independent assemblies had been held for years. With the lyceum bureaus, which had previously done much of the booking for the independents, now selling entire chautauqua circuits, it had become increasingly difficult for local committees to independently book the quality and quantity of talent necessary to hold an independent assembly. Furthermore, the efficiency of the commercial bureaus made possible programs comparable to the independents at significantly less cost to the community. In 1914, ten years after Vawter's first attempt at circuit chautauqua, fifteen commercial chautauqua bureaus provided chautauquas to 2,400 communities. Independent assemblies were held in six hundred communities that year, although there had been 1500 independent chautauquas annually at the height of the independents' popularity.[39]

The summer of 1924 is considered the pinnacle of the chautauqua phenomenon. It is estimated that up to 12,000 communities hosted chautauquas in 1924.[40] That year, known as circuit chautauqua's "jubilee year," was followed by a steep decline in both attendance and community commitments for upcoming seasons. In 1925 there were fifteen bureaus operating fifty circuits across the U.S.; in 1930 five bureaus operated fifteen circuits. It is estimated that fewer than 300 communities hosted chautauquas in 1932. After 1932, the commercial bureaus in the United States[41] ceased operation and fewer than twenty communities continued to hold (independent) chautauqua assemblies.[42]

The decline of the chautauqua movement has been the topic of extensive discussion. In recent years, scholars have largely attributed it to broad cultural shifts such as changes in public taste, economic climate, and technological advances. Interestingly, the Great Depression, while coinciding with the decline of the circuit chautauqua movement, is not directly blamed for the decline by either modern scholars or first-hand observers.[43] Those with closer connections to the movement, both temporally and in terms of involvement in the chautauqua business, pointed primarily to problems within the chautauqua movement. In all likelihood, both opinions have merit. Scholars evaluating the movement from a distance of fifty years or more may have greater insight into societal trends that were not at all clear to the observer of the 1930s. Conversely, someone with firsthand knowledge of the chautauqua movement may have assigned great significance to events and trends that seem inconsequential to the outside observer.

Technological and infrastructure improvements are often blamed for circuit chautauqua's ultimate failure. Scholars point especially to the increasing popularity of radio and the improvement of roads in the rural United States. Keith Vawter was quick to dismiss the effect of radio on circuit chautauqua, writing, "I still insist that the radio did not materially affect lyceum and chautauquas, but rather the advent of country clubs and dancing mothers."[44] The term "dancing mothers" is a reference to a Broadway play and film by the same name about a woman who embraces the jazz-age lifestyle and moves to Europe, leaving her husband and daughter behind.

Less attention is paid to the exponential increase in newspaper publication during the 1920s and 1930s, though it certainly affected circuit chautauqua programming. The independent assemblies, like the lyceum before them, had initially centered on lectures. As more rural Americans gained access to timely national news, much of the appeal of the chautauqua lecture was lost. Chautauqua reacted by booking fewer lectures in favor of programs emphasizing entertainment.

This change in programming is often cited as a major factor in chautauqua's rapid decrease in popularity. While the circuit bureaus were unsurpassed in their ability to bring major intellectual, political, and cultural figures to rural Americans, they were ill-equipped to compete with the various entities dedicated solely to bringing entertainment to these communities. Harry Harrison, manager of the Redpath-Chicago circuit, wrote that carnivals intentionally followed his circuit in the later years.[45] Russell Johnson asserts that after 1925, local movie theaters deliberately scheduled their most attractive offerings to compete with chautauqua week.[46] Aside from carnivals and other traveling shows that made no claim to educational merit, by the mid–1920s the major bureaus found themselves competing with a number of smaller bureaus offering shorter, less expensive chautauquas filled with entertainment acts. In 1923 the All-American Circuit presented a three-day "Chautauqua Festival and Jubilee." This chautauqua consisted of just eight events, only three of which were lectures. Of these lectures, two were travelogues by speakers whose advertised credentials included pleasing accents. One concert was given by Brown's Jubilee Singers, and the Rocky Mountain Warblers performed twice. The latter was a male quartet that did impersonations, sang, and performed on various percussion instruments. The remaining two events of the All-American chautauqua were dramatic productions by the Wales Players.[47] The All-American Circuit program seems to have been typical of those produced by the smaller bureaus of the 1920s. While retaining the basic chautauqua format and advertising itself as "a canvas-covered temple of joy and inspiration," the All-American Circuit's offering did little to advance the goals set forth by the major bureaus in the previous decade.[48] Nevertheless, these small bureaus competed — with increasing success — with the well-established circuit organizations. This was especially true in smaller communities or those with limited capital, where cost was perhaps more important than quantity or quality of offered chautauqua events.

Just as the independent assemblies had blamed the commercial circuits for lowering the quality of the chautauqua movement, the major bureaus blamed the smaller chautauquas for damaging the reputation of the circuit chautauqua. In truth, however, it is unlikely that the Midwest could have sustained the number of circuit chautauquas operating by 1924, no matter their quality. The market had become so saturated that it was not uncommon for a community to host two chautauquas in one summer, one sponsored by the county and one by the town. In areas where the chautauqua movement was most popular, patrons in the early 1920s could choose from several chautauquas within a reasonable traveling distance. In 1924, the circuit chautauqua movement reached critical mass in most of its target regions; both the talent pool and the audience population had been stretched too thin.

Keith Vawter divested from the circuit chautauqua business in 1926. By 1927 Charles Horner and Harry Harrison had begun to do the same.[49] Crawford Peffer's Redpath–New York–New England circuit fared better than most, and Peffer was convinced his bureau would survive through the 1930s. Despite Peffer's optimism, the Redpath–New York–New England circuit closed after the 1932 season.[50] In 1933, C. Benjamin Franklin of Associated Chautauqua attempted to launch a circuit, but it failed after its first engagement of the season.[51]

Those independent chautauquas that had managed to fend off competition from the circuits were able to survive for some time after the circuit chautauqua movement failed. Mediapolis, Iowa, for instance, hosted a six-day independent chautauqua in 1944. The Redpath Lyceum Bureau, which had continued to produce winter lyceums throughout the circuit chautauqua era, booked lyceum acts through the 1940s and also supplied lecturers, musical acts, and other entertainers for a variety of clients. In recent years, communities throughout the United States have hosted independent chautauquas reminiscent of those of the early twentieth century, and the Chautauqua Institution in New York has been in continuous operation since its inception.

II
Chautauqua Musicians

In thirty years of involvement in the circuit chautauqua movement, the Redpath bureau alone employed approximately six thousand acts.[1] This figure includes both musical and nonmusical acts, and acts involved in both lyceums and chautauquas. While it is not possible to know the exact number of musicians involved in the movement, an approximate number can be figured using the data available for 1924, which was the peak year of the circuit chautauqua movement. In that year there were fifteen major bureaus operating fifty separate circuits in the United States.[2] The average chautauqua at that time was five days long and incorporated five different musical acts at minimum. Thus, counting solely those chautauquas operated by major bureaus, at least 250 musical acts were touring the circuits in 1924. This figure does not include performers in truly independent chautauquas (many "independent" assemblies relied on commercial bureaus to provide talent and thus would be included in the estimate) or minor commercial circuits. The majority of these acts were ensembles, and many would have been bands, orchestras, or choruses involving a dozen or more musicians. Thus, while the exact numbers cannot be known, it is certain that a great many musicians found employment in chautauqua.

Several paths could lead to a career as a chautauqua musician. Many of these were not dissimilar to the career paths of other musicians, while others were more specific to chautauqua. Some musicians found chautauqua work through talent agencies, while others booked through lyceum bureaus or were trained in institutions specializing in cultivating and promoting lyceum and chautauqua musical acts. Some musicians viewed chautauqua as an opportunity for exposure at the beginning of a career, while established performers used the circuits as a way to supplement income or generate publicity in the face of declining popularity. Others spent their entire careers on the circuits or were most famous for their chautauqua work.

Several educational institutions specialized in training lyceum and chautauqua performers. These institutions varied greatly in both scope and quality, ranging from those offering training by short courses more aptly described as workshops to full-fledged conservatories offering courses in music theory and history as well as applied instruction. One such latter institution was the Horner Institute of Fine Arts. Its founder, Charles Horner, had been an early pioneer of the circuit chautauqua movement and managed a large circuit under the Redpath banner. His Redpath-Horner chautauquas covered nine states, with headquarters in Kansas City, Missouri. Horner was not a musician or performer of any sort, but he recognized the need for formal training of musicians for chautauqua. Interestingly, he considered lecturing to be an inborn talent, while believing musicians could be trained.[3] This philosophy may explain why Horner's chautauqua training institution focused on music, while others offered (and usually featured) elocution and lecturing courses. In 1914, Horner joined with conductor and vocalist Earl Rosenberg to found the Horner Institute of Fine Arts in Kansas City.[4] In its first years of operation, the Horner Institute served largely as a training institute for performers on Horner's own chautauqua circuit, though it would eventually outgrow this purpose and outlive the circuit chautauqua movement.

The Horner Institute offered applied lessons in piano, voice, and violin. Students paid tuition based on ability level, major professor, and frequency of private lessons. All students enrolled in applied lessons also took courses in harmony, counterpoint, and music history. Chamber ensembles were available for advanced string players, as were coached accompanying opportunities for advanced pianists. The Horner Institute's promotional brochure clearly states that the institute's primary objective was to train those who intended to pursue music professionally, though it adds, "if they have the means to study the fine arts for cultural advancement they will be encouraged to remain for that purpose."[5] The faculty of the Horner Institute was initially drawn from local professional musicians acquainted with Rosenberg, who had held various positions in Kansas City, including conductor of the Kansas City Symphony Chorus. A partial listing of faculty during the tenure of Rosenberg and Horner follows:

Piano	*Voice*	*Violin*	*History/Theory*
Floyd Robbins	Earl Rosenberg	Forrest Schulz	Forrest Schulz
Clara Blakeslee	Roland White	Hans Peterson	Floyd Robbins
Anna St. John	Margaret Von Glaubetz		
Harriet Olin	Winifrede Repp		
Pearl Wideman			

During the period in which the Horner Institute's primary focus was providing musicians for Horner's circuits, the faculty and curriculum were dominated by applied music, especially voice and piano. The Horner Institute was successful beyond its original purpose, however, and in 1926 Horner agreed to absorb the failing Kansas City Conservatory of Music and Art, renaming the merged organization the Horner Institute Conservatory of Music. By the end of Horner's involvement, the Horner Institute had an enrollment of more than 3,000 students.[6] The Horner Institute eventually became the music department of the University of Kansas City, which is now known as the University of Missouri-Kansas City Conservatory of Music.

The Horner Institute was an unusually large, stable, and active chautauqua training institute. In general, organizations dedicated to the training of chautauqua performers were more akin to workshops in scope and, not being directly linked to any bureau, were often more concerned with attracting tuition-paying students than with producing working chautauqua musicians. For instance, prolific chautauqua and lyceum actor Elias Day ran an institution, the Elias Day School of Lyceum Art, which advertised itself as "not in the interest of any one lyceum bureau or group of bureaus." Day operated several terms, ranging from four weeks to eight weeks, with instructional time of up to fifteen hours per week. Less expensive courses consisted of two lessons per week over a span of six weeks. One of the school's booklets stated, "Mr. Day does not teach vocal culture in his classes, but his interpretation of concert manners, both of vocalists and instrumentalists, will be found of exceptional value."[7]

Day's instruction in concert manners may seem odd, but it was not unique. Esther Gaskin Williams, pianist for the Eureka Jubilee Singers, stated that her group received extensive instruction from the Redpath bureau in stage manners, but no musical coaching. According to Williams, Redpath worked with the Eureka Jubilee Singers for a month before the group gave its first chautauqua performance, although that instruction was confined to "what to do with our hands and how to walk out and stand and bow together, sit together."[8]

By 1915, Day had expanded his school to offer instruction in piano, voice, organ, all orchestral instruments, and public school music. In fact, a 1915 advertisement for the rechristened Lyceum Arts Conservatory lists eighteen instructors of music and only four instructors of drama. The Lyceum Arts Conservatory was billed as "a thorough education in music and dramatic art to prepare for concert work or teaching" and promised "exceptional opportunities to those who are talented."[9] The school, however, made no guarantee of future employment, and it remained unaffiliated with any lyceum or chautauqua bureau.

Some training institutions more closely resembled talent agencies, and indeed many of them functioned as such. The Boston Lyceum School conducted a two-year program for beginners seeking a diploma, as well as a "finishing school for lyceum and chautauqua attractions." The school also offered help in arranging programs and "general coaching," and listed six musical companies available for lyceum and chautauqua work.[10] It is unclear whether these groups were formed from a pool of Boston Lyceum School students or alumni or if the management of musical attractions was entirely separate from the school's educational mission.

Ellison-White opened a school for lyceum and chautauqua performers in 1918. Located in Portland, Oregon, the Ellison-White Conservatory of Music offered courses in music and dramatic expression. The conservatory seems to have existed primarily to train Ellison-White performers, although advertisements for short-term workshops indicate that at least those activities were open to musicians not seeking chautauqua work.

The Lyceum Magazine regularly published a directory of "schools and colleges" for platform performers in the back of the magazine. The list of schools was small and relatively stable, including the previously discussed Horner Institute of Fine Arts and the Lyceum Arts Conservatory. Also included was the California School of Artistic Whistling in Los Angeles, which advertised "whistlers fitted for concert, lyceum and chautauqua work."

There were also agencies dedicated not to training but to promoting and securing work for chautauqua musicians. The Chicago Bureau Agency of Music, for instance, provided musicians and small ensembles for lyceum and chautauqua work, and also small orchestras for festivals and other community events. The agency dealt only with musical acts, rather than booking lecturers, dramatic acts, or complete chautauquas or lyceum courses. The Dunbar Chautauqua Bureau, managed by brothers Ralph and Harry Dunbar, supplied independent chautauquas with all manner of acts, including musicians. The bureau, which replaced the Independent Chautauqua Department of the Redpath bureau when Redpath opted to focus entirely on its own chautauqua circuits, advertised that its musicians "transform the 'I don't like classic music' and the slapstick applauders into music lovers." In an introductory letter, Harry Dunbar, president of the bureau, trumpeted the originality of his musical offerings, announcing that "we have several companies that *do not* play the 'Sextette from *Lucia*,' the 'Quartet from *Rigoletto*' and the 'Prison Scene from *Trovatore*' with sounding brass and tinkling cymbal, but have brought out other less venerable and less frazzled art gems."[11]

An advertisement in the June 1920 issue of *The Lyceum Magazine* read, "Ralph Dunbar offers long seasons and splendid opportunities to young American singers, players, and cultured advance agents (either ladies or gentlemen), with his opera companies, presenting *Carmen* (in English), *Robin Hood*, *Mikado* and *Chocolate Soldier*, respectively. Not a repertoire company but four complete organizations appearing [on] tour at leading theaters, auditoriums, convention halls, etc." Dunbar also operated the Dunbar American School of Opera, which ran an eight-week course in Chicago to train singers for Dunbar's productions. While it does not appear that attending the course was a prerequisite for employment with Dunbar, advertisements for the school note that its creation was spurred by Dunbar's inability to find enough suitable singers to fill his many operatic companies.

Recall that many circuit chautauqua performers spent winters touring the lyceum circuits and were managed by lyceum bureaus. Many of the circuit chautauqua bureaus, most notably Redpath and Coit-Alber, were affiliated with lyceum bureaus and drew some chautauqua talent from the ranks of lyceum performers. The drawing-card attractions on a chautauqua circuit would often be acts who booked through the bureau only for summer chautauqua work, while the lesser-known acts would be those who used the lyceum agents to book dates year-round for chautauquas, lyceums, state fairs, and other engagements managed by lyceum bureaus.

In some cases there was no intermediary organization — either educational or promotional — between the performer and the bureau. Performers sometimes approached bureaus directly, and bureaus would occasionally advertise in trade publications to fill specific needs for performers. Impresarios and circuit mangers placed advertisements in trade publications such as the *Lyceumite* in search of specific instruments, voices, or ensembles to perform in the "tented temples of music." One advertisement in *Lyceumite and Talent* read, "Artist Wanted: Vocalist, entertainer, or instrumentalist who can play two or more instruments wanted to join high class concert party for tour of western Canada season '10 and '11." Such advertisements were common, as were advertisements placed by performers (and agencies working on their behalf) looking for chautauqua work.

Successful chautauqua performers sometimes became impresarios as they advanced in years, forming acts designed to either replace them or to capitalize on their success by imitating a proven formula. Ralph and Harry Dunbar, who had made names for themselves as lyceum bell ringers and have been credited with popularizing bell ringing among American audiences,[12] formed several lyceum and chautauqua acts bearing the Dunbar name. One brother or both or other relatives sometimes performed in these groups, but often acts labeled "Dunbar" were so named only because they were created or managed by one of the brothers. Several quartets of bell-ringers toured the chautauqua circuits under the Dunbar banner, as did various other musical acts. Ralph Dunbar promoted musical acts for major vaudeville circuits as well as lyceum and chautauqua and was also involved in the production and promotion of comic opera. Groups bearing his name ranged from jubilee singers to Hussar bands, and were drawn from a constantly changing pool of young

Advertisement showing the geographic territories of the various Vierra's Hawaiian groups.

musicians. A group bearing the name "Dunbar's Male Quartet and Bell Ringers," for instance, may have had entirely different personnel from one year to the next or from one venue to another.

Dunbar's White Hussar's were originally a vaudeville act and became one of the most popular acts of the circuit chautauqua movement. The demand for the White Hussars was great, and Dunbar was quick to create groups to fill it. Gay MacLaren, a dramatic reader who toured with one White Hussar group on the Redpath circuits, stated, "Every circuit wanted them. But this didn't worry Dunbar. He always had an extra supply of White Hussars and could send them out at a minute's notice in companies of from eight to twenty five."[13] When saturation of White Hussars reached the point that communities were likely to realize that multiple groups were using the name in close proximity, Dunbar created the Black Hussars so that communities would not argue about who had hosted the "real" White Hussars on a given day. Similarly, chautauqua performers and promoters Albert and George Vierra simultaneously operated six Hawaiian groups on the chautauqua, lyceum, and vaudeville circuits.

In 1926, Ralph Dunbar offered sixteen acts for chautauqua engagements. They included musical groups first made popular on the Keith and Orpheum vaudeville circuits, groups with a prior history of chautauqua work, a comic opera by Victor Herbert (*Sweethearts*), for which the community would need to supply an orchestra (or pianist), and two of Dunbar's jubilee groups: Dunbar's Dixie Chorus and Dunbar's Tennessee Ten. In the foreword to this 1926 attractions list, Dunbar reminds the reader of his previous vaudeville success and hopes that his experience "will assist me now in creating some new and progressive ideas for the chautauqua — at least I shall make a heroic effort in that direction with these attractions, which will be produced at Chicago."[14] While he produced and managed his chautauqua acts from Chicago, Dunbar's main office was located in New York.

Salaries for chautauqua musicians varied significantly from bureau to bureau and among acts within each bureau. Headlining musical acts could command extraordinary salaries and benefits such as private, custom-built train cars, while lesser-known acts faced low wages, uncertain futures, and difficult traveling conditions. Circuit chautauqua bureaus encountered the same realities of the music business as any booking agency, including slim profit margins and tense negotiations with performers' unions. These difficulties were amplified by the logistics of moving every act to a new city nearly every day, often in rural areas where travel could be unpredictable.

Katharine La Sheck's 1913 contract with Redpath seems to be typical of contracts secured by lesser-known musicians. Nineteen thirteen was La Sheck's third season with the College Singing Girls, alternately known as the College Girls, a female vocal quartet. The quartet contracted with Redpath for a seven-week season beginning in July, with La Sheck and the other members receiving $32 per week. This represented a substantial raise over the 1912 season, during which La Sheck had received $20 per week for a full twenty-week season. It is unclear why La Sheck's 1913 contract began in July, since April was the standard start date for chautauqua circuits. It is also notable that La Sheck's contract, while guaranteeing seven weeks of performances, required La Sheck to keep her schedule open without guarantee of payment through September 15 (nearly four weeks beyond the guarantee) for bookings made at the bureau's discretion.[15] Similar conditions favoring the bureau appear in contracts of other musicians, often requiring performers to commit to a far longer engagement than the contract guaranteed and thus shielding the bureau from financial damage in the event of an unsuccessful circuit or unsatisfactory act.

Major bureaus could set their own terms with most musicians—especially singers—due to a glut of musicians applying for nearly every opening. Charles Horner remarked that at the peak of the circuit chautauqua movement "there was no dearth of applications. If we needed a hundred new singers, for instance, perhaps as many as a thousand applications were heard."[16] The chautauqua job market was considerably better for most instrumentalists. A 1913 editorial in *The Lyceum Magazine* stated, "Young people who confine their musical education to theory, piano, and voice are limiting their possibilities. There is always an oversupply of singers and an undersupply of orchestral musicians. The lyceum, chautauqua, and entertainment fields each year call for more musical organizations. Those who will learn to play violin, clarinet, cornet, flute, saxophone, trombone, horn, cello, etc., will find increasing demand for their services. The supply is short. Young ladies who are good orchestral players are especially hard to find while pianists wait in rows."[17]

A Coit Lyceum-Northern Ohio Territory price list for musical ensembles for the 1916–1917 lyceum season lists prices ranging from $50 to $250 per performance. Even among similar groups, prices varied considerably. The most expensive groups were the Chimes of Normandy Company, a large ensemble performing choral and orchestral repertoire, and the Cord-Rummell Recital Company, which consisted of two vocalists, a violinist, and a pianist. The Lyndon-Gordon Company, by contrast, could be booked for $50. Newspaper reviews indicate that the group was a duo, with Gordon giving dramatic readings and Lyndon specializing in "negro dialect selections."[18]

A Horner-White Concert Bureau talent listing for the 1924–25 lyceum season lists Rosa Ponselle, a soprano at the height of her career with the Metropolitan Opera, as available for $1750. The lowest-paid musicians on Horner-White's advertised roster were soprano Idelle Patterson and violinist Caroline Powers Thomas, listed as available for $350 each or as a duo for $450. It should be noted that these rates are exceptionally high for lyceum performers and that Horner-White's roster comprised established, sometimes famous, classical musicians. Even the lowest-paid Horner-White musicians had established reputations beyond the chautauqua movement. Idelle Patterson had recorded with Victor, and Caroline Powers Thomas had toured as a soloist with Sousa's band.

The high fees paid to famous musicians in chautauqua were used as advertising fodder by bureaus looking to recruit new musical talent. One advertisement stated that Alice Nielsen "spent two seasons traveling in her private car from Florida to Canada and incidentally earned $30,000 a year singing for the crowds that gathered in the tented temples of music." It continued: "Singers, instrumentalists, readers, concert and dramatic performers find more opportunities for long, pleasant and profitable engagements in this field than in any other." While the information regarding Nielsen's chautauqua career is largely accurate (Nielsen is discussed later in this chapter), the implication of the advertisement seems to be that Nielsen's situation was typical for a chautauqua musician. This was certainly not the case.

In 1926, the seven-member Royal Gypsy Orchestra was engaged by the Redpath bureau for a fifteen-week chautauqua season at the rate of $385 per week. The Royal Gypsy Orchestra would give seven prelude concerts and seven evening concerts per week, and would be required to furnish their own costumes.[19] In contrast, Julia Claussen's contract[20] with Redpath for the twenty-week chautauqua season of 1916 stipulated that she would be paid $13,000 in installments of $650 per week plus 40 percent of single-ticket admission receipts[21] for her performances in excess of $24,000. Claussen would give six performances per week, compared to the fourteen (seven evening concerts and seven afternoon preludes) required of less famous musicians. Redpath also agreed to furnish Claussen and her assisting performers with a private rail car in which to travel.[22]

The chautauqua bureaus' relationship with musicians' unions, both local and national, was complicated by the nature of the chautauqua movement. Bureaus employed a great number of musicians, both full-time and seasonal. While many of these musicians performed exclusively for chautauqua and lyceum and booked solely through chautauqua bureaus, others devoted most of their year to more mainstream musical organizations, such as theater orchestras and opera companies.

It does not appear that union membership was either a requirement of or a hindrance to chautauqua employment. Bureaus did, however, have to weigh the cost of paying union salaries against the drawing ability of an act and the availability of less expensive nonunion alternatives. This was especially an issue for larger ensembles, which were often simultaneously the most popular and most expensive attraction on a chautauqua circuit. Travel and lodging expenses alone for a large musical ensemble would account for a significant portion of a circuit's talent budget, and it was not financially feasible for bureaus to pay union wages on top of these expenses for more than a few of the most popular large ensembles.

Bandleader A.F. Thaviu recognized the precarious situation of the unionized large ensemble and sought to reach a compromise with the American Federation of Musicians (AFM), of which he and his band were members. He had led a series of popular bands in chautauqua and had been successful at expositions, fairs, and in independent tours as well. His band was large by chautauqua standards, and he feared that the band's size coupled with its union affiliation would make chautauqua engagements cost-prohibitive. Thaviu's goal was to make union acts competitive with nonunion groups in seeking chautauqua work, and also allow the chautauqua bureaus to set salaries of union musicians at a level reflecting the added travel expenses inherent to circuit chautauqua. To this end, Thaviu wrote to Harry Harrison telling of his efforts to convince the AFM to reduce the minimum salary of chautauqua musicians, announcing his intention of addressing the national convention with his proposal, and urging Harrison to write to the union supporting Thaviu and his efforts.

It is unclear whether Thaviu's efforts bore fruit. He launched his campaign in 1922, not long before shrinking profits would force chautauqua bureaus to reduce the size of musical ensembles to the point that bands the size of Thaviu's no longer appeared on the circuits. While no evidence of a successful union-chautauqua bureau compromise over pay scales exists, efforts such as Thaviu's underscore two important points concerning the relationship between the union and the bureaus. First, the chautauqua bureaus did deal with the union, although not exclusively. Second, union pay scales represented an obstacle to chautauqua engagement, especially for larger ensembles.

Union membership was never a requirement for employment with any major chautauqua bureau. In fact, the Redpath bureau worked with clients to provide specifically nonunion talent on at least one occasion. In 1926, the Phoenix Hotel in Lexington, Kentucky, had been boycotted by the local musicians' union due to a disagreement with the hotel's chief executive officer, who was also president of the firm operating the Lexington Opera House. This boycott impaired the Phoenix's ability to book musicians for events held at the hotel, including its large New Year's Eve celebration. The manager of the Phoenix contacted the Redpath bureau (Redpath was well known in Lexington, having provided the city's chautauqua for many years) in search of a small nonunion orchestra to play the event. Harry Harrison replied that the bureau could send the Adriatic Tamburica Orchestra for between $100 and $125, plus room, board, and train fare from Chicago to Lexington and back. The Tamburica Orchestra was engaged for the celebration, and the hotel manager later wrote to Harrison to express approval of the group.[23]

Once a musician found employment through a chautauqua bureau, the musician entered into an involved and close relationship with bureau management. The chautauqua bureaus' need to present their product as wholesome and educational meant that most bureaus exerted substantial control over their acts. Bureaus exercised control over musical programming at the point of choosing to hire an act and deciding where to place the act on a program. Once an act was on the circuit, its performance was constantly evaluated by the platform superintendent, a position which will be discussed later in this chapter. Furthermore, the bureaus kept strict guidelines for the appearance and conduct of "talent" while on the circuits, both onstage and off.

While rules set forth by employers for employee dress and behavior — especially in the entertainment industry — were not uncommon in the early twentieth century,[24] the rules governing performers for the major chautauqua bureaus were inordinately involved and enforced. Dress codes varied by community, and it was not uncommon for a bureau to send a memorandum to talent stipulating specific dress to conform to local sensibilities. In one instance, the Redpath bureau sent notice to talent that a particular community was very religious, offering as evidence the fact that the town had no movie house and no theater. The memorandum went on to advise women not to wear décolleté gowns or short-sleeved dresses.[25]

The Redpath bureau had strict policies against both drinking and smoking, in public and in private. When any Redpath employee (the policy applied to performers as well as those working behind the scenes) was rumored to have broken these rules, Redpath launched a thorough investigation. Witnesses, often bar employees, would be interviewed by Redpath personnel. If proof of a transgression was found, the bureau's policy was to terminate the employee. In practice, it was not unusual for employees to be given a second chance, but never a third.[26]

Rules forbidding specific behaviors and styles of dress were common to many musical venues of the time.[27] Because of chautauqua's favored place among entertainments in the minds (and pocketbooks) of community leaders, chautauqua bureaus were also obliged to attempt to regulate some of the more abstract qualities of their talent. A pleasing appearance and sociable demeanor were often cited in advertising and in internal bureau communications as important positive attributes. True to the bureaus' emphasis on crafting and maintaining a certain image, performers' looks and demeanor were commonly referred to as "wholesome." The Redpath bureau even quantified these qualities in reports under the label of "personality." Redpath was also careful that its performers conformed to accepted gender roles of the era, and it noted deviations in the form of aberrant dress or behavior in internal correspondence.[28]

Quality of performance was also monitored closely while a performer was on the circuit. This evaluation was conducted by the platform superintendent, an employee whose job it was to remain in a community for the duration of a chautauqua (usually arriving several days before to supervise site preparations and advertising), serving as the highest-ranking bureau official at the chautauqua and as liaison between the bureau and the community. The platform superintendent filed daily reports with the bureau, detailing receipts, weather, crew behavior, audience reception, and talent performance. Performers were assigned letter grades, and these grades could be explained in a comment box next to the letter. It seems that most acts performed satisfactorily most of the time, with the most common complaint about musical acts being failure to fill the allotted time slot.[29]

Several lengthy memoirs written by circuit chautauqua lecturers and managers survive. Only one account by a musician, however, has been found. Written by clarinetist Erwin Harder, it chronicles the 1912 Redpath-Chicago tour of Bohumir Kryl's band. Harder never refers to the band or the bureau by name, but gives tour dates that correspond to the 1912 Redpath-Chicago circuit. Harder also gives biographical details of his conductor that indicate it must have been Kryl, specifically that the conductor was a sculptor who had created a particular statue known to be Kryl's. Programs from the 1912 Redpath-Chicago circuit indicate that Bohumir Kryl and his band were the featured act on the fifth day (of seven) of that circuit. Kryl's band consisted of twenty-six musicians and gave sixty performances in thirty cities on a circuit beginning in Tennessee, traveling through Kentucky, and closing in Indiana.

Harder indicated that many of the musicians in Kryl's band were Europeans, including several Germans and Italians. The band was based in Chicago and consisted of forty musicians while in that city. The musicians' pay scale was reduced when on tour, owing to the added expense of traveling, which was paid for by the conductor out of the money paid to the band by the chautauqua bureau.[30]

Band members were responsible for room and board, and also for laundering and care of their own uniforms. Much of Harder's memoir chronicles the challenges faced by him and his two roommates as they searched for accommodations in small towns whose boardinghouses were already filled by chautauqua-goers. Harder also lamented the food available to musicians. Specifically, Harder was not fond of Southern food, celebrating the band's crossing into Indiana as deliverance from "the biscuit zone." He also noted that the Italians in the band were greatly troubled by the lack of Italian food in chautauqua towns.

Harder mentions several incidents of drinking, and he notes rampant gambling among band members. This indicates that Redpath was not overly concerned with monitoring the band, which may have been a result of the band's relative autonomy. Since Kryl's band already had a leadership structure in place and performed together year-round, Redpath may have trusted the band's leadership to manage band personnel independent of the bureau. It could also indicate lax enforcement of rules due to an embryonic management system on that circuit as a whole, as this was one of Redpath-Chicago's earliest circuits.

From Harder's account, it seems several of the musicians in Kryl's band struggled to save money while on the circuit. While acknowledging that this insolvency could often be blamed on gambling, Harder mentions many expenses levied on the musicians that also contributed to financial hardships. For instance, he notes that the musicians were occasionally made to pay a surcharge out of pocket for a sleeping berth on an overnight train and that they had to have uniforms laundered quickly, resulting in an additional fee for a rush order.[31] Harder notes that some musicians ceased staying in hotels and slept in a tent on the chautauqua grounds intended to house equipment, and that a number of the musicians "did not save twenty dollars on the whole trip."[32]

Musical companies may have fared worse than other performers when it came to hotel accommodations. Larger groups were treated with distrust in many hotels, and instrument cases were checked for contraband. Musicians, at the mercy of performance circuits and train schedules, were in no position to complain when placed in undesirable rooms or told to "double up." These problems were exacerbated by the fact that chautauqua week was generally very busy for hotels, and musicians were often competing with their audience for lodging. In 1916, Bohumir Kryl wrote to the Redpath bureau asking that a tent be supplied for his brother Frank's band. The band found hotel accommodations spotty and expensive, he said, and cited Jaroslav Cimera's band as precedent for bureau provision of a tent for musicians. As Cimera's band was also managed by Redpath, it seems likely that the bureau did in fact supply at least one large musical act with its own sleeping tent.

The records of the Redpath bureau support the notion that it was difficult for some chautauqua musicians to remain financially sound while on the circuits. Correspondence between the bureau and the Dixie Chorus indicate that at least one musician required frequent advances on his salary to cover debts. The bureau recorded the debt and eventually required the musician to sign a contract for extended bookings beyond the contract of the Dixie Chorus with groups to be named (possibly created) later.[33]

Harder's busy performance schedule seems to have been typical for chautauqua musicians. The Florentine Musicians, who toured the chautauqua circuits under the management of Coit-Alber, gave chautauqua performances on 76 days in 1916. Between June 12 and July 24, they performed at 43 chautauquas on the Coit-Alber circuit through Ohio, Michigan, and Pennsylvania. This schedule allowed for no days off and no dedicated travel days. One day after the Coit-Alber circuit ended, the Florentine Musicians embarked on a tour of independent chautauquas, likely also booked by Coit-Alber. From July 26 through August 31, they performed at 23 independent assemblies in Iowa, Illinois, Ohio, and Missouri. Several of these engagements were for two or more days, a common occurrence in independent chautauquas. The schedule allowed for three open days in August, giving the Florentine Musicians a total of four days off during their eighty-day chautauqua season.

Ability of Chautauqua Musicians

An editorial in the *Lyceumite* opined that "the platform has exploited too many passé celebrities" and that platform work represented "the last pull on the pursestrings [sic] of the public."[34] The author felt the situation was improving, but that the reputation of the platform was tarnished by a string of aging performers—especially musicians—selling an inferior product for a cut-rate price to rural audiences who had little or no point of reference by which to judge the performers against their reputation. Clay Smith wrote the following in his monthly column devoted to chautauqua music: "The music in our field has improved wonderfully in the past fifteen or twenty years. Mind you, I say the music, not the musicians. Our standard of artists is not nearly so high, but the material used is much better, newer, more interesting and of a much wider variety."[35] If audiences shared the editorialist's opinion that they were being supplied with inferior performances by performers past their prime, they do not seem to have expressed that sentiment in print. Local reviews of chautauqua performances—especially by headliners—were nearly always laudatory. This phenomenon can likely be explained by the pressure placed on local newspapers to support the chautauqua unconditionally in the name of supporting the community.

While it may have been true that some aging performers saw the chautauqua circuits as a way to extend their careers beyond what would be tolerated in urban circles, not all of the famous musicians on the circuits were past their prime, nor is it accurate to assume that headliners put less effort into chautauqua or took chautauqua work less seriously than their other endeavors. Famed contralto Ernestine Schumann-Heink performed sporadically on the Redpath circuits from 1913 through 1919. Born in Austria in 1861, Schumann-Heink began her career in Dresden and performed regularly with the Metropolitan Opera of New York, the Royal Opera House, Covent Garden (where she sang under Gustav Mahler), and at the Bayreuth Festival. Though she was never contracted for a complete circuit, she filled many dates for Redpath, and her chautauqua performances were highly publicized. In 1916, for instance, she performed at eight chautauquas. A single-admission ticket to one of her chautauqua concerts cost $1.00 — half of the price of a season pass for the entire chautauqua and double the next most expensive single-admission ticket on the Redpath-Vawter circuit. (Vawter charged $.35 for single-admission tickets to most acts, and $.50 for the circuit's regular headliners, Quintano and his band.)

Despite the relatively high ticket price, Schumann-Heink was highly sought after as a chautauqua performer. Her performances were well received and well attended (crowds in excess of 1,000 were reported by Redpath platform superintendents) and there is no indication that she either intentionally or unwittingly gave inferior performances on the circuits. To the contrary, Schumann-Heink appears to have been conscientious about her chautauqua performances. Harry Harrison, who traveled with Schumann-Heink acting as manager for her Redpath engagements, wrote that the contralto experienced anxiety to the point of physical illness before her chautauqua concerts, just as she did for operatic performances. Harrison also wrote of Schumann-Heink's great concern for her reputation as both a musician and an attraction, claiming that once, when inclement weather caused a performance in Ohio to sell far fewer single-admission tickets than anticipated, Schumann-Heink offered to pay the difference between the community's investment of one thousand dollars and the box office receipts for the evening. When Harrison objected to Schumann-Heink's offer, she supposedly replied, "Never let them lose money on you."[36]

Ernestine Schumann-Heink (Library of Congress, Prints & Photographs Division, LC-DIG-ggbain-30114).

There appears to have been some conflict between Schumann-Heink's career as an international opera star and her work on the chautauqua circuits. Correspondence between Schumann-Heink, her New York management (primarily the Hensel & Jones agency), and Harry Harrison of the Redpath bureau reveal tense discussions regarding Schumann-Heink's chautauqua and lyceum bookings. In a telegram to Harry Harrison dated July 21, 1919, Schumann-Heink wrote:

WILL YOU STOP AT ONCE YOUR ADVERTISING ME FOR YOUR LYCEUM COURSE AND TELL ALL THE MANAGERS THAT YOU MADE A BAD MISTAKE YOU SPOILED MY TOUR AND BUSINESS FOR NEXT SEASON AND I POSITIVELY WONT STAND FOR IT YOU VERY WELL KNOW I GAVE YOU ONLY ONE TOWN IN IOWA TO MY PRICE BEFORE I GIVE IT TO MY LAWYER CLEAR THE SITUATION AT ONCE.[37]

The correspondence surrounding this incident is vast. Schumann-Heink's contract with Hensel & Jones would expire before the 1920 chautauqua season, and Schumann-Heink had expressed discontent with Hensel & Jones to Harrison. She had tentatively agreed with Harrison to perform at the Marshalltown, Iowa, Redpath chautauqua, as the local committee had indicated that the community would not be likely to sign a guarantee of financial support if she did not perform. In February of 1919, Harrison wrote a memorandum to the various Redpath offices stating that they were not to advertise Schumann-Heink as a Redpath artist or book her for chautauqua performances. Subsequent letters indicate that Schumann-Heink's future with Hensel & Jones was uncertain and that Redpath agents believed Hensel & Jones to have a relationship with the Coit-Alber chautauqua bureau, fearing that Coit-Alber was on the verge of assuming management of Schumann-Heink's chautauqua engagements.

Despite Harrison's exhortation that Redpath agents not advertise Schumann-Heink for the 1920 chautauqua season, it is clear that one or more Redpath representatives did just that. In fact, an agent from Hensel & Jones wrote to Harrison on 24 March 1919, indicating that Redpath agents were "selling Mme. Schumann-Heink in direct competition with ourselves." In April of 1919, Harrison himself was guaranteeing Schumann-Heink's availability for 1920 chautauqua dates. After receiving Schumann-Heink's telegram (it is telling that previous letters from Hensel & Jones were largely ignored) Harrison again asked Redpath agents not to book her until further notice. In a letter dated 4 August 1919, Harrison referred to the situation as a "fine mix-up" and noted that Schumann-Heink had decided to stay with Hensel & Jones. Harrison closed the letter with, "Let the chips fall where they will, but I would decidedly not carry the thing on any further, and of course it would be absolutely useless for me to see Hensel & Jones. They are 'madder' than a rattlesnake at the Redpath bureau."

By January of 1920, the dispute had not been settled. Redpath was willing to turn their bookings of Schumann-Heink over to Hensel & Jones, but Hensel & Jones wanted more money than Redpath had contracted for. Harrison felt that Schumann-Heink would overrule her management out of loyalty to him (they had a long working relationship, and Harrison had defended Schumann-Heink when accusations of pro-German leanings had been leveled against her during World War I) and to the chautauqua movement, stating, "I still have enough faith in the old girl to believe that she will absolutely do the square thing, regardless of what Hensel & Jones have to say in the case." It is unclear how the situation was finally resolved. With the date in question rapidly approaching, Keith Vawter, the manager in charge of Redpath operations in Iowa, had agreed to paying Hensel and Jones $1500 for Marshalltown despite the initial contract with Schumann-Heink for $1250, and he asked Harrison if he would be able to reimburse Vawter for this loss. Harrison encouraged Vawter to appeal to Schumann-Heink directly on the matter, in hopes that she would insist that Hensel & Jones honor the original contract.

Failing that, Harrison volunteered to discuss the matter with her personally, "although I would rather be shot than have any more dealings with the old lady."[38] Harrison did, in fact, have several more dealings with Schumann-Heink, through various managers, for years beyond the dispute.

Harrison's belief that Schuman-Heink would "do the square thing" was probably well founded. Schumann-Heink's chautauqua performances were not motivated solely by financial gain, as evidenced by her willingness to suffer financially in order to preserve her relationship with a chautauqua community. Nor did her chautauqua performances occur in the twilight of her career. In the summers of 1913 and 1914, for instance, she performed in chautauquas and at the Bayreuth Festival. While Schumann-Heink was neither passé as a performer nor indifferent to the quality of her chautauqua work, the perception that well-known musicians used the circuits to make money while giving inferior performances certainly existed. Furthermore, lesser-known chautauqua musicians were often viewed as second-rate performers, both within the chautauqua and lyceum movement and by outside critics. In the absence of live recordings of circuit chautauqua musical performances it is difficult to assess the musical ability of chautauqua performers or to compare them to competitors in other venues. (Several recordings were made of popular chautauqua lectures, yet there is no indication that musical acts were recorded live at chautauqua events. Many of the more popular chautauqua musical acts did release studio records, however.) A study of musical acts on the circuits, and of those who chose not to participate in circuit chautauquas when given the opportunity, will provide insight into the musical ability (as well as the public perception of musical ability) of chautauqua musical acts.

The Redpath bureau managed tours for musicians and musical groups that did not appear on either the chautauqua or lyceum circuits. These musical acts, which included the Chicago Symphony Orchestra, were not interested in or suited for chautauqua or lyceum tours, but rather opted for shorter tours in other venues, such as universities and large churches. John Philip Sousa and his band appeared at several of the more prominent independent assemblies and performed at the Chautauqua Institution, but he never made a complete chautauqua circuit. Sousa was acquainted with Charles Horner and Harry Harrison, two of the major players in the circuit chautauqua sphere. Correspondence between Harrison and Horner indicate that Horner had successfully booked Sousa for extended engagements at the rate of $8000 per week (including twelve performances) prior to 1919, and that Harrison was attempting to engage Sousa's band for the first week of 1920 in New Orleans for $8800. It is unclear whether the New Orleans concerts came to fruition. Records show Horner was concerned that Harrison, having presumably never dealt with a band as large — or scheduled as tightly — as Sousa's, underestimated the amount of planning such a booking would entail. Letters and telegrams to Harrison are full of exhortations to book appropriate venues well in advance and to consider the train schedules before signing a contract, indicating that Horner may have believed Harrison to be out of his league dealing with an organization like the Sousa Band.[39]

It is telling that major musical groups such as the Chicago Symphony Orchestra and the Sousa Band had relationships with chautauqua organizations and toured sporadically in the summers without committing to a complete circuit tour. The opportunity certainly existed. Sousa was courted by the major bureaus during the most successful years of the circuit chautauqua movement, when it was financially feasible to hire large ensembles.[40] The reluctance of groups like Sousa's band and the Chicago Symphony Orchestra to participate in circuit chautauqua could be interpreted as an indictment of the quality of chautauqua music or of the reputation of acts already associated with the movement. In the case of Sousa, however, this interpretation would be unjustified. There is no indication that Sousa sought to avoid association with the chautauqua movement. His participation in prominent independent assemblies and the Chautauqua Institution contradicts the assumption that Sousa disdained the musical reputation of chautauqua. It should be remembered that, although this study, along with most recent chautauqua scholarship, differentiates between independent and circuit chautauquas, this distinction would not have been made by the majority of the public. Thus, it is highly unlikely that Sousa would have seen the independent chautauquas as positive publicity while avoiding negative associations with circuit chautauqua, as the audience and media would not have made the distinction.

Performers in every phase of life and career traveled the chautauqua circuits. For some, chautauqua was an entrance into life as a full-time professional musician. Composer Howard Hanson, for instance, joined a Redpath concert company at the age of fifteen, playing piano and cello. Some years later he toured the Redpath Premier circuit with star lecturers Glen Frank and Opie Read. Hanson forged a close relationship with Redpath manager Charles Horner, and the two remained friends long after Hanson ended his relationship with Redpath.[41] Other musicians, especially those who toured the circuits as children or young adults, pursued nonmusical careers after leaving chautauqua. Some chautauqua musicians were best known for their chautauqua work, while others viewed chautauqua as secondary to a previous or concurrent career in another musical venue.

Vocal quartets were very popular in the chautauqua movement. Most were single-gender groups of young singers who often doubled on instruments. Some groups were formed by chautauqua impresarios, and some had

II. Chautauqua Musicians

worked or studied together prior to embarking on their platform careers. One of the longest lived vocal quartets in chautauqua was the Weatherwax Brothers, who toured full-time, performing at chautauquas in summer on the lyceum circuits in winter, from roughly 1910 through 1921, with a two-year hiatus while younger brothers Tom and Lester played in a military band during World War I. The Weatherwax Brothers sang and played trumpet quartets, using two Bb trumpets and two smaller Eb cornets.

Like most chautauqua acts, the Weatherwax Brothers did not regularly provide programs for their performances. Redpath did publish sample programs in some Weatherwax brochures, including the following numbers:

Dixie	
De Sandman	Protheroe
Serenade*	Harrison
The Goblins	Parks
Good-night Beloved*	Pinsutti
Diadem	
Sunset	Van de Water
A Flag Without a Stain	
National Airs*	
Good-night	Buck
*instrumental	

Readings were interspersed between musical numbers. Two of the brothers were advertised as readers, with Lester specializing in pathos and William giving comic readings. Anecdotal evidence indicates that the Weatherwax Brothers strongly favored American composer Dudley Buck. This is not unusual. Buck's work was popular throughout chautauqua as it was considered accessible yet musically worthwhile. It is notable that, according to relatives, the Weatherwax Brothers did not compose music for their act, and generally performed commercially published arrangements. This was also the norm for chautauqua quartets, as most comprised young, relatively untrained musicians.

The Weatherwax Brothers had been performing together as amateurs for over a decade before signing on with Redpath. While they lacked formal training, their years of prior experience and the stability of their roster (an advantage of being a family group) set them apart from most chautauqua quartets, as did their age. When the Weatherwax Brothers stopped touring in 1920, the oldest brother, William, was 47, and all of the brothers had married, establishing families in their home state of Iowa despite their constant touring. Interviews with family members indicated that the Weatherwax Brothers once traveled with their wives and young children while on the chautauqua circuits in Florida with Redpath. This seems highly unusual and it is unclear

(Left to right) Tom, Lester, Asa and William, The Weatherwax Brothers Quartet (author's collection, gift of Fred Crane).

whether Redpath subsidized travel for the family members; but it does indicate that life on the circuits was not always as trying as the experiences related by Harder.

The account of Dorothy Phillips Kohl indicates that her group, the Phillips Sisters Orchestra, had extensive musical coaching prior to embarking on a chautauqua tour. The sisters studied at Simpson College in Indianola, Iowa, and had musical directors rehearse them in preparation for their chautauqua tours. It is unclear who paid for this instruction, although the group was under Redpath management. It is possible that the extra instruction was necessitated by the sisters' youth; the younger sisters were still in high school during their chautauqua careers. The Phillips Sisters Orchestra played from commercial arrangements, some of which were heavily altered by the music directors for the group.[42] Interestingly, it seems the Phillips Sisters also danced — a rarity in chautauqua. They wore Scottish costumes for most of their chautauqua careers and danced the Highland Fling as part of their program.

The Phillips Sisters and Weatherwax Brothers were unusual in the extent of their preparation prior to joining a chautauqua company. Many quartets were hastily formed by managers who sometimes booked groups without a clear idea of the personnel involved. Harold Plotts of Des Moines, Iowa, approached chautauqua impresario Harry Bland about joining a musical company in order to make money while awaiting the results of his state dental

The Phillips Sisters Orchestra (author's collection, gift of Fred Crane).

board exams. Potts was an amateur violinist and singer who participated in the glee club and orchestra while in college, but he had no individual training in either voice or violin.

Bland hired Potts on the spot to replace a member of Bland's Wesleyan Quartet, a novelty quartet whose baritone was "going sour." Bland and Potts traveled together the next morning to meet the quartet in Oklahoma. Potts joined the quartet immediately and gradually learned the music through sporadic rehearsals while on the circuits. The group was successful enough that they were asked to sign on for the following lyceum season, but Potts declined, having received word that he had passed his dental board exams.[43]

Katharine La Sheck began her full-time musical career with Redpath and parlayed her chautauqua experience into a career as a singer and professor of voice. La Sheck was born Rachel Katharine Lasheck in Iowa City, Iowa, in 1891.[44] Her father, an immigrant from Bohemia, moved the family several times while Katharine was in high school. She finished high school in Revere, Massachusetts, where she sang in several amateur and school groups. La Sheck's first musical engagement under professional management came as a member of the Ideal Quartet, a touring women's quartet managed by a small

The College Girls (author's collection, gift of Fred Crane).

firm out of Boston. The group performed around the Boston area, but did not embark on any long-term tours or perform in high-profile venues. La Sheck and other quartet members spent most of their time pursuing other professional and educational interests, as the Ideal Quartet was a decidedly part-time and local endeavor. At this time La Sheck was still known primarily as "Rachel," and had not yet altered the spelling of her surname. Once she began her chautauqua career, she preferred to be billed as "Katharine La Sheck," opting to use her middle name and altering the spelling of her surname, feeling that "La Sheck" sounded French and was thus a more desirable name for a singer than the Bohemian "Lasheck." It should be noted that in her native Iowa, newspapers insisted that the name change was not an attempt to distance herself from her Bohemian roots but rather a capitulation to the constant misspellings and mispronunciations of the Boston media.[45]

La Sheck's entry into the chautauqua field was spurred by her sister Adelaide, who contacted the Redpath Lyceum Bureau of Boston on Katharine's behalf in 1910. Adelaide stated in her letter that her sister was a talented contralto interested in chautauqua work, preferably in the Midwest. The bureau responded that the upcoming season was already booked.[46] There must have

The Marigolds (author's collection, gift of Fred Crane).

been further communication between the bureau and the singer, however, because La Sheck signed on with Redpath for a chautauqua tour in 1912. Redpath seems to have paid no heed to La Sheck's preference for Midwestern work, as she spent much of her early chautauqua career in New England. This lack of concern for a performer's preference was the rule with Redpath rather

"Come Hear the Marigold's [*sic*] Sing," the most popular of the Marigolds' opening numbers (Katharine La Sheck Papers, Iowa Women's Archives, the University of Iowa Libraries, Iowa City).

than the exception, especially when dealing with young, unknown, and easily replaced singers.

La Sheck's initial chautauqua engagement, and most of her chautauqua career, was with a group known as the College Girls. The group originally consisted of four female singers accompanied by seasoned lyceum and chautauqua performer Walter Eccles. At this point the group was usually billed as Walter Eccles and the Four College Girls, although the name would change as more members were added to the group. Several newspaper accounts of early College Girls performances often noted La Sheck's unusually deep voice, sometimes referring to her as "the female baritone." The College Girls' repertoire would be considered typical for a circuit chautauqua vocal quartet, consisting of older popular and folk songs, comic songs, light classical arrangements, and sacred music when required for Sunday performances. The College Girls also danced and played mandolin and xylophone. This instrumental doubling was normal and often expected of circuit chautauqua quartets.

The College Girls toured the chautauqua and lyceum circuits for the Redpath bureau, and were even booked through Redpath for a tour of the Panama Canal Zone in 1913. Although the group was very popular, it suffered from internal disagreements that would eventually cause La Sheck and two other members to leave and form a new group, known as the Marigolds, in 1915. The Marigolds were managed by La Sheck and booked through the Redpath bureau. Unlike the College Girls, the Marigolds had no outside musical director. Perhaps because of this, their repertoire was largely devoid of classical numbers and heavily favored popular songs. The Marigolds began each performance with one or two signature songs introducing the group and often closed with a patriotic song. The most popular of the Marigolds' opening numbers was "Come Hear the Marigold's [sic] Sing." The manuscript copy of this song housed in the Katharine La Sheck papers is inscribed, "Written by Luke [illegible] Gluck, a snow shoveler." The manuscript also included a short "Ultra Modern Song," obviously intended as a joke at the expense of atonal music.

La Sheck left the Marigolds, and the chautauqua and lyceum platforms, in 1920. She settled in Buffalo, New York, where she performed in local opera and oratorio productions and was a regular broadcast radio personality. In 1944 she returned to Iowa, joining the faculty of the University of Iowa to teach voice and elementary music until her retirement in 1959. Nearly all of La Sheck's formal musical training took place during or after her chautauqua career. She had little professional experience prior to signing on with Redpath, yet she was able to parlay her chautauqua experience into a successful commercial and academic musical career. Although she did not go on to great musical fame, La Sheck was able to use circuit chautauqua to enter the world of full-time professional music.

In the peak years of the chautauqua movement, large bands toured with nearly every major circuit. While the bands, like all chautauqua acts, could vary greatly in size and quality from one circuit to the next, several of them were — or would become — famous beyond the chautauqua and lyceum movements. A.F. Thaviu was able to make a name for himself and his band on the chautauqua circuits, in time becoming one of America's premiere wind bands.

Thaviu was born Alexander Tevye Feiman in Zvenigorodka, Ukraine, in 1875. He emigrated to the United States as a teenager, eventually settling in Chicago. He played cornet and cello in several Chicago-area groups before forming his own band in 1905. By this point, he had adopted the name "A.F. Thaviu," combining an anglicized "Tevye" with his remaining two initials. Thaviu's early band was not exactly a standard wind band; it included at least four strings and a vocalist. His first wind band was the nineteen-piece Thaviu's Oriental Band, which performed in Turkish costume, although their repertoire was primarily standard American wind band fare (a sample program includes two numbers out of eleven labeled "Oriental," and also includes chautauqua staples such as the sextet from *Lucia* and quartet from *Rigoletto*). After 1910, Thaviu's band was no longer advertised as "Oriental" and had abandoned the Turkish costumes in favor of the pseudo-military uniforms common to professional wind bands of the time. Thaviu's band enjoyed a long career in chautauqua and, after divesting from the movement, continued to perform year-round at state fairs, amusement parks, and many venues in their home base of Chicago.[47]

Thaviu's career in many ways parallels that of Bohemian cornetist Bohumir Kryl. Kryl, touted as "the world's greatest cornet virtuoso,"[48] began his career outside of the chautauqua movement but rose to prominence as a circuit chautauqua soloist and bandleader. Despite his considerable acclaim as a cornet soloist and the popularity of his recordings and compositions for brass instruments, Kryl is best remembered as a conductor, and more specifically as a conductor on the chautauqua circuits.

Kryl was born in Prague in 1875, and immigrated to the United States at the age of fourteen. Upon arrival in the United States, he settled in Chicago, where he studied both music and sculpture. In 1894, he moved to Indianapolis where he established himself as a sculptor. Although he was well regarded as a sculptor and had been commissioned for a high-profile project for the city of Indianapolis, Kryl had come to the U.S. primarily in hopes of becoming a cornet soloist. To that end, when John Philip Sousa's band came to Indianapolis, Kryl sought an audience with Albert Bode, cornet soloist with the band and former star of Patrick Gilmore's band. Bode was impressed by the young Kryl and invited him to join Sousa's band. Within the year, Kryl had replaced Bode as cornet soloist with the band.[49] Several contradictory biographical accounts of Kryl's life were published during the twentieth century. Specifically, there is debate as to the circumstances surrounding Kryl's appointment to the Sousa band. Also, some sources, notably Howard

II. Chautauqua Musicians

Left: Cartoon of Bohumir Kryl by Fred Craft (author's collection, gift of Fred Crane).
Right: A.F. Thaviu in "Oriental" costume (author's collection, gift of Fred Crane).

Schwartz's *Bands of America*, cite Kryl's chautauqua career as being considerably shorter than evidence from chautauqua bureau records suggests.

Kryl served as soloist for several prominent American bands, including the Chicago Marine Band and the Innes Band. In 1903, he was appointed assistant conductor of the Inness Band, and in 1906 he left to organize his own band, in which he filled the positions of both conductor and soloist. Kryl's band gave lyceum performances in that same year and was performing in chautauquas, traveling with eight opera singers, by 1909.

Kryl was unimposing in stature, overweight for most of his career, and did not fit the image expected of an American bandmaster at the turn of the century. Perhaps realizing this, Kryl crafted a stage persona unlike those of his contemporaries. His conducting was emotional and enthusiastic, and his appearance was far less militaristic than his contemporaries. Although, like most bandmasters of the time, he wore a uniform, Kryl's was relatively subdued and rarely involved the elaborate decorations common at the time. He let his hair grow, and his shock of coarse blonde hair became his trademark. His promotional photographs often showed him alone in brooding poses, as opposed to those of his peers, which typically invoked military imagery and featured the conductor in front of the entire band.

Thaviu's Oriental Band (author's collection, gift of Fred Crane).

Although he was best known for his band, Kryl toured with several other musical groups. He performed in lyceums in the winter of 1914 with his two daughters, Josephine (violin) and Marie (piano), as Bohumir Kryl and Company. His daughters studied music in New York and London as children and made concert tours in their early teens. During World War I, Bohumir Kryl held a paramilitary position with the U.S. Army, similar to that held by Sousa with the navy. Though the exact nature of this appointment is unclear (a C.G. Conn publication referred to Kryl as "bandmaster of all the military camp bands in the county") it is likely that he served as an unpaid leader of a reserve band in or near Chicago.

Kryl organized many musical groups, including the Chicago Novelty Quartet, the Chicago Orchestral Choir, Kryl's Orchestral Sextette, and the Roumanian Orchestra. All of these groups were managed by Redpath. A study of Kryl's work as an impresario yields insight into the discussion of the ability level of chautauqua musicians. Once Kryl had established himself and his band as headliners on the chautauqua circuits, many groups bearing his name appeared under the Redpath banner. It seems Redpath trusted Kryl to supply quality acts without the usual strict Redpath oversight, and by 1919 Kryl was taking advantage of that relationship. In that year, several disputes arose between Kryl and Redpath involving audience and platform manager displeasure with acts managed by Kryl.

The Redpath bureau records regarding these disputes are incomplete;

they include copies of letters to Kryl from Redpath and letters to Redpath from Kryl, but not letters about Kryl from concerned chautauqua and lyceum communities to Redpath and its agents. Even without this information, the situation is clear. By 1919 Kryl was acting as producer for a number of musical acts and lacked either the time or the inclination to oversee them personally. In this way, he resembled the Dunbar brothers: his name was associated with groups of vastly varying quality and preparation that were apparently booked on chautauqua and lyceum circuits based on their association (however tenuous) with an established chautauqua performer. There is some indication that Kryl and the Dunbars had a business relationship by 1920 and that Redpath was not happy about this, as the bureau had previously been disappointed by low-quality acts bearing the Dunbar name.[50] Whether or not Kryl's ensembles' decline in quality was due to an association with Dunbar, correspondence shows audience dissatisfaction with several Kryl groups in the 1919 and 1920 chautauqua seasons and the winter lyceum season bridging them.

Promotional photograph of Bohumir Kryl (author's collection, gift of Fred Crane).

A letter to Kryl from the Redpath home office during the 1919 chautauqua season regarding Kryl's Spanish Orchestra states, "I do not see how we can advertise six girls and then deliver only three of them. We have had enough grief this year on account of substitutions."[51] A letter from Crawford Peffer of Redpath-New York to Kryl dated March 8, 1920, regarding an unnamed Kryl ensemble states, "I had so many kicks with regard to this company that I made a thorough investigation and among other things found out that you personally gave the company no rehearsals with the personnel as it came to my territory." Peffer then notes, as he had previously written to Redpath headquarters, that two new members were added to the group with no rehearsal whatsoever before their first performance. Peffer continues: "One of our committees will not pay the fee and to another we are sending an attraction to make [g]ood. All of this is going to cost me about $250, to say nothing of the places which were dis-satisfied."[52]

Of the many instances in which a Kryl organization disappointed a chautauqua or lyceum audience, the 1919 incarnation of the Kryl Saxophone Sextette is likely the most significant. In a letter to Kryl dated October 2, 1919, Keith Vawter writes, "You say that you know the Saxophone Sextette was all right musically. I believe they had the ability to put up a better program than they did. I also believe they had the ability to have dressed better and look more like white men than they did. We have to judge them on what they do rather than on what they can do." Setting aside Vawter's jarring comment about the group's dress and appearance, his comment on the Saxophone Sextette's underachievement is significant, as this was one of the musical groups on the circuit chautauqua attended by Sinclair Lewis in 1919.[53] Lewis was no great fan of the circuit chautauqua. In his 1920 bestseller, *Main Street*, written during the summer in which Lewis would have heard Kryl's Saxophone Sextette, he describes circuit chautauqua as a "combination of vaudeville performance, Y.M.C.A. lecture, and the graduation exercises of an elocution class." It is a stretch to lay the blame for Lewis' disdain for chautauqua entirely at the feet of Kryl's Saxophone Sextette, but it is worth noting that the music he experienced at the Mankato, Minnesota, chautauqua was subpar even by circuit chautauqua standards.

Rather than defend the quality of his groups (being an excellent musician himself, Kryl may have realized such a position was indefensible), Kryl routinely went on the offensive, placing blame on the audience, the committee, and even the Redpath bureau. After an engagement at Neilsville, Wisconsin, during which the Kryl Orchestra "made fools of themselves," Kryl accused the local committee of cruelty, stating, "I really would not believe that such hard-hearted people are living."[54] In a letter to L.B. Crotty, a Redpath manager, Kryl writes, "Sorry that you folks have it in for my companies this season. There must be some reason for this I am sure. Wish I knew it."[55]

The Redpath bureau and its managers appear to have been unusually enmeshed with Kryl financially. Legal proceedings related to a dispute between Kryl and Jaroslav Cimera, former trombonist in Kryl's band who himself had a band on the Redpath circuits, show Kryl and the various Redpath agencies in a nearly perpetual state of indebtedness to one another. Cimera alleged that Kryl convinced him to buy an orchard from Redpath manager Harry Harrison. Kryl financed the majority of the transaction ($5000) personally with the agreement that Cimera's band would appear on the Redpath circuits for a number of years, with Kryl as their booking agent. Thus Cimera entered into a sort of twentieth-century indenture to Kryl, the terms of which he later disputed.[56] It is unclear why Kryl created such a complex arrangement, but Cimera was under the impression that Harrison owed Kryl $20,000 and this was an attempt to recoup some of that debt. Kryl's relationship with Cimera extended to bookings with other chautauqua bureaus, and these transactions were yet another source of dispute, this time involving Ellison-White Chautauquas, the Affiliated Lyceum and Chautauqua Association, and, of course, Redpath.

Kryl's career outlasted the circuit chautauqua movement. In

Alice Nielsen on her private railcar (author's collection, gift of Fred Crane).

the late 1940s, he conducted the Women's Symphony Orchestra of Chicago. A shrewd businessman, Kryl amassed a considerable fortune in his business ventures and in the stock market.[57] He is said to have offered each of daughters $100,000 if they would refrain from marrying until after age thirty, in order to pursue their musical careers.[58] Neither daughter lived up to the agreement. Josephine Kryl married composer Paul Taylor, and Marie married conductor Michael Gusikoff. Although Kryl was an accomplished musician prior to his chautauqua career, it was through circuit chautauqua that he acquired his fame (and much of his wealth).

While "home grown" musical celebrities like Kryl were often headliners on the circuits, the rise in popularity and credibility of the circuit chautauqua movement throughout the 1910s spurred an interest among the major bureaus in acquiring established stars from the art music world to headline the larger chautauqua circuits. Ernestine Schumann-Heink's chautauqua appearances had been risky ventures for the Redpath bureau. Redpath had no way of knowing prior to 1913 if chautauqua communities would pay a premium to bring in an opera star, or if audiences would attend in the numbers required to recoup the community's extra investment. The Schumann-Heink experiment proved successful, however, spurring the Redpath managers to pursue opera stars from New York and Chicago for full seasons of chautauqua work. In 1915, Harry Harrison of Redpath-Chicago booked Alice Nielsen for a circuit of 120 towns. The following year, he booked Julia Claussen for the same circuit.

Alice Nielsen was an American-born soprano who had begun her career in vaudeville, become a star on Broadway in collaboration with Victor Herbert, and eventually established herself as one of America's leading operatic sopranos. She was no stranger to the business side of music, having formed her own opera company during her years on Broadway. Her immense popularity and business acumen led her to sign the most lucrative contract of any chautauqua performer, including the aforementioned private railcar.

Despite Redpath's generous accommodations, correspondence between Nielsen (or her representative) and Harry Harrison reveals a strained relationship between the soprano and the bureau. Although she was contractually obligated to make a full 120-town circuit with Redpath, Nielsen attempted to cancel or reschedule several appearances. While this may have been feasible on a regular concert tour, it was not possible on a chautauqua circuit. Nielsen's insistence on cancelling a scheduled chautauqua date in Indianapolis and instead performing in Boston caused a heated exchange between Thomas Nielsen, her de facto manager, and various Redpath representatives. In a letter dated March 24, 1916,[59] Nielsen wrote, "I have fired my last gun. Miss Nielsen insists on doing Boston in Indianapolis. Please arrange accordingly. Sorry about this but the lady insists and I am not her manager."[60]

Nielsen wired Harry Harrison early in her first circuit from Greensboro, North Carolina, threatening to cancel the remainder of her performances due to the quality of pianos supplied by the bureau. Nielsen objected to the Kimball pianos used by Redpath for that circuit and insisted that a grand piano be supplied for each of her performances, beginning ten days after the date of the telegram.[61] Charles Horner wrote to Nielsen in March of 1916, asking for definite confirmation for a performance about which he had been inquiring "for a couple months."[62] Nielsen seems to have cancelled, attempted to reschedule, or avoided committing to performance dates with a frequency not usually tolerated by Redpath management.

Nielsen was between managers in the months preceding her chautauqua tour. In correspondence between Thomas Nielsen and Harry Harrison, Mr. Nielsen alternates between stating that he is acting as Ms. Nielsen's manager until a manager can be found, and stressing that he (Nielsen) is not Ms. Nielsen's manager and cannot be expected to influence her in the way a manager could. It is unclear if Thomas Nielsen and Alice Nielsen were related, although the rarity of that name would seem to make it likely. It should be noted, however, that neither of Alice Nielsen's two documented husbands used Nielsen as a last name or was named Thomas. Thomas Nielsen, therefore, may have been a brother to Alice, but this has not been verified. This lack of a manager to act as intermediary may explain the unusually adversarial tone of the correspondence between Nielsen and the Redpath managers.

Nielsen's 1915 circuit was heralded as the beginning of a new era for circuit chautauqua music. An article in *Musical Courier* trumpeted her upcoming tour as a demonstration of "the practicability of the appearance of the greatest artists in a new and rapidly developing field." The article also claimed that while Nielsen's concerts would be given in tents with a seating capacity of 2000, the canvas would be "properly stretched and sprinkled" so that "the acoustic properties [were] made superior to any hall one-half the size." In its conclusion, the article praised Harry Harrison for booking Nielsen, stating, "By his enterprise and willingness to try out new fields and educate the people to an appreciation of the best in music, Mr. Harrison is doing a much greater service for the musical world than can yet be fully appreciated."[63]

Predictions of a shift in chautauqua programming toward well-known professionals from the art music world never came to fruition. Despite the successful tours of Claussen and Nielsen, along with several other well-known singers and instrumentalists, such high-priced musical headliners would never become the norm in circuit chautauqua. This failure of the introduction of nationally known performers to significantly affect the circuit chautauqua movement would seem to indicate that circuit chautauqua's detractors might have been right in arguing that chautauqua audiences either could not distinguish between first- and second-rate musical performances or simply were not willing to pay a premium for a superior musical product.

It is true that chautauqua audiences did not seem to differentiate greatly between headliners from the operatic and symphonic spheres and those, such as Kryl, for whom chautauqua was a primary focus. To assume that audiences should have made a great distinction, however, is to assume that the famous opera singers touring the major circuits were objectively musically superior to chautauqua-focused headliners. This is an inaccurate assumption, at least when comparing headliners. Kryl's band, for instance, was consistently compared to Sousa's in quality, and Kryl himself was world famous as a cornetist.

Furthermore, when comparing like attractions, chautauqua audiences certainly did differentiate between those operatic acts formed by chautauqua impresarios using unknown talent and famous performers such as Julia Claussen.

The failure of famous art music headliners to become a mainstay on the circuits is more likely attributed to several of the same factors blamed for the overall decline of the chautauqua movement in the 1920s, as well as to logistical and economic factors specific to chautauqua. The advent of radio broadcasts of art music likely detracted from the allure of touring high-profile art music acts. Shifting American musical tastes may also have contributed, with bureaus being forced to orient programming towards emerging popular musical genres. Finally, just as the chautauqua movement reached critical mass in the mid 1920s, with more communities hosting chautauquas than the local economies could bear, it may have been the case that a similar phenomenon negated the effectiveness of high-profile chautauqua musical acts as drawing cards. Bureaus may have realized that at the height of chautauqua's popularity, the major chautauquas were already attracting the vast majority of those interested in and financially able to attend the chautauqua.

The increase of attendance generated by a famous opera singer would not necessarily be great enough to justify the increased cost of presenting the chautauqua in smaller communities. Headliners' fees were generally recouped from single ticket sales (tickets for one event, rather than for the entire chautauqua), a practice that assumed there would be those in a community who would be interested in hearing the headliner but would not attend the rest of the chautauqua. In small communities with high levels of chautauqua support and attendance, the box office receipts for single tickets might not approach the cost of bringing the famous headliner to the community. Traveling a complete chautauqua circuit required acts like Claussen and Nielsen to give performances in areas that would have sold nearly the same number of tickets without them, at a considerably lower cost to the community and bureau. For this reason, the system of scattered "special dates" for star attractions such as Ernestine Schumann-Heink and William Jennings Bryan proved more profitable for the bureaus.

Conclusion

Chautauqua was a large movement, encompassing dozens of organizations ranging from large, highly organized transnational bureaus to independent assemblies to underfunded and unstable regional operations. Even within a single bureau there was great variety in musical acts in terms of training, background, and musical ability. Bell ringers with little or no musical training traveled under the same banner as world-famous art music performers. For this reason, it is unreasonable to make generalizations about chautauqua music or musicians, as some nonmusician scholars of the movement have done. Furthermore, one cannot use the presence of lesser quality musical acts on the circuits as proof of musical illiteracy on the part of bureaus or audiences. Although the two traveled the same circuit, famous art musicians and unknown novelty acts were subject to highly disparate treatment (and payment) by the bureaus. Musical discernment on the part of audiences is evidenced by their heightened support — both in enthusiasm and in ticket purchases — for high-quality musical acts. Chautauqua music was not a monolithic entity, but rather a musical venue employing many musicians representing a variety of genres and backgrounds.

III
Musical Selection in Chautauqua

Music was integral to chautauqua from the very inception of the movement, though its role changed over time. As the twentieth century progressed and the circuit and independent chautauquas grew and eventually collapsed, both the repertoire of music performed and the perception of that music among audience members and within the chautauqua movement would evolve, influenced by changing societal conditions and divergent philosophies regarding the place and purpose of music.

Musical acts in all branches of the chautauqua movement obtained sheet music primarily from commercial sources, though some acts performed original compositions. Bureaus sometimes provided music for special events within a chautauqua, such as religious services and community sing-alongs. Furthermore, commercial publishers seized on the chautauqua movement as both a customer base and a means of advertising. While there was considerable variety in chautauqua music, musical selection within the movement was not haphazard. In fact, forces from both within and outside chautauqua influenced musical selection and performance practice.

Music at the Chautauqua Institution

While the Chautauqua Institution cultivated a reputation as an art music venue in the last century,[1] art music was not a prominent feature of the institution during the years that the "Mother Chautauqua" exerted influence on the circuit and independent chautauqua movements. Early meetings of the Chautauqua Assembly (the original name of the Chautauqua Institution) involved group singing of hymns, other religious music, and, by the last quarter of the nineteenth century, occasional art music concerts. By this time, local (independent) chautauqua assemblies, which were direct precursors to the circuit chautauqua movement, were forming across the United States. These assemblies more closely resembled the early Chautauqua Assembly, rather than the Chautauqua Institution of the twentieth century.

No precise record of music at the first Chautauqua Assembly survives. Later reminiscences of that first assembly, however, mention group hymn-singing, a lone cornet, and the performance of "Negro spirituals" (this may have been at a subsequent assembly). Chautauqua's musical offerings expanded quickly as the assembly broadened in scope and increased in duration. In its second year Chautauqua began to offer formal music instruction by three dedicated music teachers. In 1875 there was a residency by the Tennesseans and a performance by a vocal trio in addition to the group singing of hymns; 1876 featured the introduction of secular music and performances by jubilee singers, a (presumably vocal) trio, a brass band, piano, cabinet organ, and cornet.[2]

Modern scholars are quick to distinguish between the Chautauqua Institution and its namesake movements. While this distinction is important and generally valid, it should be acknowledged that the early Chautauqua Assemblies were not as far removed — especially where music is concerned — from the circuit and independent chautauquas as one might assume, based on the cultural cachet of the modern Chautauqua Institution.

Perhaps because of the Chautauqua Institution's longevity and prestige, it is the only facet of the chautauqua movement to have been thoroughly examined by a music historian. Jeanette Wells chronicled musical activities at the "Mother Chautauqua" in her 1958 doctoral dissertation, and her findings challenge preconceived notions regarding musical offerings in Chautauqua's infancy. One highlight of the 1882 season at Chautauqua was the Royal Handbell Ringers and Glee Men from London, England, who gave a series of concerts at Chautauqua between August 15 and 21. The group, which boasted a collection of 134 bells, was very popular with Chautauqua's audience.[3] The appearance of bell ringers on the program at the "mother" assembly is significant because critics of the circuit and independent chautauquas often invoked bell ringers when discussing the lack of musical value in these assemblies. In 1885 the Schubert Quartette made its debut at Chautauqua.[4] It is unclear if this was the same Schubert Quartette that performed at commercial and independent assemblies, but the possibility of reverse influences — the "Mother Chautauqua" imitating the circuits — is intriguing.

Artifacts from (and studies of) the Chautauqua Institution in the early twentieth century focus on the growing presence of world-class art music at the institution. Evidence from the broader chautauqua movement, however, indicates that less lofty music still held a place at the Institution during this time. In a 1919 article for the *Lyceum* magazine, Clay Smith asserted, "A few years ago at the great Assembly at Chautauqua Lake, N.Y., 'Silver Threads' was used by four consecutive companies and the fifth one used it twice, repeating it at night 'by request.'"[5] "Silver Threads Among the Gold" was over forty years old at the time, but its exceptional popularity and longevity is well documented. Thus, it would not be surprising to find it so frequently performed on the traveling chautauqua platform or lyceum stage well into the twentieth century. Smith's claim that it was equally popular at the Chautauqua Institution at this late date is surprising, but it is possible that "a few years ago" could reference decades before, or that Smith's claim was exaggerated.

By the third decade of the twentieth century, when events bearing the chautauqua name were crisscrossing the continent, the Chautauqua Institution had grown to the point that it had very little in common with its namesakes. *Musical America* declared the Chautauqua Institution to be "the summer music capital of the United States." George Gershwin and Arnold Schoenberg each spent a summer at Chautauqua. The New York Symphony, the Victor Herbert Orchestra, and the Detroit Symphony gave summer concerts at Chautauqua, and in 1929 Chautauqua established its own symphony; 1929 also saw the establishment of the Chautauqua Opera. By the 1930s, the Chautauqua Institution had developed a world-class summer music program with an internationally renowned faculty.

Currently, the Chautauqua Symphony Orchestra gives roughly twenty concerts per summer at the amphitheater, which has been the center of the Chautauqua Institution since its construction in 1893. Chautauqua Opera maintains an active performance schedule of new and classic repertoire, and the music festival at Chautauqua trains scores of young musicians every summer.

Music in the American Lyceum

As discussed in chapter one, the American lyceum movement predated the Chautauqua Institution by decades and was virtually devoid of music in its early years. The inclusion and proliferation of music in the lyceum movement coincided with the commercialization of lyceums and the reliance on booking agencies, rather than local committees, to provide lyceum events. Because music was inextricably linked with commercialization in the minds of those discussing and writing about the lyceum movement in the post–Civil War era, it is difficult to differentiate between opposition to music and opposition to commercialization. Whatever the root cause, it is clear that many within the lyceum movement were wary of music.

There appears to have been objection among some audience members to the inclusion of music in the lyceum as well. An editorial in the *Alden (IA)*

III. Musical Selection in Chautauqua

Times from 1879 scolded lyceum audience members who showed their lack of musical sophistication (the author claims these audience members could not distinguish between a cowbell and an Aeolian harp) by talking throughout musical performances. The author makes it clear that these are not teenagers engaging in "social misdemeanor depriving others of the treat" but rather "old senators, who usually occupy a seat well in the front, who do not whisper, but show their non-appreciation for music by talking in a loud and animated voice during that exercise."

Objections to music on the lyceum stage may have been calmed by the presence of lectures about music or involving music. Such lectures appear sporadically in antebellum lyceum programs, and are a popular feature of the later commercial lyceum movement. In the trade publication *Who's Who in the Lyceum*, musical topics are very popular among lecturers, some of whom even had musical training. For instance, the 1906 edition of *Who's Who* lists Louis Charles Elson, head of theory at the New England Conservatory, as having given about 2000 lectures on the lyceum circuits since 1890. Elson's listed repertoire included the following:

"The Songs and Legends of the Sea"
"Our National Music and Its Sources"
"Shakespeare in Music"
"The Story of German Music"
"The Troubadours and Their Descendants"
"Seven Centuries of English Song"
"Old Scottish History and Song"

Despite having given 2,000 lyceum lectures, Elson apparently left behind no programs or promotional brochures. There were, however, many other musical lecturers on the lyceum circuits, and considerable ephemera from those acts survives. For instance, Harry Vincent's "Listening to Music" lecture appears to have been a condensed music appreciation class. The promotional brochure lists the listening selections for the evening, which seem to have been performed by Mr. Vincent on the organ:

Toccata and Fugue in D minor	Bach
Fugue on "Over the fence is out!"	Paine
Funeral March of a Marionette	Gounod
Selections from the Fifth Symphony	Beethoven
Variations on an American Air	Flagler
Fantasie	Clegg
Caprice "The Brook"	Dethier
Clock Movement	Haydn
Pilgrim's Chorus	Wagner
Reverie	Johnson

Spanish Caprice	Moret
Pavane	Sharpe
Rondo d'mour	Westerhout
March of the Toys	Herbert
Dance of Death	Saint-Saens
Overture to William Tell	Rossini

A rare but interesting bit of music on the lyceum stage was the lecture with incidental music, as seen in a flyer for Fr. MacCorry, a Catholic priest who began lyceum work in 1896. MacCorry's lecture, "The Story Beautiful," was a multimedia presentation on the life of Christ in which the lecture was accompanied by 100 illustrations and at least eight pieces of music:

Hallelujah Chorus (Messiah)	Handel
Fear Not, O Israel (Jeremiah VI)	Spicker
Praise Ye (Attila)	Verdi
Noel — O Holy Night	Adam
Les Rameaux	Faure
Marche Funebre	Chopin
Regina Coeli	Stearns
Recessional (Praise Ye the Father)	Gounod

One promotional brochure states that the music would be performed by local musicians and could be altered as needed. It appears Fr. MacCorry got excellent mileage out of "The Story Beautiful"; advertisements for the production span several years and at least three different lyceum management companies, while a trade publication from 1911 claims he performed it sixty six straight nights on a summer chautauqua circuit.

As the turn of the century approached, lecture-recitals become less frequent, and pure recitals more prevalent. By the late nineteenth century, a typical small town (large cities would often have more elaborate offerings) would strive to book a lyceum season, or "course," consisting of five events. Of these, only one would be a lecture, one would be a variety evening, one would be a dramatic performance, and two would be musical acts.[6] The course offered in Decatur, Illinois, while especially elaborate, offers a snapshot of available lyceum offerings. It is twice the size of a typical lyceum course, involving ten acts, including an arctic explorer, an impersonator, the "funniest man in America," a military lecturer, a caricaturist, a magician, and four musical acts:

Lyric Ladies Quartet of Chicago
Slayton Grand Concert Company
   Max Bendix (Concertmaster, Theodore Thomas Orchestra)
   Jenny Osborn, Soprano (based out of Chicago)

III. Musical Selection in Chautauqua

Mary Angell, piano [made many piano roll recordings, also out of Chicago]
Frank Ormsby, tenor
Original Swedish Quartet [billed as "finest in the world"]
Welsh Prize Singers

An important (and difficult) question to address is, what did these musical acts look (and, more importantly sound) like? While my research has uncovered very few programs from actual lyceum performances (it appears that, especially for lyceum courses run by commercial agencies, printed programs were not the norm), there are a great many sample programs included in promotional brochures for musical acts. A sample program from the Lyceum Grand Concert Company, under the management of the Central Lyceum Bureau of Chicago, lists the following pieces:

Part One
 "Repeat Once More" by Badia.
 Tarantella by Lizst [sic]
 "Sognai" (I Dreamt) by Schira
 Polonaise for Cello by David Popper
 "Prince Ivan's Song" by Frances Allitsen,

Part Two
 "It Was a Lover and His Lass"
 Romance by Rubenstein [sic]
 "Hark Hark the Lark" by Schubert. [Possibly this is the popular Liszt transcription.]
 "On the Shore" by Neiglinger [sic]
 "How Can I Leave Thee Here?"
 Chopin Nocturne [This was likely a cello transcription.]
 Danse Hollandaise by Emile Dunkler
 "Blow Blow Thou Winter Wind"
 "Somewhere," [likely by Charles Harris]
 "Days of Youth" from *La Favorita* (1840) by Donizetti

In this example we see a program consisting primarily of art music and parlor songs. Absent from the program are novelty songs, minstrel songs, whistling, or other less lofty works that populated the American stage in the late nineteenth century. It is important to note that even compared to its sister movement, the circuit chautauqua — and certainly compared to vaudeville and other competitors — the lyceum movement was relatively free of acts that could be considered mindless entertainment. This is a nod to the educational origins of the movement as well as a strategic move to be explored later in this book.

From surviving ephemera we have a good idea regarding the content of a lyceum musical performance; what is less clear is the quality of these offerings. One historian of the movement stated, "Undoubtedly many concert companies that have been paraded before the lyceum public have been mediocre, and some have been no better than amateurs."[7] This same author also questioned the ability of some of the stars brought in by lyceum bureaus: "The greatest star from opera is available to any town that can afford to pay enough money to secure her services. Some of these stars have been and are truly great. Others are upheld by superficial publicity and clever managerial tactics."[8] It bears mentioning that many musical celebrities of the day, including Ernestine Schumann-Heink and the Sousa band, were available to communities who could afford them. But these celebrities were unlikely to travel to the small towns where most lyceum courses were held. These smaller communities most often booked what would today be considered "B-list" musical acts, often acts created for and existing wholly within the American lyceum movement. Many of them had studied at schools, such as the Horner Institute (now the University of Missouri-Kansas City Conservatory), which trained performers strictly for the lyceum and circuit chautauqua stage. It is difficult to know how competent these groups were. As mentioned before, local newspapers had a vested interest in promoting the lyceum, and the vast majority of newspaper reviews of lyceum performances were laudatory. In the absence of unbiased reviews or good recordings, it is difficult to judge these groups.

The invocation of composers and institutions central to the art music canon was common in the lyceum movement, even when the link between these pillars of the art music world and the groups bearing their names is unclear (sometimes a group would bear the name of a famous composer without having one of his works listed in its repertoire). This was also common on the chautauqua circuits, and may have been an attempt to legitimize otherwise under-qualified art music performers in the eyes of the audience. A group billing itself as the Mozart Symphony Club of New York (thus associating itself with Mozart and urban high culture), claiming to perform "three centuries of popular music," did in fact play one movement of one Mozart symphony. It is difficult to imagine the first movement of Mozart's Symphony No. 41 performed by this group, since despite the use of "symphony" in their name, the Mozart Symphony Club of New York was in fact a string quartet who doubled on novelty instruments such as the double alpine horn. Another group called itself the "Schuberts," while admitting in their promotional flyers that none of the members bore the name Schubert and there was no music by Schubert in their program. The lyceum circuits also hosted several groups with implied (but nonexistent) connections to musical institutions such as the Metropolitan Opera and the Fisk Jubilee Singers.

Regardless of their quality, these groups were always touted as "high

III. Musical Selection in Chautauqua

class," and that perception is critical to understand music in the lyceum and broader chautauqua contexts. While the late nineteenth-century lyceum movement was overwhelmingly commercial, this fact was often hidden from the public, and local lyceums were promoted as if they were still the lyceums of old. A newspaper advertisement from Eau Claire, Wisconsin, trumpeted, "The aim of those managing this course is not to make money, but to give the people of Eau Claire as much high class entertainment for the coming winter as they possibly can for as little money as they can, and pay expenses." Community leaders were still urging the formation of societies to support the lyceum at the turn of the century. In 1895, for instance, the *Atlanta Constitution* devoted most of a column to the need for more lyceums in the South, complete with suggestions for creating lyceums in small communities.

Community support was key to the success of the lyceum movement, and to gain that support, the lyceum had to set itself apart from vaudeville shows, circuses, carnivals, medicine shows, and other traveling amusements crisscrossing America at the time. It should be noted that, by virtue of opposite schedules, the lyceum movement did not compete with the chautauqua movement, and in fact the two were closely allied. The primary distinguishing factor of the lyceum movement was its emphasis on education. And while there were many arguments within the lyceum community about the educational value of music, the placement of art music on the lyceum stage was touted as an important distinction between the lyceum and its competitors.

There is no doubt that the lyceum bureau managers felt they were providing something beyond entertainment through their inclusion of art music, and there is evidence to support this belief. James Redpath's biographer attributed the bulk of America's then-blossoming music education system to the influence of the lyceum, though that seems a bit of a stretch. Doubtless, though, thousands of Americans were exposed to art music for the first time through the lyceum. Reports claim, in fact, that the American premiere of Flotow's last opera, *L'Hombre*, was performed by the Redpath English Opera Company on the lyceum circuit with "scenery and elegant costumes, and a strict adherence to the original composition."[9]

While an objective analysis of the quality of music presented on the lyceum circuits is impossible to conduct after over a century, such an analysis would be largely pointless, as the lyceum musical performances carried a meaning to the audience beyond objective performance ability. Two quotes regarding the influence of the lyceum movement on public musical tastes in the late nineteenth century are especially germane to this discussion. The first is from the aforementioned biography of James Redpath:

> Truly the lyceum concert companies have been made by the people themselves, but, at the same time, these people have been influenced by such concert compa-

nies. Instead of long-haired, eccentric freaks, the people discovered that they were listening to men and women, more frequently boys and girls, who were exactly the same kind of folks that lived in their own town.... Many an old, hard-shelled, self-confessed independent who boasted of his provincialism, and tried to laugh out of countenance that which was not of his kind, began to discover he really enjoyed the kind of a musical program that the lyceum was offering, and concert companies shortly had the right of way in the selection of lyceum courses of entertainment.[10]

A quote from the *Two Rivers* (WI) *Chronicle* is especially relevant because it does not come from within the lyceum industry: "If anyone had said that a Two Rivers audience would sit for two hours and listen to solos, duets and quartets from Donizetti, Verdi, Grieg, Flotow and as many other composers, we would not have believed such an audience could have been found."

Music's second-class status within the lyceum movement was never questioned. Statements in trade publications about music's inferiority to the lecture were couched in language suggesting that the established hierarchy of lyceum acts was part of the natural order. Even the musicians involved in the early lyceum were reluctant to defend music's value to the movement. Nineteenth-century bias against music in the lyceum persisted well into the twentieth century, to the point that lyceum courses involving music (by this time, the vast majority of courses) were denigrated as entertainments no better than cheap traveling shows.[11]

While decision-makers within the lyceum movement at the turn of the century exerted much time and effort selecting lecturers and monitoring lecture content and reception, there is little evidence that such attention was paid to music on the lyceum platform. To the contrary, several key figures in the lyceum movement placed the burden of musical quality control on the audience. Edward Amherst Ott, writing in the *Lyceumite*, contended that "as long as a poorly selected course will be bought and paid for, it will be sold. The moral and financial responsibility rests with the buyers."[12] The lyceum movement's disregard for musical oversight and reliance on market-driven programming speaks to the commercial nature of the lyceum, and points to a key difference between the lyceum and its successor, circuit chautauqua. The chautauqua bureaus, although they were commercial enterprises, used moral and pedagogical, rather than strictly economic, criteria for selection and programming of musical acts. This was due not to a fundamental difference in mission between the circuit chautauqua and lyceum movements — both espoused moral and educational principles — but to the way music was viewed in each movement. The lyceum movement was initially openly hostile to music, and music never reached a point of equality with the lecture in the eyes of lyceum managers. Circuit chautauqua bureaus, whose task it was to craft an entire week of continuous, appropriate programming, worked to integrate music as a part of the broader mission of the movement, rather than as diversion from it.

The Chautauqua Literary and Scientific Circle

The formation of the Chautauqua Literary and Scientific Circle was announced by Bishop John Heyl Vincent, cofounder of the Chautauqua Institution, in 1878. It was designed to be a four-year home study course involving a series of required reading lists. Over 8400 people registered for the inaugural class of the CLSC, as it was usually called, and 1718 of those initial students graduated from the course in 1882.[13] CLSC participants formed reading circles of friends and neighbors, sometimes with a designated teacher. In his essay, "Chautauqua: A Popular University," John Heyl Vincent discussed the formation of these groups and listed several subcategories of CLSC reading groups, including a "Chautauqua Musical Reading Union."[14]

Readings for the CLSC consisted of books assigned in their entirety, supplemented by articles published in the *Chautauquan*, a journal that also carried articles of general interest not intended for the CLSC, as well as announcements and discussion regarding the Chautauqua Institution and some independent assemblies. It was not until 1932 that the first music-related book appeared on the CLSC reading list, a biography of Mozart by Marcia Davenport. The 1933 list included a music appreciation text, after which it would be ten years before the next music book assigned by the CLSC. Overall, from its inception in 1878 until 2012, the CLSC book list has included twenty music titles.

The *Chautauquan*, by contrast, included considerably more discussion of music. Volume 1, published in 1880 and 1881, included an article on the technique and merits of solfege singing, The first article on music history, entitled "Music in Early Times," was published in volume 3 (1882–83), which also included an article entitled "Music in the Christian Era" by the same author (Prof. E.R. Ayers). It should be noted that music articles appear in the required CLSC portions of the *Chautauquan* as well as the sections of the publication intended for a general audience. Later volumes include articles on practical musical topics pertinent to the chautauqua movement such as music education and choral singing, as well as discussions of specific works (operas are popular), time periods, genres, and composers.

Music in Independent Chautauquas

In the decade after its inception, the "Mother" Chautauqua in New York spawned scores of imitators across the country, primarily in the Midwest.

These assemblies, which came to be known as independent chautauquas, had no official relationship to the Chautauqua Institution, yet provided a chautauqua experience for thousands of Americans who could not travel to New York. It should be noted that while there was no official link to "Mother Chautauqua," several of the independent chautauquas hosted graduation ceremonies for the Chautauqua Literary and Scientific Circle, and program announcements for independent chautauquas appeared in the *Chautauquan* alongside announcements for events at the Chautauqua Institution. In this, the independent chautauqua movement was closer to the Chautauqua Institution than the commercial circuit chautauqua ever would be.

Though they would often share programming strategies and even personnel with commercial circuit chautauquas and lyceums (independent chautauqua assemblies often booked musical acts through commercial lyceum booking agencies), the *independence* of the independent chautauquas makes it impossible to discuss broad trends and conventions as is common regarding its commercial cousins. Independent assemblies ranged in length from three days to two weeks or more; the New Piasa Chautauqua in Illinois lasted twenty-two days and was held on a permanent assembly grounds (complete with privately owned cabins and a hotel) modeled after the Chautauqua Institution.

Independent chautauqua communities had the ability to incorporate local musicians into their programs, and many did. Community choruses, either preexisting or created for the purpose of the chautauqua, were a common attraction of independent chautauquas. Bands from nearby colleges frequently appeared, as did municipal bands. Local musicians also gave solo and chamber recitals at independent chautauquas, and it was common for a local pianist to serve as accompanist for several — or in some cases, all — musical performances on the program. This might also include religious services, which occurred much more frequently (sometimes daily) in independent chautauquas than in their commercial counterparts. Lincoln Chautauqua System, based in Illinois, suggested in a handbook for employees that local bands and orchestras could sometimes be secured to play at the chautauqua in exchange for season passes for the musicians "and their wives and sweethearts." The Lincoln bureau felt this arrangement was beneficial financially and also an important link between the itinerant chautauqua and the local community.

Independent chautauquas also differed from commercially booked assemblies in their ability to book musical acts for longer engagements. While circuit chautauquas almost never scheduled musical acts to play the same community for more than one day, independents frequently booked talent for extended engagements, emulating the residency model of the Chautauqua

Institution. The Florentine Musicians, discussed in chapter two, appeared in both circuit and independent chautauquas in the same season. Since it is very unlikely that the independent assembly audiences would have tolerated much repetition between concerts on consecutive days, it is safe to assume that the Florentine Musicians' repertoire must have included enough material to fill six concerts with very little redundancy, in order to accommodate typical independent chautauqua engagements of three days, with each day involving two performances. Given the youth and inexperience of many chautauqua musical acts, such depth of repertoire was likely not possible for all musical talent on the circuits.

Music in Circuit Chautauqua

Preceding American cultural movements—including the Chautauqua Institution, the lyceum movement, and the independent chautauqua movement of the late nineteenth century—would shape circuit chautauqua's attitude towards and relationship with music in the movement's early years. From the lyceum movement, circuit chautauqua would inherit a business model for effectively managing and promoting musical acts. From the independent assemblies, the circuit bureaus gained an appreciation for music as a legitimate companion to the lecture in a varied program. Finally, although it came largely filtered through the lens of the independent assemblies, circuit chautauqua inherited from the Chautauqua Institution an awareness of responsibility to the audience to provide a program that was educational and in keeping with turn-of-the-century progressive ideas of morality and culture.

While the circuit chautauqua movement's original concept of music may have been heavily influenced by preceding phenomena, as the movement matured it would establish a relationship with music unique to circuit chautauqua, largely influenced by forces within the circuit chautauqua sphere. This concept of music reflected a set of values and circumstances unique to the movement, and became clearly distinct from the values of previous movements as circuit chautauqua came to prominence in the 1920s.

As chautauqua's fortunes declined in the late 1920s and early 1930s, rhetoric about music focused more on economic factors and popularity; and concerns about educational value and "uplift" (previously a driving factor in selection of acts) were diminished. This evolution of musical philosophy among decision-makers resulted in a shift in musical programming away from art music and older popular forms, and towards a more relevant and exciting musical repertoire designed to attract crowds.

Sources of Music Performed in Chautauqua

In most situations, the musical sources used by the chautauqua movement were little different than those of other commercial musical ventures of the early twentieth century. There was no musical form unique to chautauqua, nor was the distribution of musical forms and genres within it vastly different from that of competing movements of the era. Since there was very little chautauqua-specific music on the platform, and no musical attributes connecting the works performed by musical acts, the purpose of the musical analyses presented in this chapter is not to define or discuss one genre of "chautauqua music," but rather to show the breadth of the chautauqua musical repertoire.

Chautauqua musical acts performed from commercially published scores, from manuscripts, and from published songbooks. Some performers composed or arranged music specifically for their acts, while others employed composers or arrangers for this task or relied on composers and arrangers employed by chautauqua bureaus and management firms. Chautauqua's musical repertoire also included music created specifically for use in the chautauqua movement. This included music referring to the chautauqua movement, music composed for use in chautauqua religious services, and music distributed to performers for performance during chautauqua programs. This last category includes several songbooks.

Several repositories of chautauqua documents contain songbooks. These books were often used for specific events involving community singing, a practice held over from the Chautauqua Institution. They were frequently used for brief religious services incorporated into chautauqua programs (usually a vespers service on Sunday evening), although at least one bureau, Ellison-White, seems to have incorporated nonreligious community singing events into some programs.

The vespers service performed most often in circuit and independent chautauquas was the service compiled for the Chautauqua Institution or an adaptation thereof. In a rare gesture of cooperation between the Chautauqua Institution and its offspring, the editors of the *Chautauqua Hymnal and Liturgy* prepared for use at the Chautauqua Institution stated on the copyright page that the hymnal was compiled "in the hope that it would be generally used by chautauqua assemblies."[15] The *Chautauqua Hymnal and Liturgy* was in fact widely used by both independent assemblies and circuit chautauqua bureaus, as evidenced by its presence in the records of several organizations. The hymnal contains eighty-eight hymns in four-part arrangement. As in many Protestant hymnals, hymns in the *Chautauqua Hymnal and Liturgy* appear to be grouped informally by function in the liturgy, though the text

III. Musical Selection in Chautauqua

of the liturgy itself is not provided in the congregation's hymnals. Hymns are also identified by tune and indexed by first line, a common practice in hymnals of the time. The hymnal differs very little from a typical Protestant one of the era, and neither the texts nor the music appear to have been altered for use by the Chautauqua Institution in the way that was common for the Salvation Army and other groups of the time. The first eight hymns in the collection are intended for a Sunday evening service and were most likely the ones used by the circuit chautauqua bureaus for circuit performance, as Sunday morning services were not common in circuit chautauqua.

The Redpath-Vawter bureau published a short vespers service complete with songs for use on its circuits. The three religious songs used in the service ("Day Is Dying in the West," "Jesus, Savior, Pilot Me," and "Abide with Me") were published with both text and music, while the two patriotic songs ("The Star Spangled Banner" and "America") were published as text only. The provided music is arranged in conventional four-part harmony (SATB), and the texts do not seem to have been altered for use in circuit chautauqua.

The Ellison-White bureau published its own song sheet for community singing. The *Ellison-White Community Song Sheet* contained twenty-one popular and patriotic songs which appear to have been published as texts only. The song sheet—in reality an eight-page booklet—credits Walter Jenkins as director and Ruby Lloyd as accompanist, implying that piano accompaniment was available, although the piano version does not seem to have survived. The song sheet carries these instructions: "Save this booklet for use in the evening." The only known surviving copy of the *Ellison-White Community Song Sheet* belonged to chautauqua musician Katharine La Sheck, indicating that these evening community singings may have been led by musicians employed by the bureaus, rather than by local musical leaders as was common in independent chautauquas.

Most of the musical collections—in fact most of the sheet music in general—in the collections of the circuit chautauqua bureaus were not published by the bureaus or specifically for circuit chautauqua. Chautauqua bureaus often used song books from other institutions as well as commercially available collections. The records of the Redpath bureau contain the *West Virginia Institute Program and Songbook* published by the West Virginia Department of Schools for use in public school assemblies. The records also contain the collection *18 Songs for Community Singing*, a commercially available song book published by C.C. Birchard and Company. The songs are popular and patriotic in nature and are arranged for four voices (SATB) and piano. *Patriotic Songs of America and the Allies*, a commercial publication of twenty-four national airs in three-voice arrangement (SAB) with piano, is also housed in the Redpath archives.

Song books and part books for various musical ensembles are found frequently in the collections of individual chautauqua musicians. This indicates that it was common for musical acts to use music from commercially published collections. There is no indication, however, that these song books were distributed by the bureaus. On the contrary, similar ensembles employed by the same bureau most often took their repertoire from entirely different sources, with no more overlap than would be expected due to the influence of popular taste. While bureaus did occasionally distribute vocal music for events involving audience participation (Ellison-White's song sheet and Redpath-Vawter's vespers service are two such collections), there is no reason to believe that bureaus either published or distributed collections intended for performance by professional musical acts. Individual musical acts had considerable freedom to select their own music.

Many chautauqua musical acts performed music either composed or arranged specifically for the group, often by a group member or someone affiliated with the group. An advertisement for the Dunbar Company read, "Most of their music is in manuscript, not published, much of which is composed or arranged by members of the company."[16] Such an advertisement spoke to both the originality of the music performed, assuring audiences of fresh material, and to the musical abilities of the performers. The latter was especially important for groups such as the Dunbar Company, which were often composed of young musicians unknown outside of the chautauqua movement.

For some musical acts, skepticism regarding musical competence was certainly valid. Many groups, especially the vocal quartets, employed performers with little musical training or performing experience. To combat this lack of experience and musical knowledge, chautauqua acts (or their bureaus) sometimes hired musical directors. These musical directors would select, arrange, and compose music for the group, and would sometimes act as vocal coaches as well. It was not uncommon for one musical director to work with several groups employed by the same bureau or managed by the same agent. The College Girls, a popular circuit chautauqua act, employed George Madden and Clarence Pearsall (successively) as musical director. When members of the College Girls left to form a new quartet, the Marigolds, they chose not to employ a musical director. This choice coincided with a shift away from art music and towards popular, commercially published vocal quartets, possibly because the members of the Marigolds were not comfortable selecting or arranging art music.[17]

While it does not seem to have been the norm, it was not entirely unheard of for chautauqua bureaus to employ staff arrangers or composers. Thurlow Liuerance and Howard Hanson both worked as staff composers for Redpath-

III. Musical Selection in Chautauqua

Cover of "On Old Chautauqua Lake" (Library of Congress, Music Division).

Horner. Charles Horner took an extraordinary interest in the musical side of his operation, as evidenced by his employment of staff composers and by his operation of a training school for chautauqua musicians. There is no record of another bureau employing a staff composer, but many bureaus employed musical directors or music managers to select and manage musical acts.

Chautauqua musical acts routinely used commercially published sheet music. Much of this repertoire was purchased by musical acts or bureaus through retail outlets. Some publishers targeted platform performers, advertising in chautauqua trade publications and creating divisions to supply music to chautauqua acts. Commercial publishers also printed music specifically for some bureaus.

The Lyceum Magazine regularly featured a "Music Reviews" column by Clay Smith, in which the merits of new music for the chautauqua platform and lyceum stage were discussed. It appears most of the music was sent to the magazine for this purpose. Smith seems to have been honest in his reviews, noting both strengths and weakness. For instance, Misha Elman's arrangement of the Grieg "Notturno" was judged "too difficult for use by any but virtuoso players. Very high harmonics, not responding well."[18] The reviews make references to standard platform musical fare, in some situations recommending a song to replace a similar tired standard.

While most chautauqua music did not specifically reference the chautauqua movement, several bureaus did incorporate music composed for or mentioning the Chautauqua Institution. A few bureaus had songs and marches composed specifically for the bureau, citing the bureau by name. The scarcity of bureau-referencing music in collections, even among those bureaus that employed full-time composers, may seem conspicuous. This could be due, however, to the reluctance of some communities to acknowledge the commercial production of their local chautauqua.

The late nineteenth century saw the publication of several pieces of music referencing chautauqua. Some of these works clearly refer to the Chautauqua Institution, some to the lake itself, and others are vague enough to apply to either the institution or an independent assembly. Several pieces referencing chautauqua have been located in archives outside of the movement, and not in the records of any chautauqua performer or bureau. Thus it is possible that they were not intended to be performed as part of a chautauqua, although it is impossible to state with authority that they never were.

"Memories of Chautauqua" was composed by J.G. Dailey and published by John Church & Co. in 1885. From the publication date, it seems very likely that the song refers to the Chautauqua Institution, rather than to an independent assembly (it could not possibly refer to a circuit). The text, however, is vague enough that it could invoke in the listener memories of almost any chautauqua experience. Similarly, "On Old Chautauqua Lake," composed by W. Howard Doane and published in 1883, focuses on friendships formed at Chautauqua, rather than specific attributes of the Chautauqua Institution. Although there is no indication of the piece being used by any chautauqua assembly, its form would have worked well on the chautauqua platform. It was written to be performed as a vocal solo or duet, with an SATB chorus singing the refrains. This would make it especially suited for independent chautauquas, in which a community chorus was often present and audience sing-alongs were not unheard of.

Some circuit chautauqua bureaus did incorporate bureau-branded music, presumably for use on circuits in which each chautauqua was openly acknowledged to be commercial. "The Coit-Alber Chautauqua March Two-Step" was composed and published in 1916 by Frank Barone of Boston. The title is a reference to the Coit-Alber Chautauqua Bureau, a major bureau that supplied assemblies to over 150 communities in Pennsylvania, Indiana, Ohio, Michigan, New York, West Virginia, and Kentucky. The labeling of the piece as both a march and a two-step was common for similar pieces of the early twentieth century; many well-known marches of the era were published as both marches and two-steps. The extant copy of "The Coit-Alber Chautauqua March Two-Step" was published in piano score. It is highly likely, however, that the work was also published in band or orchestra form, since solo piano was rare on the chautauqua circuits.[19]

An interesting corollary to "The Coit-Alber Chautauqua March Two-Step" is the "Chautauqua Lake Waltz" from 1876. Also published for solo piano, it seems likely that the "Chautauqua Lake Waltz" was in fact intended to be played on the piano. It is also rather unlikely, due to its relative simplicity and lack of connection (other than the title) to the chautauqua movement, that this piece was performed frequently in chautauquas. Rather, it was most likely intended for home performance. The existence of another piano solo, "On the Chautauqua Lake," casts further doubt on a possible connection between these solo piano pieces and the chautauqua movement. "On the Chautauqua Lake" was published in 1871, three years before the founding of the Chautauqua Institution.

The records of the Redpath bureau contain dozens of commercially published musical scores in popular, art music, and sacred genres, including the following works:

Popular

"Aggravatin' Papa"
"The World Is Waiting for the Sunrise"
"American Violet"
"Arcady"
"After the Storm"
"Coal Black Mammy"

Art

"Triumphal March" from *Aida*
"Gypsy Love Song" from *The Fortune Teller* (Herbert)
"The Radiance in Your Eyes" (cornet solo)

Sacred

"Hallelujah Chorus" from *Messiah*
Selections from *Messe Sollennelle* (Gounod)
"Ave Maria" (Bach-Gounod)

The collection also contains a compilation of religious musical works apparently intended to constitute a complete performance. It began with *Magnificat No. 2* by American composer and organist Dudley Buck for four voices (SATB) and organ. The organ introduction is marked through, indicating that in performance the piece would begin with the vocal entrances in the fourth measure. Measures thirteen through nineteen are omitted. After the twenty-eighth measure, a piece of manuscript paper is inserted with "Dan's Bass Recital" written at the top and the first seven measures of the hymn "O Come All Ye Faithful," apparently cut from a hymnal, glued to the bottom, followed by the word "text." The recto page of the inserted manuscript paper begins with a handwritten soprano solo, "See Now the Dusk Is Falling," ending with three unison repetitions of the phrase "Ave Maria." This handwritten closing material may have been adapted from the 1912 edition of the Boosey & Company publication *Mezzo-Soprano Songs*, in which "See Now the Dusk Is Falling" was followed by Joachim Raff's setting of the Ave Maria.

Such compilations and heavily altered versions of large musical works were not uncommon in chautauqua. The archives of the Redpath bureau contain several other large works modified in a similar manner. One such work is John Stainer's oratorio *The Crucifixion*, into which the hymns "When Wilt Thou Save the People?" (Josiah Booth, 1888) and "Just As I Am" (William Bradbury, 1849) were inserted. These extensive alterations and additions seem to have been most prevalent in the religious music housed in the Redpath collection. Little consideration seems to have been given to theological integrity or textual cohesiveness, as the inserted texts seem unrelated to the primary work, and in several cases the movements of larger works seem to have been rearranged in performance. Although it is not discussed in the trade publications or in extant bureau documents, it seems probable that these modifications were done in order to make these relatively unfamiliar musical works more palatable to rural audiences.

III. Musical Selection in Chautauqua 79

Many popular compositions can be found in the surviving records of the major chautauqua bureaus. While the published works usually supply copyright information, and thus publication dates, copyright dates alone are not sufficient to place these compositions on a timeline of chautauqua performance. While they do indicate the earliest possible year a work could have been performed on the circuits, the bureaus' proclivity for programming older popular music makes the latest possible date of performance impossible to garner from publication information. Detailed programs from chautauqua musical programs are exceedingly rare. Chautauqua performers did not, as a rule, supply printed programs for audience consumption, and bureaus did not normally keep repertoire lists. Thus, much of the chronology of chautauqua musical selection is imprecise. Nevertheless, analysis of broad programming trends indicates that most of the popular music found in bureau collections was most likely performed in the later years of the movement. Much of this later popular repertoire consisted of dance-based works for modified dance orchestra, with or without vocals. It should be noted that while much of the later musical repertoire consisted of dances, there is no indication that dancing ever occurred as part of a chautauqua event, and it is unlikely that the moral climate of chautauqua permitted it.

The archives of the Redpath bureau contain a copy of "You Gave Me Your Heart," composed by Ted Snyder and orchestrated by Arthur Lange. This score was a complimentary copy, furnished by the Lyceum, Chautauqua, and Home Talent Department of the publisher, Waterson, Berlin and Snyder Company of New York and Chicago. The score included a letter from Arthur Lange, dated October 1922, explaining tempo markings, interpretation, and instrumentation. Lange noted that the piece has a "Spanish atmosphere," but he feared an actual tango would prove unpopular with audiences unaccustomed to the tango. Lange stressed the piece's flexible instrumentation. For instance, he provided saxophone parts in five different keys to accommodate the multiple combinations of saxophones used by bands in the early twentieth century. The published copy included a piano score, parts for two violins, viola, cello, bass, flute, clarinet, three alto saxophones, C melody saxophone, tenor saxophone, two trumpets, trombone, drums, timpani, and tenor banjo.

Many of the popular musical numbers housed in the Redpath records dealt with exotic subjects, most often in a superficial manner. Most of the pieces with titles invoking the exotic are in fact common American dance forms for standard dance band or orchestra. It should be noted that there is no evidence of such pieces being performed by exotic acts—those specializing in music from a particular foreign culture—but rather they seem to have been performed solely by popular acts. Examples of this genre include "Dreams of India" (fox trot), "Spain" (tango fox trot), and "Goodbye Shanghai" (Chinese fox trot). "Goodbye Shanghai" was composed by Joseph Meyer with lyrics by Howard Johnson. It was scored for three voices, strings, flute, clarinet, two cornets, two horns in F, trombone, drums, and piano. It is composed in contrasting verse-chorus form, with the verses. The first two verses are musically identical and in the key of G, while the chorus and last verse are in C. The text reads as follows:

Verse:
> Lonesome little love-sick Chinaman,
> Packing up his grip, ready for a trip
> on a great big ship.
> How he hates to leave his native land,
> after all these years. Time for sailing nears.
> He sings through his tears:

Chorus:
> Goodbye, Shanghai, across the sea I've got to fly to fair America.
> Oh my, Shanghai, sweet China girl waits there that's why a pig tail must sail and go to her.
> She wrote a note to me, said that we would
> start a tea room, Chop Suey room,
> later build a home with one two three room.
> Just sigh, if I don't get there soon I'll die.
> Goodbye, Shanghai, goodbye.

Verse:
> As the great big liner leaves the pier,
> steaming out to sea,
> there stands young Chinee, lonesome lad is he.
> Waving to the shores that disappear,
> you can hear him say, "Tho' I'm far away,
> in my heart you stay."

Chorus:
> If you hit the pipe, law catch you quick.
> Smokee opium no more.
> 'Merican police man swing big stick,
> hop head drop dead.
> Wear no more kimono made of silk,
> wear no more pagoda hats.
> Dress up like a dude in pitch black suit,
> wear a little cane and spats.

III. Musical Selection in Chautauqua

"Goodbye Shanghai" was one of many Chinese-themed popular pieces composed in the 1910s and 1920s. It is similar, both musically and textually, to compositions such as "Chinatown, Our Chinatown," "Wing Lee's Rag-Time Clock," and many other "Oriental" pieces composed for film, Broadway, and sheet music publication. The vocal music for "Good-bye Shanghai" relies heavily on "Oriental" clichés, involving parallel fourths and the rhythm Garrett dubs the "Asia trope."[20] This is the dominant rhythmic figure of "Goodbye Shanghai, serving as the basis for the introduction and the verses. The orchestral accompaniment is rhythmically simple and incorporates considerable chromaticism, the former being a characteristic of dance band arrangements of the era and the latter a common tool of composers writing popular music in an Orientalist vein.

The text of "Goodbye, Shanghai" incorporates several stereotypical depictions of Chinese culture and of the relationship between Chinese-Americans and broader American society. The protagonist is referred to synecdochically as "a pig tail." Reducing the Chinese man to his pigtail was a dehumanizing tactic common in Chinese-themed American popular compositions of the time.[21] The final verse of "Goodbye, Shanghai" abandons the narrative of the protagonist and his love, instead offering instructions to new Chinese immigrants. The immigrant (possibly the protagonist) is warned to "smoke opium no more." Chinese culture and opium were often linked in songs of the early twentieth century, although rarely this explicitly.[22] Finally, the immigrant is urged to abandon the kimono (conflation of Chinese and Japanese culture was also very common in American popular culture at this time) and pagoda hat, dressing instead in American fashions.

"Goodbye, Shanghai" represents a vein of popular music rarely seen in circuit chautauqua until the late 1920s. Its lyrics are at odds with the movement's ideals concerning racial and economic equality.[23] It was also a relatively new composition (copyright 1921) by the standards of popular music on the chautauqua circuits. The fact that a piece of recent popular music of questionable moral or educational value was included in the Redpath bureau's repertoire speaks to the increased emphasis on entertainment in the late 1920s and early 1930s, as circuit chautauqua struggled to compete with traveling shows and other musical venues whose sole or primary concern was entertainment.

Music publishers seized on the market for sheet music created by the circuit movement. Not only did it provide many performer/consumers with published music, but the nature of circuit chautauqua as a musical venue and its focus on rural audiences also meant that through circuit chautauqua, publishers could reach a broader audience. Several publishing companies created divisions specializing in chautauqua music. In addition to providing sheet music to chautauqua performers, these divisions also provided programming consultants, custom arrangements, and even in-house accompanists and coaches to help performers select and learn purchased music.

M. Witmark and Sons, a leading publisher of popular and stage music throughout the late nineteenth and early twentieth centuries, entered into the chautauqua business in 1915 by establishing "Department C," a comprehensive publishing and consultation services catering to lyceum and chautauqua performers. Witmark offered those performers engaged by lyceum or chautauqua bureaus a selection of sample works from its catalog gratis, including:

"In Pillowtown"	Elliot
"If"	Vanderpool
"Who Knows?"	Ball
"Spring's a Loveable Lady"	Elliot
"Beyond the Sunset"	Tours
"Evening Brings Rest and You"	Bishop
"There's a Long, Long Trail"	Elliott
"Too-Ra-Loo-Ra-Loo-Ral, That's an Irish Lullaby"	Shannon

Witmark offered to customize packages for any voice or combination of instruments, and invited musicians to visit the Witmark offices in New York and Chicago to work with musical consultants and staff accompanists.

"There's a Long, Long Trail" was labeled "the song of melody that captured the chautauquas." Witmark ran full-page advertisements in lyceum and chautauqua trade publications offering "There's a Long, Long Trail" to "any recognized artist." [24] He required the musician to send a business card stating bureau affiliation or a program from a lyceum or chautauqua performance, and would then send the "recognized artist" an arrangement of "There's a Long, Long Trail" for any solo voice with piano, several vocal duet combinations, vocal solo with band, vocal quartets (male, female and mixed voices) orchestra in the key of F, G, Ab, Bb, or C, cornet solo with orchestra or band, or trombone solo with orchestra or band in published form. The publisher also offered an arrangement for vocal trio, brass quartet, or saxophone quartet in manuscript form. Furthermore, Witmark offered custom arrangements of "There's a Long, Long Trail" for any ensemble at the request of a recognized chautauqua or lyceum musical act. Witmark's heavy promotion of a song seen as a chautauqua favorite, and the company's willingness to provide (and advertise) free sheet music to chautauqua performers, indicated that circuit chautauqua was viewed as an effective means of advertising sheet music. Circuit chautauqua programs, as a general rule, did not include the printed advertisements common to musical programs of the time (though advertising was commonly seen in independent chautauqua programs). It is not known whether it was common (or permitted) for performers or platform superintendents to announce the commercial availability of a performed arrangement.

It appears there was some controversy surrounding the practice of performers accepting payment in exchange for programming music that publishing houses wished to promote. This practice had been in existence long before the chautauqua movement and was common among traveling musicians in the years before radio became the primary disseminator of new music. In the chautauqua and lyceum fields, however, it seems the overriding sentiment was disdain for the blatant commercialism of the practice and the apparent disregard for education and uplift, the supposed pillars of chautauqua programming.

A 1920 column in *The Lyceum Magazine* argued, "Every number rendered on a lyceum or chautauqua platform should be of such merit and of such distinctiveness, should fill such an important niche in the contour of the program, that its place could not be easily filled by any other number.... The musician who receives remuneration for the including of any special number in the program is not possessed of the vision which entitles him to remain in this work."[25]

The September 1914 issue of *The Lyceum Magazine* included the soprano solo with piano "If I Knew You and You Knew Me" by James MacDermid. The song includes no explanatory note, and does not appear to be an advertisement for a publisher. In fact, no publisher is listed, although a British copyright is listed. It is unclear why this particular song should have been published in *The Lyceum Magazine,* as it does not appear to have held any special significance to the lyceum or chautauqua movements, nor was it unusually popular on the circuits.

Attitudes About Music

As discussed previously, attitudes within the chautauqua movement proper concerning music were generally more positive than those within the lyceum movement. Circuit and independent chautauquas involved music heavily from their inception, and as such did not suffer the difficulties of integrating music into an established, lecture-based format as did the lyceum. Furthermore, chautauqua presented itself as a cultural outlet as well as an educational movement. This emphasis on culture, which was inherited from the Chautauqua Institution and its descendants and not present in the lyceum movement, made music an essential part of chautauqua's identity. Chautauqua needed music — good music — to distinguish itself from competing traveling shows and to solidify its relationship with the communities it relied on for financial support.

Not only were chautauqua decision-makers more supportive of music than their lyceum counterparts, they were also more invested in presenting an appropriate musical product. The major chautauqua bureaus, especially, took great interest in the musical side of their programs, carefully screening prospective musical acts and debating various musical issues as they related to the circuit chautauqua movement. These debates, which are documented in trade publications and in the correspondence of chautauqua bureau managers, center around discussions of which types of music were appropriate for the platform, and what the purpose of music should be in the chautauqua context.

Those within the movement seem to have seen a great difference between art and popular music. Trade publications and inter-bureau communications clamor for more or less popular or classical music, with little acknowledgement of the spectrum of music between these labels. As with many aspects of the circuit chautauqua movement, the connotations of a particular musical genre and the audience's perception of the music and musicians were often as important as the reality of the music programmed. For this reason, performers and their managers were reluctant to let published programs speak for themselves, instead often choosing to explicitly label musical acts. Art music acts were often advertised as "real" or "authentic classic music" with the performer's musical pedigree clearly stated. Popular acts were often advertised as "fun" or "diversions."

While this dichotomy between art and popular music was at the forefront of many discussions regarding music in chautauqua, the reality of chautauqua programming was more nuanced. Many of the movement's musical staples, especially the vocal/instrumental quartets and small orchestras, performed a repertoire consisting primarily of light classical and older popular music. Ralph Dunbar, an influential chautauqua performer and impresario, emphasized his ability to provide music between the contested extremes of popular and "classic" music in his advertisements. An advertisement for one of his namesake ensembles stated, "Ralph Dunbar is neither a long-haired 'fad,' who pretends to abhor everything but Beethoven and Brahms, nor a fiddler of tunes."[26] Dunbar and his many successful chautauqua musical acts are important to remember when considering the selection of music for chautauqua performance, as Dunbar's success speaks to a reality that was rarely acknowledged in the decades of debate surrounding popular versus art music on the circuits.

Others within the chautauqua movement railed against the idea of chautauqua managers as arbiters of musical value. Henry Roney, a longtime pro-

III. Musical Selection in Chautauqua

ducer of chautauqua musical acts (many labeled "Roney's Boys"), wrote the following:

> What is "classical" music, and what is "popular?" Where draw the line? Who decides? You and I and Professor Stick-de-houtz, and Madame Parley Voux Tiddledewinks may get together and vote ourselves the heavenly elite and final adjudicators on all questions of musical merit and standards. In ponderous theses we can show why a fugue differs scientifically from a funnel, and explain how counterpoint and counterpane happen to be two differentiated breeds of cats. And because we have brought on gray hairs and amnesia digging into the absurdities and monstrosities of diminish sevenths and concealed fifths, we resolve ourselves into a "St. Cecilia's Society of the Holy Anointed" (limited), proclaim our taste to be the true and only one, and sit down and calmly await our crowns.[27]

It is interesting that Roney invokes the St. Cecilia Society. This group, formed in Charleston, South Carolina in 1766, was in fact an influential early arbiter of America's musical taste. It seems likely that Roney was reacting negatively to the St. Cecilia Society as it existed during his lifetime, by which time it functioned more as an exclusive social club than a musical society.

Arguments over the purpose of music in chautauqua were directly linked to arguments concerning the type of music appropriate for the platform. Those who felt music's purpose was to elevate the audience's tastes or to provide some educational or moral benefit argued that art music was the preferred genre for chautauqua. Those in the industry who were more concerned with financial viability expressed concerns that too much art music would hurt attendance, and that popular music served a purpose by attracting a broader audience to the chautauqua. Finally, the more pragmatic among bureau officials worried that many chautauqua musical acts simply did not possess the level of musical proficiency required to perform high-quality art music, and thus argued primarily for music that fit the abilities of the performers the bureaus were able to hire.

Pianist Luella Keller, writing in *Lyceum*, spoke to chautauqua committees directly: "Committeeman, the day for shying at classical music is passing. If you continue to put all entertainment on your course and put on no music of high appeal, you are not doing your duty to your community." Keller argued her position by pointing to the success of the Century Opera Company of New York, which offered operas in both English and the original language, targeted to audiences unfamiliar with opera.[28]

B.C. Boer, a platform superintendent, argued that it was because of music's obligation to elevate the popular taste that overly technical art music should be avoided. In his article, "Keep Unpopular Music Off Popular Programs," he declared "not only that the musical programs should be varied so as to relieve the audiences part of the time from 'classical agony,' but that a great percentage of the classical music has no proper place upon the chautauqua or lyceum platform at all." Boer was not alone in objecting to much of the art music on the platform. His rationale, however, was unusual. He went on to state, "The great object of the [music] profession now, as I can see it from a layman's point of view, is to arouse and to stir up in the Great Depraved, by the use of music, those very better and more noble emotions to which the aforementioned Great Depraved finds itself unable to give vent in that particular manner. That this very thing can be and often is accomplished cannot be gainsaid." While admitting that music could and did accomplish this goal, Boer felt that classical performers tended to be self-absorbed, performing music they found challenging with little or no regard to audience interest. He continued: "With that, then, as the great object of the profession of music, I am ready to assert that the musician who stands up before an audience of plain human beings and gives a demonstration of pure technique has utterly confused the means with the end and is not true to his profession."[29]

A.A. Thornburg, a musician with the Castle Square Entertainers, argued that the typical lyceum or chautauqua audience lacked the musical education to appreciate a lengthy program of classical music, and that such programs should be avoided. In an article in the *Lyceumite and Talent*, he stated that only "about two percent" of the population of a small town has a musical education, and that "we may talk all we want about uplifting the people to a higher musical level; it will never be done by putting on long concerts of Beethoven, Myerbeer [sic], Wagner, Verdi, Chopin, etc., but by starting children to studying music." Thornburg advocated the inclusion of some art music into a program, but did not believe small-town audiences possessed the musical sophistication to enjoy an entirely classical program. He wrote, "There is no audience, no matter how unmusical, but what will appreciate a certain amount of the best music, yet is a mistake to give an audience a two hour program of classical music, unless the audience is a select musical audience. Where will you get a select musical audience in a small town? The population is too small."[30]

Frank Morgan believed that art music was beyond the understanding of the lyceum or chautauqua audience: "I am as anxious as anyone to hasten the day when high-class music will be appreciated by the masses, but it is useless to try to elevate people musically if we remain on a musical platform so high above them that we cannot reach them." Morgan did not believe the performers' ability level was at issue, stating, "I still insist that one's success depends more (mark the exact words), more upon what is sung, played or read, than how one does it." He combines his two principal arguments—that art music is over the audience's heads and that the performers' ability is largely irrelevant — by stating that "a large majority of the most distinct successes is by companies of the popular class, and even by those with comparatively uncultivated voices."[31]

The May 1916 edition of *Lyceumite and Talent* featured a transcript of a roundtable discussion of chautauqua committee members from across the United States. In a section entitled "Art and the Musician," an unnamed committee member stated, "Our people always say they want something popular; but we find that the best music, played by high grade artists, is the most popular. When we engage a concert company of players who are not famous and not strong as individual performers, we arrange in advance for a program that is not above the capacity of the players, and when they do medium class music very well the people like it; but high grade music played by people who are not capable of comprehending it becomes a punishment alike to the critics and to the unmusical listeners, so we have this as our rule — high grade music only by high grade players; middle music by people of lesser experience; and low class music never."[32] The committee member expressed an unusual awareness of and sensitivity to the ability of the chautauqua performers available.

While musical selections within individual chautauqua performances were generally chosen by the performers, it seems that bureaus occasionally felt compelled to intervene in order to avoid stagnation in programming or over-repetition of favorite songs. Clay Smith once devoted his regular column in *Lyceum* to the topic of musical diversity on the platform. Smith asserted that several years previously, chautauqua bureaus had been forced to ban several over-performed works from the chautauqua stage, including "Silver Threads Among the Gold." He also mentions a "double ironclad ban on the dear old threadbare 'Sextette' [from *Lucia di Lammermoor*]." While it is unclear exactly which bureaus enacted such bans or how strongly they were enforced, bureaus were likely justified in their concern. The sextette from *Lucia*, specifically, is mentioned so often in chautauqua literature that the casual observer might wonder if the piece was connected to the movement in some mysterious way. A Boulder, Colorado, manager was purported to have warned performers, "We have only one request to make of you. Desist from using the 'sextette.' We have all been Lucia-ed to death."[33]

Critical Response to Music

Analysis of critical response to circuit and independent chautauqua musical performance reveals a striking difference between local critiques of individual acts and evaluations of circuit chautauqua music as a whole written for national publications. Local reviews were generally vague and avoided harsh criticism, while evaluations of the broader state of circuit chautauqua music — and of the movement as a whole — were often much more critical. It is tempting to dismiss this disparity simply as a lack of musical education on the part of the local critics, to believe that these reporters were unable to appreciate a superior performance or recognize musical inferiority. This assumption, however, ignores a complex set of circumstances surrounding the critics, both on a local and national level.

Local newspapers exerted great influence on small-town culture in early twentieth-century America. A negative review in a respected local newspaper could be disastrous for any recurring event. Circuit chautauqua was not affected as directly by this influence as were traveling plays or carnivals, since the chautauqua itself was guaranteed not to lose money. Of course, the financial loss from an unsuccessful chautauqua was shouldered by the community guarantors, who might refuse to guarantee the chautauqua for the next year. In this way, local newspaper coverage could affect the likelihood that the chautauqua would return.

Chautauquas were often considered status symbols for rural communities. The ability to hold a chautauqua showed the community was solvent enough to make the guarantee, and that its citizens were educated enough to recognize the need for the chautauqua as a cultural opportunity. Furthermore, neighboring communities competed to host the best possible assembly. As discussed previously, there was considerable variance between chautauqua bureaus in length, quality, and cost of supplied programs. Communities that could afford a more well-known chautauqua than those hosted by neighboring towns would often highlight this fact in advertising leading up to the event.

In areas where several communities would host chautauquas in close proximity, it was common to see the chautauqua advertised by both the community name and the name of the bureau (for instance, "come to the Cedar Rapids Redpath Chautauqua"), while this type of advertisement is less common in areas with fewer competing chautauquas. In light of this relationship between the chautauqua and the community's image, the local newspapers' reluctance to speak ill of the chautauqua is not surprising.

Reviews in local newspapers tended to focus on headlining musical acts, and the reviews often featured lengthy discussions of performers' personalities, biographies, and nonmusical attributes such as costumes and appearance. A local review of the Kaffir Boys made no specific musical observations, noting only, "The program rendered by the African Boys delighted all. It was exceedingly unique in its nature." The remainder of the review discussed the weapons displayed on stage, the boys' appearance, and their individual personalities.[34] One local review reads more like an advertisement, and may have been derived from one. A reporter for the *Thomson* (IL) *Review* wrote:

III. Musical Selection in Chautauqua 89

The Music Box Girls not only is a fun-loving group of entertainers but includes brilliant musical artists capable of doing justice to the best works of the masters. One of the specialties of the company is the adaptation of great compositions to modern tastes. The Music Box Girls are carrying on the splendid chautauqua tradition of bringing the great musical compositions to all the country and presenting them so that they can be understood and enjoyed by everyone. During the last quarter of a century, other agencies have been helping in the crusade for making good music popular. The great increase in musical knowledge through use of graphophone [a recording/playback device that used wax cylinders as the recording medium; the author appears to have used "graphophone" as a generic term for devices capable of reproducing sound] and radio, attendance at concerts and study at universities has given a field for organizations which can interpret in an artistic way the most appealing music of classic works and the most worthwhile of popular present day productions.[35]

One of the more detailed, while still self-consciously positive, reviews of a chautauqua musical performance was written in the *Coshocton Weekly Times* of Coshocton, Ohio, by reporter S.W. Sibley. Sibley's review of the Wesleyan Singers discusses multiple performances given by the act at the local chautauqua. He remarked that overall "the quartet is well balanced and each voice is particularly adapted to the part he sings." Sibley noted, "[P]erhaps the first tenor's tone had a slightly uncouth and strained effect and made suspect the so-called falsetto in the high tones, if not a decided thinness of tone. [This] may have been due to the fatigue of travel or some off-day condition, for he got bravely over it, and a more magnificent first tenor is seldom heard." Sibley's rush to excuse the tenor's flaws is striking, and such mitigation returns later in the review in a discussion of the baritone's performance. Sibley writes, "The first bass is characteristically baritone. A certain velvety quality of voice, while it has its charm, slightly mars the tone." Sibley's choice of "velvety" to describe a timbre he clearly viewed as undesirable seems intentionally muddled.

Sibley's description of a quartet labeled "Wesleyan," with a struggling baritone, is strikingly similar to Plotts' account of his entry into chautauqua (as discussed in chapter two, Plotts replaced a struggling baritone in Bland's Wesleyan Quartet mid-season). Sibley's review, however, was written when Plotts was a child, and Plotts' brief chautauqua career occurred after he had finished dental school. Thus, unlikely as it may seem, there must have been two separate instances of male quartets with struggling baritones using the name "Wesleyan" touring the chautauqua circuits. Sibley discussed each member of the quartet individually and, with the exceptions noted above, in positive terms. He finished by reviewing the act as a whole, stating, "The blend of the quartet is fine, its harmony good and the ensemble perfect. They are equally at home in serious or comic, plain song or artistic, sacred or secular music. Their enunciation was excellent. They were very agreeable and responded to many encores. The Wesleyans have a repertoire of 125 pieces, of which at least 80 are committed. The gentlemen all have interesting personalities."[36]

One local review began with a broad positive assessment, yet most of the specifics mentioned were negative: "The Mathisen Concert Party was very good. The soprano singer in this company was about the best of it and her work made the company really what it was. However it is too small for concert work and in putting on the Bohemian girl was handicapped by lack of numbers." The review continued by lamenting the excess of patriotic music performed, noting that audiences had grown tired of patriotic music by that time (1919).[37]

It should be noted that the absence of objectivity in local newspaper reports was not unique to chautauqua. A 1920 article in *Music Supervisors' Journal* warned of the damage being done by newspapers, particularly in "country towns and smaller cities," heaping undeserved praise on young performers. The author believed that such reviews spurred untalented youth to pursue stage careers until "some big daily critic who doesn't know them from Adam tells the truth. Then comes indignation, heart aches, and with the women, tears."[38]

As chautauqua's popularity declined, it seems it became more acceptable for local newspapers to criticize the movement. An article in the August 7, 1930, issue of the *Terril* (IA) *Record* spent eleven paragraphs criticizing several local assemblies held that summer, and questioning whether the benefit of a chautauqua was worth the cost to the community. It described the assembly at Odebolt as "a total failure" and noted that "as a whole the programs were not up to the standard of chautauqua years ago." The article noted that some of the communities mentioned were either considering or had already decided not to host a chautauqua in 1931, and the author seemed to sympathize with those decisions.[39] This article represents a distinct departure from earlier local coverage, in which unconditional community support of the chautauqua was openly advocated.

Critiques of chautauqua music in national publications were generally less positive, if not less vague. The laudatory generalizations of the local reporters were replaced by negative stereotypes of chautauqua music on the national level. An article in the *North American Review* described art music in circuit chautauqua as Chopin, Beethoven, and Tchaikovsky played on "an old piano that is moved every seven days in a baggage-car while the audience sits enthralled and demands four or five encores."[40] Prominent chautauqua and lyceum trade publications were often the harshest critics of chautauqua music; one editorial proclaimed the platform to be the realm of washed-up musical celebrities surviving on reputation alone.[41]

Conclusion

Historically, circuit chautauqua's relationship with music was influenced most by the independent chautauqua movement, which in turn derived its incorporation of music from the Chautauqua Institution. Although the lyceum movement was in many ways the predominant influence on circuit chautauqua (especially in the areas of business and logistics), circuit chautauqua's relationship with music was far more akin to that of the independent chautauqua movement. Chautauqua's musical repertoire was far from homogenous. Musical acts performed music spanning several centuries, ranging from art and sacred music of the Baroque era to popular dance music. This music reflected — and evolved along with — musical tastes of the era, and the repertoire of a given chautauqua musical act would likely not be exceedingly different from that of a similar act performing in another venue.

While most of the music performed in chautauqua consisted of relatively standard fare, programming of circuit chautauqua music was influenced by forces specific to the movement. For instance, managers had to take into account the musical ability of the players and the itinerant nature of the venue, and balance these challenges with their desire to program high-quality music in order to maintain the movement's reputation as a cultural and educational outlet. This balance was complicated by conflicting ideas about the purpose of music in circuit chautauqua, which led to debates surrounding the proportion of art and popular music on the platform. By the end of the circuit chautauqua movement, economic pragmatism generally outweighed philosophical rhetoric in the eyes of bureau managers, and the proportion of newer popular music on the circuits increased significantly.

Audience perception of platform music, especially as expressed in local news media, was significantly influenced by the idea that the chautauqua was good for the community and thus should not be openly criticized. This allegiance to the chautauqua ideal waned in later years, and the public, through local newspapers, began to look at chautauqua music — and the movement as a whole — more critically. This criticism had always existed in the national press, where opinion of the value of circuit chautauqua music was often negative. The relationship of the chautauqua movement to its music acts as a lens through which the history of the movement itself may be viewed. Circuit chautauqua's philosophy of music was initially heavily influenced by preceding phenomena, and evolved as the movement came to prominence. The abandonment of hard-fought musical principles in favor of ticket sales in the late 1920s and early 1930s shows the desperation of a movement in steep decline. The reluctance of the audience to critically assess chautauqua's musical product speaks to the reverence given the movement by the community; and the disparity between local and national media coverage of the movement underscores differences in perception between chautauqua's largely rural audience and its urban critics. It is for this reason that the study of music in chautauqua is particularly valuable. The music itself was often unremarkable, but the way the music was viewed from within the movement, by the audience, and by the critics speaks volumes about the chautauqua movement as a cultural institution.

IV
Musical Programming in Chautauqua

Programming a chautauqua was a deliberate — and often formulaic — endeavor. Commercial circuit bureaus began with programming patterns that had been successful in the independent chautauqua movement and adapted them to the singular needs of circuit chautauqua. While the bureaus orchestrated programming on the event level by scheduling acts in time-tested patterns, musical programming decisions *within* each performance were most often left to the performers.

The records of the Redpath bureau contain hundreds of promotional brochures advertising musical acts. While some of these brochures were produced by Redpath or other agencies for musicians with whom the bureaus had contracts, many were produced independently by the acts and sent to bureaus in hopes of acquiring a contract. Potential chautauqua musical acts could be called upon to audition by performing their entire program, rather than selected works, and would be expected to present at the audition a program ready for public performance.[1] This indicates that, at least on the individual performance level, each act had considerable input in programming. The bureau made programming decisions not by dictating what pieces individual acts would perform, but by choosing which acts to hire and where to place them on a program. Thus, considerable pressure was placed on prospective chautauqua acts to create a suitable program prior to soliciting bureaus.

Event-Level Programming

In circuit chautauqua, it was the bureau's responsibility to assemble several days of programming in a manner suited to the platform. Each bureau had specific programming conventions and restrictions to consider, along with broader concerns about striking a balance between education and entertainment. To discuss programming in the context of bureau-specific conventions, it is necessary to analyze programs from bureaus representing opposite ends of the circuit chautauqua spectrum. For this purpose, programs from the Redpath bureau were chosen to represent major bureaus, while programs from Radcliffe Chautauquas were used to represent smaller bureaus.

The Redpath bureau is arguably the best case study for a major bureau because of its prominence in the circuit chautauqua community, and also because of the relative completeness of extant bureau records. Programs analyzed for this study include two generic programs used by Redpath, programs from Mt. Pleasant, Charles City, and North English, Iowa, and one program from Canandaigua, New York. The earliest program analyzed is the North English, Iowa, program of 1910, and the latest is from Canandaigua, New York, from 1931. The 1910 program was chosen rather than 1904 or 1907 because the earliest Redpath chautauquas were experimental in nature and geographically limited in scope, thus making the earliest Redpath programs less useful for detecting standard patterns that may have developed within the bureaus.

Nineteen hundred and thirty-one was well into the decline of the circuit chautauqua movement, and near the end of Redpath chautauquas. The 1931 program is from Crawford Peffer's Redpath–New York–New England circuit, which survived through 1932, several years past the divestment of the major circuit chautauqua managers in the Midwest. Just as it seemed inappropriate to draw programming conclusions based on the very earliest Redpath chautauquas, this analysis does not include the program from the final 1932 Redpath–New York–New England circuit.[2] Rather, the study ends with a program from 1931, when Peffer was still confident in circuit chautauqua's ability to weather the 1930s and programming was not yet influenced by the inevitability of the movement's collapse.

Of these six chautauquas, two were five-day events, one lasted six days, and three lasted seven days. While it is true that chautauquas in general shrank in scale after 1925, this trend is not necessarily reflected across the spectrum of Redpath chautauquas, as this sample shows. The Redpath bureau was considered by many — and certainly considered itself — to be the flagship organization of the chautauqua movement, and communities who chose Redpath chautauquas were generally highly supportive of the chautauqua, even in the declining years of the movement. The same is true for Ellison-White, Midland Chautauquas, and other major bureaus. The statistical decline in length of the average chautauqua is due more to the increase in smaller chautauquas presented by bureaus catering to less affluent or less supportive communities than to shortening of programs offered by the major bureaus.

Radcliffe Chautauquas specialized in providing chautauquas to smaller (or less supportive) communities and produced shorter events. Radcliffe chautauqua programs are discussed in the study for comparison to the major bureaus' programming practices. Radcliffe programs analyzed for this study include those from Corbin, Kentucky; Maquoketa, Iowa; St. Augustine, Florida; and Las Cruces, New Mexico. The Radcliffe bureau was chosen for study in this section because of the availability of several complete programs spanning the most successful years of the circuit chautauqua movement.

In general, independent assemblies involved more events and were more likely to program events throughout the day, including morning activities for adults. For instance, mornings were popular for choral rehearsals, and it was common in independent assemblies for a chorus of community members to give concerts in the closing days of the chautauqua. While the early independent chautauquas offered many events, both the proportion and raw number of musical performances at these assemblies tended to be smaller than was common on the commercial chautauqua circuits. This was likely due to the broader scope of the independent assemblies, tied as they were to specific communities. Independent chautauquas often featured Bible studies and lectures conducted by local religious leaders, events that would not travel well on a chautauqua circuit. Other events appearing only on independent chautauquas included cooking lessons, speeches by local politicians (Allerton, Iowa, designated "Republican Day" and "Democratic Day" in its programs) and community social gatherings. Furthermore, independent assemblies, especially in the early years of the movement, often involved activities related to the Chautauqua Literary and Scientific Circle. These activities rarely involved music, creating one more nonmusical event common on independent chautauqua programs but seen elsewhere in the chautauqua movement.

The 1899 program for the Allerton Chautauqua Assembly of Allerton, Iowa, lists 81 events over the course of 9 days. The assembly involved a total of fifteen musical events, including eight rehearsals of the assembly chorus. It appears the only traveling professional musicians hired for the chautauqua were an unnamed jubilee group that performed on each of the first four days of the assembly, once in concert with the Boy Band of Brighton (likely from Brighton, Iowa). After the departure of the jubilee group, the assembly chorus assumed responsibility for concerts, performing two "grand concerts" and one concert labeled "war song."

Day-Level Programming

In general, commercially produced circuit chautauquas concentrated musical programming and lectures in the afternoons and evenings. Mornings most often featured programs for children, and these children's programs did not, as a rule, involve professional musicians. Children did participate in musical activities led by the "Junior Girl," who was most often a childcare professional on summer break. Children's activities often included performances on the chautauqua platform, including pageants and mock weddings, which could involve music.[3] Although independent chautauqua assemblies frequently held choir rehearsals during the mornings with the goal of a community chorus performance at the end of the assembly, there was no such event in circuit chautauqua, and the "Junior Chautauqua" performances, while involving music, were not primarily musical in nature.

Musical events and lectures were primarily reserved for afternoons and evenings for several reasons. Crowds would be bigger after standard work hours, as those who were not able to use vacation time to attend the chautauqua (newspaper advertisements often suggested this as the ideal situation) could attend evening events after work. The program could not be adjusted to account for the weekend due to the nature of the circuit, and thus every day of a chautauqua had to be programmed as if it were a weekday. The nature of a chautauqua circuit dictated that any day's program would occasionally fall on a Sunday, causing scheduling conflicts for any morning program. In addition, those traveling a great distance to the chautauqua site would find an early morning event difficult to attend. Finally, the independent assemblies had set a precedent by featuring professional musicians and lecturers in the afternoons and evenings, and using mornings to showcase local talent. It is natural, then, that the commercial bureaus, who dealt solely with the professional performers, would structure their chautauquas in a similar fashion. Presumably, communities could have supplied local talent for morning programs to augment commercial chautauquas, but such events are not listed in any official programs.

Afternoon circuit chautauqua events usually began at 2:30 or 3:00 pm. Each of the representative Redpath programs analyzed in this section began with a musical event on the afternoon of the first day. All but one of the Redpath chautauquas began the second afternoon with a concert (the exception, from 1929, featured a magician as the sole afternoon event) and only one chautauqua began the third afternoon with a non-musical event (in this case, a lecture as the sole afternoon event). In both of the aforementioned exceptional programs, the non-musical opening act is followed by a play. Plays were lengthy events by chautauqua standards; one play would usually take the place of two other events on a chautauqua schedule. Further analysis within this chapter will show that bureaus generally followed clear programming patterns of alternating musical and lecture events, and that aberrations from these patterns were often caused by the insertion of plays into a format not designed for them.

IV. Musical Programming in Chautauqua   97

The fourth and fifth days of every Redpath program in the sample began with a concert. Most of these concerts were followed by lectures. These afternoon lectures were generally on lighter or pragmatic subjects and were often billed as "popular lectures." The same was often true of afternoon musical performances, the earlier musical event being consistently shorter and often lighter in character than the evening performance.

In circuit chautauqua, especially in the movement's mature years, it was most common for a musical ensemble to perform both the afternoon and evening concerts on a day's program. This is perhaps circuit chautauqua's most dramatic musical departure from the patterns established by the earlier independent chautauqua movement. Independent assemblies would often contract with one "headliner" musical ensemble to perform evening concerts for several consecutive days, if not the duration of the assembly. Afternoon "prelude" concerts would be performed by local musicians or lesser-known professionals. Early circuit chautauqua managers attempted a modified version of this strategy. For instance, Vawter's 1904 program kept the same musical acts in each community for several days. As the time and distance between circuit stops decreased, it became impossible for any act to spend more than one day in a community. For this reason, it became the norm in circuit chautauqua to feature a different musical act each day, and for that act to perform both the afternoon and evening concerts.

Afternoon concerts were considerably shorter than those performed in the evenings. Harry Harrison stated that these "prelude" concerts could last anywhere between fifteen minutes and an hour,[4] while Victoria and Robert Case wrote that these preludes lasted twenty to forty minutes.[5] The term "prelude" had several meanings in the circuit chautauqua movement. While it could refer to any musical performance prior to a lecture, it was often used specifically to denote shorter afternoon concerts in particular. Most afternoon concerts were allotted thirty minutes according to published programs. The contrast between afternoon and evening concerts is best exemplified by an analysis of programs from both events.

The New York City Marine Band toured with the Ellison-White bureau throughout the western United States in 1914. Their afternoon concert program for that tour was as follows:

Stars and Stripes Forever	Sousa
Overture: *Poet and Peasant*	Suppé
Sextet from *Lucia*	Donizetti
Trio from *Faust*	Gounod
—-Intermission—-	
Selections from *Tales of Hoffman*	Offenbach
Selections from *Madame Butterfly*	Puccini

The Rosary   Nevin
Medley: Popular Airs[6]

The band's evening program was as follows:

March from *Tannhäuser*   Wagner
Overture: *William Tell*   Rossini
Quartet from *Rigoletto*   Verdi
"La Donna è Mobile" from *Rigoletto*   Verdi
— Intermission —
Selections from *il Trovatore*   Verdi
Selections from *The Firefly*   Friml
American Fantasies   Herbert[7]

Although both concerts feature operatic transcriptions, the evening concert includes one more selection from grand opera. The afternoon concert begins with Sousa's "Stars and Stripes Forever" and ends with a medley of popular songs, while the evening concert is bookended by the relatively heavier march from *Tannhäuser* and *American Fantasies*. The use of "Stars and Stripes Forever" to open the afternoon concert may have had more to do with the concert's function of opening the day's program than with the programmer's desire to open the concert with a march. Although neither concert was especially short or placed considerable emphasis on popular music of the day, the evening concert would likely have been longer (it is impossible to know for sure, due to the vagueness of the term "selections") and did draw more from the grand opera and tone poem traditions.

Fink's Hussars Militaire, one of several musical Hussar groups touring the chautauqua circuits, published an undated sample program sheet to be sent to booking agents and local committees. This sheet gives two separate sample programs, one suited for afternoon and one for evening. The afternoon sample program consisted of seven pieces:

"Choral March"   Chambers
Overture: *Il Guarany*   Gomez
"Meditation"   Morrison
Cornet Solo
   (a) "Fancies" Fiesta Polka   Perkins
   (b) Stabat Mater   Rossini
"Now I Lay Me Down to Sleep"   Walbridge
"Crème de la Crème" Fantasia   Moses-Tobani
"Star Spangled Banner"   Sousa [*sic*]

The evening sample program consisted of nine musical works, two of which appear in the afternoon program as well:

IV. Musical Programming in Chautauqua

"Glory of the Trumpets" March	Brockenshire
Overture: *William Tell*	Rossini
"The Old Church Organ"	Chambers
Euphonium Solo	
(a) "My Old Kentucky Home" Air Varie	Goldman
(b) The Rosary	Nevin
"The Glow-Worm" Idyl	Lincke
(a) "Hark the Herald Angels Sing"	Mendelssohn[8]
(b) "It Came Upon the Midnight Air"	Gabriel
"Crème de la Crème" Fantasia	Moses-Tobani
Nibelungen March	Wagner
"Echoes from the Metropolitan Opera House"	Moses-Tobani
"Star Spangled Banner"	Sousa

While it was not unusual at that time for musical groups on the chautauqua circuits and elsewhere to end a program with "The Star Spangled Banner," and thus it is not surprising to see that piece on both programs, the repetition of "Crème de la Crème" seems contrary to the circuit chautauqua idea of two distinct concerts per day. It should be noted, however, that this concept of two entirely different performances by the same group on the same day is supported primarily by the literature, as very few extant programs of specific chautauqua musical events have been found. This is not to say that the notion of two distinct concerts is incorrect or not the norm, but of only two programs discovered in the course of this project listing both afternoon and evening concerts, one contains a repeated number.

Most Redpath chautauqua evenings began at 8:00 pm, usually with a concert. The evening concert was sometimes the final event of the day, but it was often followed by a lecture. The last event of the day would sometimes be an "entertainment" comprised of music, costumes, drama, and light lectures around a central theme. This event would often take the place of the evening lecture and concert, and thus would constitute the entire evening's program. Exotic acts were frequently featured as "entertainments" in circuit chautauqua. Redpath's 1929 Premier Circuit included full-evening entertainments by the Cossack Chorus and Vierra's Hawaiians. The Cossack Chorus's performance was billed as a "gorgeous singing pageant and entertainment supreme." The program for Vierra's Hawaiians, dubbed "A Night in Hawaii," was billed as "the most ambitious spectacle ever attempted in chautauqua."

The Raweis, a popular and long-lived act on both the chautauqua and the lyceum circuits, offered an entertainment entitled "The New Zealanders in Song, Story and Picture: From Cannibalism to Culture." The program involved Wherahiko Rawei, a Maori raised by English adoptive parents, his

A chautauqua performance of *The Mikado* (author's collection, gift of Fred Crane).

wife, Hine Taimoa, and their daughter, Rae. The Raweis sang, gave demonstrations of Maori customs, and gave a lecture billed as "an illustrated trip through the North Island."[9] Although the promotional flyer for "The New Zealanders" does not elaborate on the specifics of the musical aspect of the performance, the Raweis did publish a musical program to accompany one of their lyceum acts. Selections included music from across Polynesia, from New Zealand to Hawaii, the sextet from Donizetti's *Lucia di Lammermoor*, and a "Polynesian version" of the hymn "Calvary." (Presumably this is a reference to "At Calvary," by William Newell and Daniel Towner.)

The archetypal Redpath chautauqua daily program opened the afternoon with a musical event followed by a lecture, and resumed in the evening with another musical event — often a larger program by the very same act that had performed in the afternoon — that either concluded the evening or was followed by a lecture. Mornings during a Redpath chautauqua usually involved activities for children, or were left open for logistical reasons. Twenty-one of the forty-three days represented in the Redpath sample follow the pattern of *morning-music-lecture-music-[lecture]* exactly.

The Raweis (author's collection, gift of Fred Crane).

The Radcliffe programs analyzed for this section were more uniform than Redpath programs of the same period. Much of this uniformity can be attributed to the scope of the bureau. Radcliffe was a smaller organization managing fewer circuits. Radcliffe chautauquas, at three days in length, were also considerably shorter than those produced by the major bureaus. None of the Radcliffe chautauquas included in this study presented events in the morning. Newspaper advertisements for Radcliffe chautauquas indicate, however, that local committees sometimes provided morning programs for children. The three earliest Radcliffe chautauquas studied followed nearly identical programming patterns. The first afternoon began with a concert followed by a lecture, while the evening began with a lecture followed by a concert. The second day began with a lecture, followed by a concert. The evening program consisted of two lectures followed by a concert. The third and final day consisted of an afternoon concert followed by a lecture, and an evening lecture followed by a concert. The only aberration from this pattern occurred on the last evening of the 1919 Las Cruces, New Mexico, chautauqua. In that case, the evening began with a lecture followed by a concert, rather than a concert followed by a lecture.

Later Radcliffe chautauquas, much like their Redpath counterparts, show a struggle to integrate plays into the established daily formula. Plays most often occurred on the second day of a Radcliffe chautauqua and displaced the concerts normally scheduled for that day. For instance, the second day of the 1924 chautauqua in St. Augustine, Florida, consisted of only one lecture and a play. The second day of the 1926 chautauqua in Corbin, Kentucky, involved two one-act dramas followed by a lecture in the afternoon, followed by another lecture and a three-act play in the evening.

Alternation between musical events and lectures seems to have been the norm for bureaus across the United States and throughout the era of circuit chautauqua. Harry Harrison cited this practice of opening each segment of a circuit chautauqua day with music, stating, "We pre-luded." Harrison claimed that "to pre-lude" became a standard term in the chautauqua business for preceding a lecture with music, and that the vast majority of lecturers supported the practice, believing the musical prelude helped set the proper tone for the lecture.[10]

Drama carried with it a stigma that originated long before the chautauqua era. Rural Americans—especially the leaders of rural communities—associated theatre troupes with the lowest forms of traveling entertainment. Medicine shows and traveling troupes might visit the town, but these strictly commercial ventures were not supported by or associated with the community's religious and social leaders. A chautauqua reflected upon the character of those who had invited (and usually financially guaranteed) it. The unseemly connotations of theatre made bureaus cautious about programming strictly dramatic acts for several years. It was not until 1913 that Crawford Peffer booked the Ben Greet Players (also billed as the Shakespeare Players for their chautauqua tours, possibly to add legitimacy to the venture) to tour his circuit performing Shakespeare's *Comedy of Errors*.[11]

Music Drama in Chautauqua

Opera did not carry the stigma of drama and was a fixture on the chautauqua circuits from the early years of the movement. When an opera was staged on the chautauqua platform, it was always in the evening and usually the only attraction on the evening program. It was common for individuals or small groups from the opera company to give a recital for the afternoon program, or for the opera orchestra to give a short concert. Opera companies would occasionally be prepared to present an oratorio or a recital of sacred songs in lieu of an opera if the performance fell on a Sunday and prevailing local sentiment dictated it, but this varied by bureau.

In consideration of the chautauqua venue, operas were heavily altered. Casts of a dozen or fewer were used for even the most elaborate works, and most often the accompaniment was either a piano or an instrumental group traveling the same circuit as the opera company. For instance, a Redpath circuit featured Bohumir Kryl's band as a stand alone concert in the afternoon, and as the pit orchestra for the Denton Grand Opera Company's production of Flotow's *Martha* in the evening. Similarly, the Redpath-Vawter circuit of 1913 used Thaviu's International Band to accompany Thaviu's Grand Opera Stars in the conductor's adaptation of *The Lovely Galatea* by Franz von Suppé.

In 1922 the Tooley Opera Company offered several productions for the chautauqua platform. The largest was a six-person company performing Gonoud's *Faust* "with complete scenery, costumes and lighting effects." Smaller groups included the Tooley Comic Opera Quintette, which performed a program of selections from comic operas, and the Tooley Operatic Quartet, which performed "an afternoon prelude in picturesque colonial costumes and a tabloid form of *The Mikado* at night." Presumably "tabloid" is intended to mean "condensed" in this situation, rather than the connotations more common today.

Alterations to opera were not merely necessitated by the physical chautauqua venue or the available performing forces; in some situations operas were altered to conform to chautauqua values. Gay MacLaren, longtime chautauqua elocutionist and play-reader, recounted a chautauqua production of Bizet's *Carmen* in which the women were employed at a dairy rather than a cigarette factory, and Carmen made her entrance carrying a milk pail.[12]

During chautauqua's peak years we begin to see opera and oratorio share the stage with musical comedy. A 1924 brochure for Stark's Musical Comedy Revue and Light Opera Association lists three operas (*Maritana* by William Wallace, Balfe's *Bohemian Girl*, and *The Lily of Killarney* by Julius Benedict) and three musical comedies (*Killarney's Wild Irish Rose*, *Arline*, and *The Gipsy Girl*) in its repertoire. *Killarney's Wild Irish Rose* is described in the brochure as a revue and as "a real snappy up-to-date Broadway production."[13]

A 1926 brochure for the Blue Danube Light Opera Company touts a new operetta, composed specifically for the platform by Sandor Radanovits, a Chicago-based producer affiliated with Redpath who created many art music acts for the lyceum and circuit chautauqua stage. The operetta, entitled *In*

Romany, chronicled the adventures of an American naval officer in a European gypsy encampment. A newspaper announcement of a lyceum performance of *In Romany* noted that the operetta lasted roughly one hour, with the rest of the Blue Danube Light Opera Company's evening performance devoted to "recital work, consisting of mixed quartets, trios, duets and solos."[14] The promotional brochure for *In Romany* also notes that it will be followed by a concert. It is interesting to note that although he composed it specifically for circuit performance, Radanovits chose to make *In Romany* so short as to necessitate a concert afterward. This may have been to accommodate tight travel schedules. It was relatively easy to cut individual numbers from a concert program in order to shorten a performance to catch a train, while abbreviating a dramatic work was more difficult and more likely to alert the audience to the performers' rush. Chautauqua audiences, though they must have been aware that performers were often on exceptionally tight schedules, resented performances that were cut short and complained if a performer seemed preoccupied with time.[15] Thus, Radanovits may have crafted the performance in order to present a cohesive yet flexible evening.

In the declining years of the chautauqua movement, musical comedy appeared on programs with increasing frequency. A 1930 Redpath program featured a new musical comedy, *A Night in Arabia*, performed by the Lucille Elmore Revue. In 1926, Ralph Dunbar offered several musical comedies for lyceum and chautauqua booking, including *Going Up*, a "farce comedy with music" by Otto Harbach and Louis Hirsh. *Going Up* was advertised a requiring a cast of fifteen, but only a piano for accompaniment. Dunbar's attractions for 1926 also included a one-act musical comedy, written especially for chautauqua by Dunbar himself, entitled *The Music Shop*. Dunbar advertised *The Music Shop* as a ninety-minute "vehicle containing the usual amount of chautauqua program material." Also available was Victor Herbert's comic opera *Sweethearts*. Dunbar advertised that *Sweethearts* could be performed by a cast of nine, that it was especially suited for performance in a tent, and that "an orchestra would of course add, but *Sweethearts* would be effective with only piano accompaniment and I doubt if many in the audience would feel the absence of the other instruments."

Performance-Level Programming

Although some acts were clearly presented as "concerts," the term was often used loosely and is not terribly useful to indicate the actual nature of the performance. What, precisely, was involved in a typical concert on the chautauqua circuits? The real challenge for the researcher lies here, as published chautauqua programs did not list individual works performed. Fur-

IV. Musical Programming in Chautauqua 105

thermore, there are few indications of circuit chautauqua musical acts distributing programs for a performance to the audience. This lack of occasion-specific programs combined with the absence of live audio recordings from circuit chautauqua musical events prompt the researcher to rely on other sources for information regarding specific programming. These sources include sample programs sent to bureaus and printed in publicity materials, programs provided by the acts for performances at lyceums, fairs, and other events, and unpublished set lists.

MacLaren states that musical acts did not usually supply printed programs and that this allowed musicians to shorten or lengthen a performance in order to accommodate for scheduling problems such as a speaker's arrival at the tent being delayed (in which case the musical "prelude" act would be lengthened) or, as previously discussed, tight evening train schedules.[16] Although chautauqua audiences did not expect to be given a printed program at a performance, it appears that at least some lyceum audiences did. The Redpath Collection at the University of Iowa contains many detailed programs from lyceum performances, as do many of the smaller archives and personal collections of chautauqua performers. There was considerable overlap between rosters of circuit chautauqua and lyceum performers, and many acts were managed by the same bureau for both chautauqua and lyceum seasons. Many of those who performed at Redpath chautauquas, for instance, booked winter performances through the Redpath Lyceum Bureau, and copies of programs from those lyceum performances (as well as school assemblies, fairs, and other occasions booked through Redpath) were kept on file by the bureau. The principal flaw in using sample programs and programs from non-chautauqua venues is that these programs do not represent concerts constructed with the need to produce two different concerts per day in mind. These programs are likely more representative of an evening chautauqua performance, rather than a shorter, lighter afternoon performance or a musical prelude to a lecture, both common occurrences in chautauqua. While these programs cannot tell us exactly what the program of an act's chautauqua performance would be, they do give a reasonable indication of the repertoire and overall aesthetic of the act.

The largest source of sample programs and set lists, the collection of the records of the Redpath bureau, makes no distinction between performers who toured on the chautauqua circuits, those who sent audition materials but were not hired, and those who were engaged by the Redpath bureau strictly for lyceum work. For this reason, it was necessary to first determine which performers actually toured the chautauqua circuits before analyzing the available sample programs. This process was initiated by cataloging one hundred forty-three complete chautauqua programs gleaned from various library and historical society collections and newspapers. Forty-two of the programs were produced by commercial chautauqua bureaus. These forty-two chautauqua programs listed one hundred sixty-nine distinct musical acts. It should be noted that there were several instances of different incarnations of the same act under different names. For instance, Vierra's Hawaiians and Vierra's Royal Hawaiians were two different acts, although they shared common management and incorporated several of the same personnel.

Most of these one hundred sixty-nine acts can be placed, by analysis of sample programs or advertising materials, into one of five categories. The first category, novelty, comprises groups that billed themselves as novelties or that placed great emphasis on non-musical aspects of performance and non-musical abilities of the performers. Examples of non-musical aspects include dramatic reading, costume dramas, juggling, magic, and giving "chalk talks." The term "chalk talk" refers to a lecture accompanied by real-time illustrations, often done on a chalkboard, by the lecturer. Chalk talks were very popular on the chautauqua circuits, especially in later years. While the presence of one dramatic reader with an ensemble or the use of costumes in performances does not conclusively brand an act as a novelty, in situations where several (or all) members of a group are advertised first as dramatic readers or the beauty of the costumes is emphasized over the nature of the music, the group is rightly categorized as a novelty. Other groups were labeled as novelties by their managers and were sometimes billed as novelties in program brochures. Finally, it is important to note that no group was labeled as a novelty based on analysis of a sample musical program, as none of the groups in the novelty category provided sample programs to the Redpath bureau. This failure to provide details regarding the music performed is another hallmark of the novelty acts.

The second category of musical acts on the chautauqua circuits comprises the exotic acts. This category is perhaps not as straightforward as it might seem; there are several factors to consider beyond national origin when assigning the "exotic" label. As was the case throughout the United States in the early twentieth century, many chautauqua musicians, especially those in the wind bands and orchestras, were not originally from the United States. This fact would become a sticking point in the years surrounding World War I, and smaller chautauqua bureaus would try to capitalize on the major bureaus' reliance on foreign musicians by labeling their own bands and orchestras as "American." Harrison discusses the stigma against foreign bands in *Culture Under Canvas*. These musicians, however, performed a repertoire not specifically linked to their cultures of origin. Exotic acts on the chautauqua circuits usually included a cultural indicator in their name. Examples include the Russian Cossack Chorus, the Spanish Serenaders, and the Alpine Singers and

IV. Musical Programming in Chautauqua

Yodelers. These groups often performed in costume and performed works from their identified culture and, occasionally, standards from the light classical and popular repertories. Loseff's Russian Orchestral Quartet performed selections including Russian folk songs, pieces from the Russian art music repertory, Italian opera transcriptions, and popular numbers including a fantasia on "My Old Kentucky Home."[17]

Popular acts were least prevalent in the sample. This is not to say that popular music was rare on the chautauqua circuits. On the contrary, popular music was a staple for many of the quartets and novelty acts engaged by commercial circuit bureaus. One chautauqua musical act made a point of taking requests during its afternoon performance for numbers to be performed in the evening. The leader of the group kept a record of the most often requested pieces. His list of the nineteen most requested pieces was reproduced by Allen Albert in his article, "Tents of the Conservative." The list contained the following pieces: "Annie Laurie," "Love's Old Sweet Song," "The Palms," "One Fine Day" from *Madame Butterfly*, "Goodbye" (Totsi), "My Heart at Thy Dear Voice" from *Samson and Delilah*, "Aloha Oe," "Song of the Evening Star," "Absent," "I Hear You Calling Me," "Cujus Animam" from *Stabat Mater*, Minuet in G (Beethoven), Melody in F (Rubenstein), "Humereske," (Dvořák), Largo from *Xerxes* (Handel), "Pilgrims' Chorus" from *Tannhäuser* (Wagner), "Spring Song" (Mendelssohn), "Meditation" from *Thais* (Massenet).[18] This list of the most popular selections in the repertoire of an unnamed quintet reflects a common phenomenon among chautauqua musical acts: while popular music was common on the circuits, it often fell to performers of light classical, exotic, or other genres to provide popular tunes by integrating them into their acts.

There were very few acts whose repertoires consisted solely or primarily of popular music. Those groups who did perform popular music primarily or exclusively usually employed a recognizable theme to the act and limited musical selections to (or at least emphasized) those fitting the theme. For instance, the Four College Girls performed medleys of popular college fight songs and songs about college life and sports, as well as standard popular songs of the era. Jubilee singers also sang popular songs around a central theme, that of African American folk music.[19] Another such group, the Old Home Singers, was a musical company formed by Charles Horner, manager of Redpath-Horner, to capitalize on nostalgia for popular music of the past. The Old Home Singers, discussed at length in Chapter VI, sang popular songs from the 1850s while dressed in period costumes.

A number of art music performers toured on the chautauqua circuits. These acts included opera companies, wind bands, small orchestras, choirs, vocal soloists, violinists, and flexible groups presenting chamber music. Art music performers often supplied sample programs or repertoire lists and were presented in serious poses in advertisements. These acts were often "headliners" of their circuits, occupying the most desirable and well-attended spots on the program.

It was not uncommon for the orchestra of an opera company to perform a prelude concert in the afternoon prior to the evening's opera. This is not surprising, considering the chautauqua tradition of musical attractions performing twice each day and the logistical problems associated with staging two operas per day. These orchestras were usually billed by the title of the opera. For instance, the Gondoliers Orchestra appears often in chautauqua programs. This was not a specific group — there were likely several orchestras using the name "The Gondoliers Orchestra" simultaneously — but rather denotes the orchestra touring with a company performing Gilbert and Sullivan's *The Gondoliers*.

Of course, a sizeable number of musicians on the chautauqua circuits do not fit squarely into any of the above categories. Many acts combined several genres of music or were advertised and billed so vaguely as to render accurate categorization impossible. There was, however, a combination of genres so popular in circuit chautauqua as to necessitate a separate category. Chautauqua's idea of "classic music popularized, popular music dignified"[20] is exemplified by the abundance of musical acts performing a combination of what could be termed "light classical" and "heavy popular" music. The Edna White Quartette, an instrumental group composed of two trumpets, a trombone, and euphonium, published a partial repertoire list divided between "classic" and "popular" pieces, also noting that the group was prepared to offer a "very lovely sacred repertoire." The most telling aspect of this program is the group's "popular" repertoire, which included works by Verdi and Donizetti along with pieces more akin to the standard popular repertory of the era:

Sextette from *Lucia*	Donizetti
Quartette from *Rigoletto*	Verdi
Raymond Overture	Thomas
Scherzo	Caronara
Morning, Noon and Night	Suppè
Medley	Herbert
Kerry Dance	Molloy
Bells of St. Mary's	Old English
Washington Post	Sousa
Barcarolle (from Tales of Hoffman)	Offenbach
I Hear You Calling Me	Marshall
Carmena Waltz	Wilson

IV. Musical Programming in Chautauqua

Negro Spirituals
Sliding Jim (Trombone)
Serio Comique (Novelties)

This combination was especially favored by vocal/instrumental quartets, themselves a staple of the circuit chautauqua movement. The Oxford Company, a group formed and coached by chautauqua and lyceum impresario Elias Day, published a sample program consisting of two halves. The first half comprised popular pieces, while Gilbert and Sullivan's *Mikado* comprised the second half:

Part I

Bridal Chorus (from *The Rose Maiden*)	Cowen
Love's Trinity	Reginald DeKoven
The Miller's Wooing	Eaton Fanning
Yesterday and Today	Charles Spross
Seven Nursery Rhymes	H. Walford Davies
Stacato [*sic*] Etude	Rubenstein

Part II

Comic Opera: *Mikado*	Gilbert and Sullivan

Extant sample programs have been located for forty-five of these confirmed circuit chautauqua musical acts. It is difficult to generalize about a "typical" circuit chautauqua musical program for many reasons, not the least of which is the total lack of detailed programs for novelty acts. Because of this lack of representation of novelty acts in the program sample, as well as the overrepresentation of extant art music programs relative to the number of art music acts on the circuits, it is impossible to make assumptions about programming trends based on available sample programs. Rather, it is necessary to discuss musical programming on a genre-by-genre and, ideally, act-by-act basis.

As previously mentioned, no extant programs have been found detailing the musical content of a novelty act on the chautauqua circuits. From descriptions and advertising ephemera it is possible, however, to discern what often occurred during a novelty musical performance, even if we cannot know precisely what music was performed and in what order. The Dearborn Concert Party, for instance, advertised its program as "pleasing entertainment, consisting of ensemble numbers of harp, violin, and flute; vocal trios, duets, vocal trios in Spanish costume accompanied by mandolin and guitars, and sketches. Their individual work consists of American harp solos, Irish harp and Irish character songs, whistling solos with short talks on birds, violin solos, and readings."[21] While this description is not as informative as a sample program, it does give an indication as to the breadth and character of the group's performances.

One novelty musical act, the Van O. Browne Novelty Trio, did provide sample programs to the Redpath Lyceum Bureau. The trio performed under the bureau's management on the lyceum circuits, but it does not appear on any of the commercial chautauqua programs analyzed in this study. A later group led by Van Browne, known as the Van Browne Entertainers, toured with Acme Chautauquas in 1921. The Van O. Browne Novelty Trio seems to have provided a more subdued program than those described by other novelty groups, although it is impossible to assert this definitively, given the lack of programs for comparison. The Van O. Browne Novelty Trio's program for a benefit concert at a Congregational church in Wauwatosa, Wisconsin, follows:

"Come Where the Lilies Bloom"	Thompson
Overture: *Modiste*	Herbert
Male Trio	
(a) "Bells of St. Mary's"	Adams
(b) "Nights in Dixie"	
Novelty Rag Pictures[22]	Mr. Browne
Flute Solo—"The Whirlwind"	Kranz
Duet—"Awake Dearest One"	Ball
Duet—"Call Me Back, Pal o'Mine"	Dixon
Accordion Solo—Prison Scene from *il Trovatore*	Verdi
Male Trio	
(a) "Round the Fire"	
(b) "Tomorrow"	
Flute and Clarinet Duet	
(a) "Angel's Serenade"	Braza
(b) "Three o'Clock"	
Tenor Solo	
(a) "I Don't Know How I Do It"	Herbert
(b) "Pretty as a Picture"	
Novelty Piano Solo	Mr. Browne
Saxophone Solo (selected)	Mr. Dalin
Impression of Edwin Boothe in Bulwar Lytton's Poetical-Romantic Drama *Cardinal Richelieu*	
Bass Solo (Selected)	Mr. Dalin
Male Trio, sacred, "The Recessional"	De Koven
Novelty Trio, instrumental, popular	
Closing Good Bye	Male Trio[23]

Another program from 1920, which appears to have been altered by someone affiliated with the group includes an added "up to date magic— including a 'study' of the ancient Hindoo [sic] art of 'crystal gazing.'"

Travesty on "Comin' Thro' the Rye"	G. O'Hara
Accordion Solo	Selected

IV. Musical Programming in Chautauqua

Hawthorne	H.A. Vander Cook
Master Impersonation of Edwin Booth as "Cardinal Richelieu"	
[handwritten] Up to Date Magic including a "study" of the ancient Hindoo art of "Crystal Gazing"	
Original "Operatic Burlesque"	
The Holy City	F.E. Weatherly
The Rosary	E. Nevin
Military March "National Emblem"	E.E. Bagley[24]

The Browne program consists of many short selections, a pattern common to circuit chautauqua performances regardless of genre. A program from the 1913 American tour of the Russian Balalaika Orchestra, a popular exotic act on the circuits, consisted of fifteen short pieces:

Tzarina	Russian Folk Song
Butterfly Valse	W.W. Andreeff
Beer-Berry	Russian Wedding's Song [sic]
Russian Folk Song	
(a) Echo of the Forest	
(b) On the River	
Rondo Capriccioso	Saint-Saens
Passe-Pied	Delibes
Souvenir Valse — The Moscow	W.W. Andreef
Jocelyn	Godard
Serenade	Pierne
— Intermission —	
Finale	
(a) Romance	Rachmaninoff
(b) Gavotte et Musette	Tar Sulin
Tshardasch	W.W. Andreeff
Mosquito Dance	Russian Folk Song
Gatschino Valse	W.W. Adreeff
The Volga's Boatmen Song	Russian Folk Song
The Bright Moon	Russian Dance[25]

The program consists primarily of Russian music, but also includes non-Russian works from the Western art music repertory. The Russian Balalaika Orchestra, like many large ensembles of the era, sometimes toured with a singer. In 1915, the orchestra performed with soprano Pauline Donalda. A 1913 program lists Gregory Besrodny as violin soloist, while other programs list no soloists aside from the conductor, Alexander Kiriloff, who also performed as featured balalaika soloist. It seems natural to conclude that the inclusion of Western standards might be due to the employment of non-Russian singers and instruments other than the balalaika. An analysis of programs, however, does not support this theory. There is no significant difference in the proportion of non-Russian music between programs featuring non-balalaika soloists and those programs performed exclusively on balalaikas.

Popular acts, as previously mentioned, often programmed entire concerts (or their entire repertoire) around a central theme. The College Girls, who toured with impersonator and entertainer Walter Eccles, were a staple of the chautauqua and lyceum circuits. The group, like many circuit chautauqua acts, weathered several changes in both personnel and focus throughout its existence. A 1908 promotional brochure lists ten members performing in various ensembles including a Scotch quartet, a Spanish-themed guitar group, a dramatic troupe, and a drum corps. Later incarnations of the College Girls are smaller and more focused on the theme of college, although non-musical performances, particularly by Eccles, remain. An undated program of Walter Eccles and the Four College Girls (the most popular and longest-lived incarnation of the College Girls) under the management of the Redpath Lyceum Bureau contains the following musical numbers:

Medley of College Songs	Arr. Pearsall
"The Miller's Wooing"	
Telephone Song from *Havana*	
"The Raggedy Man"	
Mandolin Quartet	
Duet from *Hansel and Gretel*	
Medley of Scotch Songs	
"Rose of my Life"	Rose
"Ching a Ling a Loo"	Hoffman
Song	
"The College Boat Race"	Kobbe
"Foot Ball"	Gilman
"Hiram Soule"	Gilman
Dutch Character Song	
Motor Song	
"The Soldier Boy"	Pearsall

Several pieces on the program reference the group's primary theme (college), although the program also contains several popular and ethnic caricature songs having nothing to do with college. This is a common pattern for acts specializing in popular music on the chautauqua circuits. Also included in the program were several non-musical events, most of which served as vehicles for Walter Eccles' impersonations and oratory.

The Schumann Quintet, a group comprising two violins, a cello, and two pianos, provided two sample programs, one for "those desiring purely classical expression" and one for "committees desiring more popular classics." The "purely classical" program consisted of ten pieces as follows:

Overture to *The Marriage of Figaro*	Mozart
Andante from "Pastoral" Symphony	Beethoven
Concerto for Violin, first movement	Beethoven
Invitation to the Dance	Weber
Hungarian Rhapsody No. 12	Liszt
Concerto for Cello	Saint-Saens
"Caro None" [sic] from *Rigoletto*	Verdi
"Cradle Song"	Brahms
Agnus Dei	Bizet
Waltz from *Dornröschen*	Tchaikovsky

The program of "popular classics" included eight works:

Overture to *Der Freischütz*	Weber
Selection from *Tannhauser* [sic]	Wagner
Aria, "a fors e lui" [sic] from *Traviata*	Verdi
Cello Solo	Schumann
Nocturne	Chopin
The Loreley (Paraphrase)	Nesvadba
Liebesfreud	Kreisler
Hungarian Rhapsody No. 2	Liszt

An undated program from a performance in Daytona, Florida, of the Music Makers Quartet, a brass/vocal quartet, shows a typical mix of light classical and relatively subdued popular songs:

Prelude — "If I Had My Way"	
March — "Honey Boy"	
Overture — *Inspiration*	
"A Chip of [sic] the Old Block"	
Medley of Remick's Hits	
Trombone Solo — "Wings of the Morning"	
Priests' March from *Athalia*	Bebe
Saw Specialty	
Barcarolle from *Tales of Hoffman*	Offenbach
"The Typical Tune of Zanzibar"	
Cornet Solo — Selected	
Humorous Song	
Medley of Operatic Airs	
"Mosquitoes"	
March — "The Music Makers"[26]	

In 1910, the chautauqua committee at Charles City, Iowa, took the unusual step of printing souvenir programs specifically for a performance by contralto Ernestine Schumann-Heink. Schumann-Heink performed with an accompanist, Katherine Hoffman, and shared the program with a piano soloist, Sara Suttel. The program lists eighteen short pieces, with Schumann-Heink being featured in thirteen and the remainder performed by Suttel. At first glance, the program seems to indicate that Schumann-Heink and Suttel would perform a selection from each numbered grouping. However, sections II and IV are labeled "piano soli" and section V is labeled "Five English Songs." This would seem to indicate that each piece listed on the program was to be performed that night. If this was the case, the program would have been exceptionally long. However, a program consisting of five short pieces would be much shorter than the norm for an evening performance as described by Harrison and exemplified by the evening programs discussed earlier in this chapter. The program follows:

I

a. Arie [sic] from *Sapho* — Gounod
b. Arie [sic] from *Samson and Dalilah* — Saint Saens
c. "O Rest in the Lord" (From *Elijah*) — Mendelssohn

Mme. Schumann-Heink

II

Piano Soli —
  a. Three Etudes — Liszt
  b. Scherzo — Liszt

Miss Sara Suttel

III

a. Gretchen Am Spinnrad — Schubert
b. Haideroslein — Schubert
c. Erl-Konig — Schubert
d. Das Erkennen — Loewe
e. Wiegenlied — Herrmann

Mme. Schumann-Heink

IV

Piano Soli
  a. Dance-March — Suttel
  b. Gnomenreigen — Liszt
  c. Campanella — Paganini-Liszt

Miss Sara Suttel

V

Five English Songs
  a. The Rosary — Nevin
  b. O Let Night Speak of Me — Chadwick

c. Danza	Chadwick
d. His Lullaby	Bond
e. Love in a Cottage	Rudolph Ganz
Mme. Schumann-Heink[27]	

Sunday presented a special problem for circuit chautauqua operators. Independent chautauqua committees had freedom to schedule programs to fit the needs of their communities, while circuit chautauqua communities had little flexibility in this regard. Independent assemblies, especially in the eastern United States, were often affiliated with religious groups, and as such could supply religious speakers, services, and sacred music for religious holy days that would fall within the chautauqua week. Commercial bureaus contracted with committees that were most often composed of local business leaders or a broad spectrum of community (including religious) leaders, but circuit chautauquas were not, as a rule, engaged by specific religious groups. Deferring to the religious sensibilities of an entire community was not as feasible as catering to the needs of one sponsoring religious group, and circuit chautauqua bureaus struggled to create a Sunday program acceptable to a variety of belief systems.

This problem was compounded by the nature of the circuit chautauqua system, which did not guarantee that the same program would regularly fall on a Sunday. For instance, if a chautauqua circuit began in community A on a Sunday, the Sunday acts from community A would be the Monday acts for community B, and would not perform again on a Sunday until community H, assuming a tight circuit with venues less than one day of travel apart. It was not possible, then, for the bureaus to designate one group of acts as the Sunday program, since each act on the circuit would most likely be performing every Sunday.

The first step in assuring that a circuit chautauqua program complied with prevailing sentiment regarding Sundays was to avoid direct time conflict between chautauqua programs and church services. This primarily necessitated leaving Sunday morning free of activities. Bureaus did not usually program musical performances or lectures in the mornings, reserving mornings for children's activities or local events. It was not difficult, then, for circuit chautauqua bureaus to clear Sunday mornings, as doing so most likely involved nothing more than suspending the children's chautauqua for a day. Children's chautauquas were not a drawing card of the week and were usually held every day (aside from Sunday) throughout the event; so suspending the children's chautauqua in deference to Sunday would not cause a major disruption to the program or draw complaints from the ticket-buying community.

The approach to Sunday afternoon and evening programming varied from bureau to bureau and changed through the years. Early circuits were more likely to conduct religious services on Sunday evenings, often based on the vespers published for use at the Chautauqua Institution. These services were conducted in addition to other programming, which may or may not have been sacred in nature. The 1913 chautauqua in North English, Iowa, produced by Redpath-Vawter, offered a Sunday program consisting of an afternoon performance by the Lilliputian Entertainers followed by a lecture by Robert Vessey, former governor of South Dakota. The "Chautauqua Vesper" service was added to the program at 4:30 P.M., a time left open for dinner on other days. The evening program began with the Lilliputian Entertainers, and concluded with a lecture entitled "The Rich and the Poor" by Hugh Orchard.[28] The addition of the vespers service did not disrupt the program and could have been inserted into any of the daily programs.

While some chautauqua bureaus used the vespers service prepared and published by the Chautauqua Institution (this was done with the blessing of the institution, as indicated in the published services), the Redpath-Vawter bureau published its own short vespers service for use during its chautauquas. The service began with "Day Is Dying in the West," a hymn composed for and most commonly associated with the Chautauqua Institution, followed by a short prayer by the leader and the "Our Father" by the audience. Next came the hymn "Jesus, Saviour, Pilot Me," by Edward Hopper and John Gould, followed by a responsive reading of Psalm 103. This was followed by congregational singing of "The Star Spangled Banner" and "America."[29] The final hymn was "Abide With Me," by Henry Lyte to the tune "Eventide" by William Monk, followed by a spoken benediction.[30]

There is no indication in the 1913 North English program that either the music or lectures were altered to accommodate for Sunday. It was not unusual, however, for bureaus to combine a vespers service with sacred musical programs, religious lectures, or both. The 1915 program for North English, also produced by Redpath-Vawter, presented a "high grade musical" by the El Dorado Grand Opera Company to begin Sunday afternoon, followed by a "business talk" by lecturer S.A. Baker. Like the 1913 program, a vespers services is inserted during the dinner break (this one at 4:15). The evening program consisted solely of "oratorio music" by the El Dorado Grand Opera Company; there was no lecture or other event in the evening.[31]

It was also common for chautauqua bureaus not to alter the program schedule at all, but rather to assure audiences that the scheduled acts would provide lectures and music appropriate for Sunday. The program for the 1922 Midland Chautauquas circuit was generic, listing events in the program by "First Day," "Second Day," etc., rather than specifying dates. Doing so allowed Midland Chautauquas to produce one program for distribution to the entire circuit, rather than producing programs for each community. At the end of the program was the statement, "All Sunday programs appropriate to the day."[32] Such a statement indicated that Midland either considered each act on the program to be appropriate for Sunday in its usual state, or that each act could alter its program to be appropriate for Sunday if needed.

The program for the Sunday evening performance of the Independence Concert Band at the Independence, Kansas, chautauqua was labeled a "sacred concert" and featured a variety of sacred and secular music, as well as two lectures by Thomas Elmore Lucey. Lucey was billed as a "globe-trotting poet-humorist" and traveled the chautauqua and lyceum circuits extensively. The combination of local amateur musicians and a paid circuit lecturer is very common for independent chautauquas such as the one at Independence. It should be remembered that the Independence Concert Band, being local and, presumably, performing at only one chautauqua per year, was in a better position to tailor its program to the assigned Sunday time slot. Still, three of the eight musical works on the program were thoroughly secular. Of course, the use of secular instrumental music in programs labeled "sacred" was not unusual or new; the precedent had been set by the Parisian Concert Spirituel in the early eighteenth century. It is impossible to know whether the chautauqua committee at Independence intentionally scheduled a local instrumental act on Sunday night in order to avoid the controversy of performing secular texted works on that day. Regardless of the reasoning, the ability to make such decisions was an advantage that independent chautauquas held over their commercial counterparts.

A 1916 program from Bohumir Kryl's band, while not a chautauqua performance (it is dated May 28 and was a multiday engagement and thus too early and too long for chautauqua), may shed light on Kryl's programming strategy for Sundays. The band gave two concerts on that day, both labeled "sacred." Each concert was divided into two parts consisting of four numbers each. Despite their sacred labels, each of the Kryl concerts was dominated by secular music. While Kryl did program *Providence,* a "sacred fantasia" by Tobani based on tunes from hymns and oratorio, as well as a cornet solo arrangement of the "Inflammatus" from Rossini's *Stabat Mater* (performed by Kryl himself) and an unnamed hymn, the majority of works chosen for these programs were standard concert fare, including a divertimento on Chinese melodies, Tchaikovsky's *1812 Overture* and a medley from Flotow's *Martha*. For these concerts, Kryl's band appeared with a vocal soloist, Helen Cafarelli. The soprano performed one song on each of the two concerts; neither of her selections was sacred in nature. Thus, at least in this situation, even music with text was not confined to religious subjects despite the sacred label.

As the chautauqua movement declined, bookings became fewer and scheduling became less tight. With fewer dates to fill, it was possible for even the major bureaus to build a day off into the circuit schedules. Considering the accommodations often needed for Sundays, it was logical to make Sundays the "dead day" on the schedule, and this is precisely what bureaus often did in the late 1920s. Of course, each of these approaches assumes that the host community is predominantly Christian, that they worship on Sunday, and that they are willing to accept musical and dramatic performances of any kind on Sundays. There were certainly communities for which these assumptions would prove false. For instance, in the eastern United States there were chautauquas produced by and for Jewish communities. There were also communities throughout the United States in which the predominant form of Christianity forbade non-church activities of any kind on Sunday. These communities were unlikely to contract with a circuit chautauqua bureau because of the inability of the bureaus to accommodate their needs. Such communities therefore were likely to produce their chautauquas independently rather than host a commercial circuit chautauqua.

The Chautauqua Musical Experience

Although the lack of detailed programs for many chautauqua musical acts makes it impossible to reconstruct an entire week's program, it is possible to approximate the musical experience of an average chautauqua-goer using available evidence. The first step in musically reconstructing a "typical" chautauqua was to select a program intended for wide distribution — that is, one produced by a major bureau for a large circuit. It was also important that the selected program be a "base" program free from added "star" attractions, musical or otherwise. To ensure that the program reflected the base program offered by that particular circuit, the printed program used was selected from the generic programs published by bureaus which could be printed with the name and chautauqua dates of any community on the circuit. For these reasons, the 1929 Redpath De Luxe (by the late 1920s, it was not uncommon to see Redpath circuits labeled "deluxe" or "premier" rather than bearing the name of the bureau manager or location of bureau headquarters) program was chosen as the basis for reconstruction of a circuit chautauqua musical experience.

The program lasted seven days and involved six musical acts in ten performances. Not surprisingly, detailed programs from chautauqua performances of each of the six acts do not survive. The Filipino Collegians published a sample repertoire in the group's advertising brochure, while the Redpath bureau published a program to be distributed at lyceum performances of the

IV. Musical Programming in Chautauqua 119

Cathedral Choir. It appears the remaining four musical acts on the 1929 Redpath De Luxe circuit left no programs from which to extrapolate possible chautauqua programs. However, this is not entirely the case, as the group labeled "Edna White and Her Trumpeters" (despite the "trumpeters" name, the group was in fact a brass quartet involving two trumpets, a trombone, and a baritone horn) in the Redpath program appeared under at least two other monikers in lyceum and other venues. Programs from this group performing under the two other names survive and can be used to create possible programs for morning and evening chautauqua performances. The third day of the chautauqua involved an afternoon concert by the Jackson concert artists and an evening performance by contralto Lorna Doone Jackson. Programs do not survive for either act. For purposes of this study, similar acts were selected for which programs do survive. A short program of the Rahm Family Concert Orchestra was used in place of the Jackson Concert artists, and a program from a chautauqua performance of Edna White, contralto, was substituted for Lorna Jackson's solo evening performance. Finally, two chautauqua playlists—one from an afternoon concert and one from an evening performance—found in the records of the Krantz Family Concert Company,[33] are substituted for missing programs of the Blue Danube Orchestra. Using these substitutions, it is possible to create an approximation of the musical experience of an audience member at the 1929 Redpath De Luxe chautauqua.

The chautauqua began with a popular concert by the Filipino Collegians, which might have included "The Indian Love Call," "Blue Skies," "Miami Shore," and the popular Philippine march "Katikas." The evening concert would have included sketches about Philippine life interspersed between musical numbers including "The Philippine Overture," Schubert's "Serenade," and *Philippine Bolero Overture*. The evening concluded with a lecture by Montaville Flowers entitled "What Young America Is Thinking."

The second day of the 1929 De Luxe circuit was indicative of the late 1920s programming shifts discussed earlier, in that it involved neither music nor a lecture. The afternoon consisted of a performance of "magic and mystery" by escape artists Mardoni and Company. *Sun-Up*, billed as the "great drama of the Carolina mountains" performed by a "New York cast," was the evening offering.

The third afternoon began with a prelude concert by the Jackson Concert Artists, which likely resembled this program presented by the Rahm family:

Coronation March	Meyerbeer
Intermezzo	Mascagni
Trombone Solo	
Prize Song	Wagner
Violin Duet	

Intermission	
Calif of Bagdad	Bieldica
Cornet Solo	
Spring's Awakening	Bach
Miserere from *Il Trovatore*	Verdi
Pizzicata Polka	Strauss

The prelude concert was followed by a lecture-recital of poetry by Anne Campbell entitled "Everyday Poetry." The evening "grand concert" by Lorna Doone Jackson would have been rather substantial, being the only offering on the evening program, and was probably similar to this program by Edna White:

Aria "O Don Fatale"	Verdi
"She Never Told Her Love"	Haydn
"Come and Trip It"	Handel
"When Love Is Kind"	
"In an Old Fashioned Town"	Squire
"Good Morning Brother Sunshine"	Lehman
"The Brownies"	Leoni
Sanctuary	LaForge
Three Chinese Mother Goose Rhymes	
Christ in Flanders	Stephens

The fourth afternoon of the chautauqua began with a prelude concert by Edna White and Her Trumpeters. Based on other programs and the group's published repertoire list, such a program likely included the following:

Quartet from *Rigoletto*	Verdi
Medley	Victor Herbert
Trombone Solo	
"I Hear You Calling Me"	Marshall
Barcarolle from *Tales of Hoffman*	Offenbach

This concert was followed by a travel lecture by aviator Denis Rooke. Edna White and Her Trumpeters also gave the evening musical performance, which was most likely more serious in nature than that of the afternoon:

Faust Fantasy	Gounod
Serenade	Schubert
Romance	Rubinstein
Cavatina	Raff
Nocturne	Mendelssohn
Intermission	
Pomp and Circumstance	Elgar
Valse in A Minor	Brahms
Prelude	Rachmaninoff

IV. Musical Programming in Chautauqua

"To a Wild Rose"	MacDowell
Pilgrims Chorus	Wagner

The evening concluded with a lecture by Governor Nellie Tayloe Ross, the first female governor in United States history.

The fifth afternoon of the chautauqua began with a concert by the Cathedral Choir, which likely included:

Processional — The God of Abraham Praise	Noble
Savior, When Night Involves the Skies	Shelley
Soprano Solo	
Sanctus	Gounod
Baritone Solo	
No Other Guide Have We	Tachesnokoff

This concert was followed by a lecture by Theodore Graham entitled "Making America American." The evening concert of the Cathedral Choir featured a musical program entitled *The Chimes of Brittany*.

The only afternoon event on the sixth day of the chautauqua was a concert by the Blue Danube orchestra, which likely resembled this program by the Krantz family:

Fanfare	J. Worth Allen
Light Cavalry Overture	Suppé
Violin Solo	
"Annie Laurie"	Scott-Parker
Dramatic Reading	
Bell Solo	
Bells of St. Mary's	Adams
Intermission	
Sophien March	Lorenz
El Capitan	Sousa
The Rosary	Nevin
Cornet and Violin Duet	
Medley	Sunday
Stars and Stripes Forever	Sousa

The Blue Danube Orchestra's evening concert functioned as a prelude to a lengthy lecture by Frederick Snyder. This inversion of musical programming — placing the "grand concert" in the afternoon and the prelude in the evening — was not entirely unheard of. The Krantz family's archive contains an "evening prelude" program from an engagement with Redpath:

Weiner Welt March	Hoch
Violin Solo	
"When You and I Were Young"	Goldman

College Days Medley
Dramatic Reading
Quartet — "Kentucky Babe"   Geibel

The seventh and final day of the De Luxe circuit involved no music. The afternoon featured animated cartoons by Beckewitz, with "electrical effects." The evening consisted of a popular Broadway comedy, *Skidding*. The absence of music or lectures in two of the seven days of the chautauqua was not typical of the circuit chautauqua movement as a whole, but it was not uncommon in the later years of the chautauqua movement, especially among bureaus that did not truncate later chautauquas to five (or even three) days.

Conclusion

While the lack of detailed program information for the vast majority of circuit chautauqua performances makes it impossible to accurately reconstruct a program for an entire chautauqua event, the extant ephemera provides a solid general description of such a program. It is possible to discern from these sources that individual musical acts were largely responsible for creating programs that would then be presented in their entirety as an audition for booking by a circuit chautauqua bureau. The bureau or committee would then construct a multiday program that fit their particular programming strategy. This would usually entail engaging musical acts to give two performances per day, the second of which was nearly always longer and often consisted of "heavier" musical selections. Musical acts on the chautauqua circuits could combine works from several genres, but usually specialized in particular styles of music. Vocal/instrumental quartets, a standard on the circuits, performed a combination of "heavy popular" and "light classical" compositions that reflected chautauqua's ideas about music and society. Finally, Sundays were problematic for circuit chautauqua managers, and several methods were employed to address programming issues related to Sunday.

V

Music Defines Chautauqua as an Educational and Cultural Institution

Chautauqua enjoyed a special place among traveling shows in early twentieth-century America. Unlike the circus, vaudeville circuit, or medicine show, it came to every community with the blessing — and more tangibly, the financial backing — of community leaders. This support was essential to the survival of chautauqua, and the bureaus were careful to cultivate and maintain an image of the movement as more than a simple diversion for entertainment-starved rural Americans. Even when the delineation between chautauqua and empty diversions was less than clear, those within the industry were insistent that chautauqua's educational and moral ideals set it apart. An article in *The Lyceum Magazine* even argued for the educational value of magic shows, stating, "It sharpens the mental facilities, develops observation and attention."[1]

The circuit and independent chautauquas were presented first and foremost as educational, emphasizing ties — both real and implied — to the Chautauqua Institution and its various educational outreach efforts. Bureaus also invoked the term "culture" in promotional rhetoric, presenting chautauqua as a much-needed link between rural communities and urban "high culture" of the era. These definitions of chautauqua served to differentiate it from competing movements and to justify the high level of community support necessary to produce a chautauqua.

Chautauqua communities were overwhelmingly rural and not especially wealthy. Promoters were often in the position of asking communities with very little infrastructure and no cultural budget to assume a significant monetary risk in order to host a chautauqua. In order to convince communities to "guarantee" a chautauqua (circuit chautauqua contracts usually required

"The Home Town Spirit" cartoon (*The Lyceum Magazine*, August 1918).

the sponsoring community to guarantee a set dollar amount of advance ticket sales, and to make up the deficit should that sales goal not be reached), promoters advanced the idea that the presence of a chautauqua, and the perceived quality of that event, spoke to the character of the community. Community leaders, religious organizations, and businesses in turn promoted the chautauqua as a means of strengthening the community and boosting civic pride. Similarly, many chautauqua-hosting communities also sought to show their support of culture through building theaters (often labeled "opera houses" to avoid negative connotations surrounding theatrical activities) for winter cultural activities, including lyceum courses. Rhetoric surrounding public support of opera houses mirrored the push to guarantee the chautauqua in these communities.[2]

It was not uncommon for local businesses to alter their regular newspaper ads in support of the coming chautauqua. It should be noted, however, that the commercial circuit chautauqua bureaus did not print advertisements in

Local newspaper advertisement encouraging chautauqua attendance (published in the *Evening* [MN] *Tribune*, Albert Lea, June 19, 1916).

their programs. In contrast, many of the independent assemblies, even those whose promotional rhetoric decried the commercialism of circuit chautauqua, printed programs containing extensive advertising from local business sponsors.

A poem by prolific chautauqua industry cartoonist Ned Woodman accompanied his cartoon entitled "The Home Town Spirit." The poem is written from the perspective of a community member who embodies the spirit necessary to support the chautauqua. It reads, in part, "I gladly sign the contract and I hustle like tarnation to bring the big chautauqua here with all its inspiration. To spread the gladsome news abroad I'm tireless in my labors. I boost the season ticket sale among my friends and neighbors."[3]

Chautauqua's public support was heavily dependent on the movement's image as an educational outlet. The early twentieth century saw an explosion of reading circles, public lectures, libraries, and other educational and self-improvement activities intended for adults.[4] An article in *Talent* contended that "anything labeled 'education' will go in the United States." The columnist noted the phenomenal breadth (if not depth) of the adult education movement, stating, "If there is anything, for example, in the line of education unadvertised as possible to secure by correspondence, from sermonizing down to sand-bagging, you may be sure it will be blazoned for patronage before the present era of prosperity is over."[5]

The sheer size of the tent, combined with the minimal cost and time commitment required to attend a chautauqua, made it the most visible and popular form of adult education available to a community. The tents were called "the canvas colleges of the common people"[6] and "the intellectual circus of America."[7] The 1910 Redpath-Vawter program included several references to the movement as an educational and cultural institution, including this: "The chautauqua is the people's university. Have you enrolled?"[8]

The invocation of the university in reference to chautauqua troubled many academics. George Vincent (son of Chautauqua Institution cofounder John Heyl Vincent), in a 1908 article defending the educational merit of the movement, wrote, "Many of my academic colleagues are not only skeptical, but derisive about the chautauqua movement, in which they profess to see a pseudo-intellectual hippodrome where all manner of absurd, grotesque, and irrational performances are conducted."[9] Academics challenged the educational value of chautauqua based not only on the presence of non-lecture acts, but also on the educational value of the lectures themselves. One professor stated that "chautauqua is not associated with the highest academic scholarship."[10]

Some of the acts that critics found objectionable due to perceived lack of educational merit could be excused based on their relative scarcity in the chautauqua program. A magician, a promoter might argue, might not be educational; but he is one act of fifteen on the program, and who would begrudge one hour of frivolous entertainment surrounded by an entire week of intellectual stimulation? With half of the program or more involving music, however, promoters were forced to address community and critical concerns about the educational value of music in chautauqua.

The role of music in the creation and maintenance of chautauqua's image is complex. The inclusion of art music in a program emphasized chautauqua's role as conduit of culture to rural areas. Even popular music — as long as it was deemed wholesome and inoffensive — was a credit to the chautauqua, as it might keep the youth from seeking amusement in less structured settings. There were, however, those who believed that the best music would always be inferior to the worst lecture in terms of educational value. To these critics, music was at best a necessary evil and at worst the downfall of the movement. Official publications of major chautauqua and lyceum organizations stressed the movement's loyalty to the lecture. The first page of the July 1916 edition of *The Lyceum Magazine* outlined "A Lyceum and Chautauqua Platform," the article consisting of fourteen pronouncements, apparently compiled by the International Lyceum Association (ILA). Although there is no direct attribution to the ILA, the "platform" references the association specifically, and one pronouncement is a mission statement for the ILA. The eleventh item of the "platform" is entitled "The Lecture Vital" and begins thus: "The Lyceum and

Chautauqua give welcome and necessary place to the musical arts, the concerter, the reader, the impersonator, the entertainer, the dramatic company, the band, the orchestra, the magician, the film and to all other exponents and vehicles of art and entertainment that conform to our standards, but recognize the lyceum lecture as fundamental."[11]

There is historical precedent for such attitudes toward music, especially among those whose focus was on the lyceum; the typical early nineteenth-century lyceum was entirely devoid of music. The addition of music to the lyceum program coincided with the commercialization — and many would argue corruption — of the lyceum movement. That certain lyceum "purists" would be critical of music in chautauqua is not surprising. Denial of music's educational merit on the platform, however, existed within the chautauqua community and persists in some modern scholarship. Russell Johnson, in an article published in 2001, categorized chautauqua acts as educational or noneducational based solely on the presence of a lecture component to the act.[12] Thus, all lectures, regardless of content, were deemed educational, while no performance, musical or otherwise, could be.

Lecture-recitals and lectures about music satisfied critics' need for obviously educational musical acts, although such acts were relatively rare on the circuits. Musical lectures were more prevalent in the lyceum, but these acts rarely appear on chautauqua programs. Pianist and composer Felix Heink, brother-in-law of Ernestine Schumann Heink and billed as the former court pianist to the prince of Schwarzburg-Rudolstadt, advertised lecture-recitals for performance at both lyceum and chautauqua events, including one entitled "Music, the Language of the Emotions." The lecture recital was billed as "decided help to those who are laboring in behalf of stimulating interest in music among the general public in their localities." The program included the following works, "interspersed with short, impressive, explanatory remarks":

Romance in F sharp	Schumann
Impromptu, Op. 90, no. 4	Chopin
Ballroom Scene from *Mirabeau*	Heink
Funeral March	Chopin
Wedding March	Heink
Military March	Heink
Reverie, "Isolee"	Heink
Minuet in A Major	Heink
Slumber Song	Heink
Grande Valse de Concert, "The Joy of Life"	Heink[13]

Pianist Edward Steckel gave a lecture-recital entitled "Music for Today" to chautauqua assemblies in the southeastern United States. Steckel's promotional materials emphasize his skills as an entertainer and the humor of his presentation. His lecture-recital included segments about "permanent" music (his term for art music and traditional folk music) as well as "familiar" music (short-lived popular music). Although no program listing specific musical works for a Steckel lecture-recital has been found, one review noted that the high point of the performance was when Steckel played "Yankee Doodle" and "Dixie" simultaneously on the piano.[14]

The junior chautauqua, a staple of many circuit and independent chautauqua events, was an opportunity to cultivate future chautauqua patrons through cultural education. To that end, White and Myers Chautauquas, a circuit bureau operating primarily in the Midwest, included music appreciation in its junior chautauqua curriculum. J. Shannon White, president of the bureau, explained the musical element of a White and Myers junior chautauqua, stating, "Every morning they gather together and listen to various selections, which they are asked to explain in their own words. Folk songs are often given. Once the children have perceived the quality of the music of the various nationalities, the next step is to translate this sense of rhythm into the graceful measures of folk dances."[15]

Winter lyceums hosted more (and more academic) lecture-recitals and lectures about music. Many of the lecturers managed by the lyceum bureaus held year-round employment and were not able to travel full-time for summer chautauqua work. They contracted with the lyceum bureaus to book local engagements for lyceums, school assemblies, and clubs. One such lecturer was Henriette Weber of Chicago. Weber was billed as the director of opera concerts, Art Institute of Chicago, and as a lecturer for the Lecture Association of the University of Chicago. Weber offered several lecture series, including a six-part series on "modern tendencies in music" and a six-part series on Richard Wagner. Sponsoring organizations could request the entire series or any combination of lectures. Weber also offered several single lectures on topics including folk music and nationalism, program music, dance forms, and music in religious worship.[16]

When a lecture about music appeared on the circuit chautauqua platform, the subject was most often the music of non-Western cultures. These lectures often included the art, folklore, history, or dance of the subject culture as well as discussion of music. Albert and Martha Gale offered lecture-recitals on both "music and myth of old Japan" and "songs and stories of the red man." In both presentations, the Gales dressed in elaborate costumes, sang, and played renditions on both Western and traditional instruments. The Gales also gave dramatized presentations of daily life in Japanese and Native American cultures on a stage strewn with folk art and artifacts.

Some musical lectures focused on the music of American subcultures, though this phenomenon was surprisingly rare considering the chautauqua movement's frequent invocation of its American identity. In 1917 Lorraine Wyman and Howard Brockway solicited single engagements for lecture-recitals based on their recently published collection, *Lonesome Tunes: Kentucky Mountain Balladry*. Wyman sang the tunes and appears to have done the majority of the lecturing, while Brockway accompanied her on the piano, playing his own published arrangements. One critic remarked, "Miss Wyman told the folks about the people in the mountains, imitated their way of singing, and then sang songs with her own witching charm."[17] Wyman's presentation of their subject seems strikingly akin to lecture-recitals on exotic cultures popular on the circuits. The Kentuckians from whom the songs were collected are referred to as "natives," their singing as "howling."[18] Wyman and Brockway were clearly presented as outside observers, their subject as an exotic other. The heavy lecture component of the act differentiates it from standard presentations of African American music, as does the fact that the performers in the Wyman-Brockway recitals were not members of the subject culture. Also in contrast to standard chautauqua performance of American folk music,[19] which most often took the guise of concerts, the Wyman-Brockway lecture-recitals were clearly presented as educational events.

Some chautauqua musical acts invoked the university without involving a strictly educational component. Musical groups such as the University Four and the College Girls incorporated college fight songs and songs about university life into their acts. They occasionally appeared in university regalia, or wearing clothing bearing the names of well-known colleges and universities. The College Girls' act was constructed around the premise that they were natives of whichever town they were currently entertaining, freshly returned from Vassar, recalling in song and story their college careers. Interestingly, none of their promotional photos invoke Vassar, but rather Michigan, Chicago, and other universities likely to be more familiar to Midwestern audiences.

As has been discussed earlier, the College Girls were a popular and long-lived chautauqua act. Though not especially educational, the act relied on the music and imagery associated with American higher education. The College Girls performed primarily in the Midwest, and it is unlikely that many in the chautauqua audiences of that region would have shared the College Girls' (feigned, as they were not actually connected with the institution either) nostalgia for Vassar. If the goal of the act was to tap into shared experience and forge a connection with the audience, the College Girls would likely have chosen one of the large coeducational Midwestern universities, whose alumni were much more likely to attend a Midwestern chautauqua. Since the College Girls were not actually alumni of Vassar, it seems strange that a group performing in the rural Midwest would choose a small northeastern women's college with which to identify. This reasoning is based, however, on the mistaken assumption that the College Girls expected the audience to identify with college life as portrayed in the act. In reality, the College Girls represented an idealized stereotype of the northeastern college experience. They presented the liberal arts education and life at a small, elite college as they would have presented a foreign culture. The audience was not expected to connect to the songs and stories of life at Vassar, but rather to experience such a life vicariously through the College Girls as a break from their rural Midwestern existence. This theme of escapism and of presenting non-Midwestern American cultures as exotic is recurrent in the literature concerning chautauqua and is addressed as it relates to music later in this chapter. Despite the importance of circuit chautauqua's reputation as an educational outlet, very few musical acts were explicitly billed as educational. Language invoking "culture," "sophistication," and "quality" is common in programs and promotional materials, and the term "education" appears frequently in reference to lectures. But acts consisting solely of a musical performance were seldom presented as educational.

It could be argued, based on the strong bias towards the lecture in chautauqua and lyceum trade publications, that musical performances were seen as an unfortunate necessity detracting from the movement's educational value and were thus indefensible as an educational asset. It is unlikely that those involved in chautauqua planning and promotion were this dismissive of music. Bureaus were very conscious of presenting music as high-quality and morally uplifting, and were wary of any music with "lowbrow" connotations. Until the very end of the chautauqua movement, when the inclusion of newer popular music was deemed economically necessary, chautauqua bureaus avoided booking jazz musicians nearly completely, and generally preferred popular music to be several years old so as to appeal to a wider audience and avoid associations with youth culture. This trend can also be seen in the selection of dramatic acts and lectures, in which certain volatile subjects, such as current national politics, were not programmed. Had the bureaus written music off as a necessary evil, it seems unlikely they would have gone to such extents to enforce standards in musical programming.

Another — perhaps more likely — scenario is that chautauqua decision-makers felt no need to justify music's educational merit, assuming the audience believed in the educational value inherent to good music. In this situation, the bureau had only to program music conforming to the audience's perception of "high quality," and the audience would infer the educational element. Of course, certain novelty musical acts were beyond justification as educational, uplifting, patriotic, or any of the associations common to musical

V. *Music Defines Chautauqua ... Cultural Institution*   131

Promotional photograph for the Kaffir Boys (author's collection, gift of Fred Crane).

acts on the circuits. These novelty acts were written off, as were the jugglers and magicians common in later years of the movement, as light-hearted breaks from the intense intellectual experience of the chautauqua, and were not central to the movement's self-definition as a cultural and educational force.

The belief in the inherent educational value of certain types of music is a complex phenomenon incorporating rural views of urban culture, American ideas about European art, early twentieth-century class dynamics, and the philosophical underpinnings of the chautauqua movement. It seems that it was not the music itself that held the educational value, but rather the culture that the music represented. Music defined as "quality" by circuit managers and accepted as such by audiences usually came from the standard western art music repertory, from exotic cultures, or from the popular repertory of years past. Older popular music served to define circuit chautauqua as a reinforcer of older values. The perceived educational value of chautauqua music was derived primarily from the movement's incorporation of art music and exotic musical acts.

Taken in the context of the movement as a whole, the educational role of exotic musical performances is clear. Exotic musical acts often involved a lecture component and discussion of the music's culture of origin. Many exotic musical acts, however, made no pretense of a lecture and were strictly recitals. Often, the music was authentic to the culture of origin and was played by native performers or those with considerable experience in the style, while the lecture component was delivered by an English-speaking "expert" with a rather superficial knowledge of the culture and its music.

Balmer's Kaffir Boy Choir of Africa was such an act. The group was formed and managed by Jason Balmer (referred to as John Balmer in secondary sources, for unknown reasons), British traveler and impresario who had, in the 1890s, formed an "African Native Choir," which he had taken on a tour of Europe and the United States, where he abandoned them to be raised by members of several African American churches.[20] Balmer formed the Kaffir Boys around 1904, and the group toured Great Britain sporadically and with many personnel changes for several years. The Aborigines' Protection Society of England campaigned against the Kaffir Boys' British tour of 1910–1911, citing the abandonment of the African Native Choir as cause for concern.[21] Despite the society's objections, Balmer and the Kaffir Boys toured Great Britain and later the United States, appearing in larger chautauquas and in urban engagements under the management of the Coit Lyceum Bureau. The group Balmer brought to the United States consisted of five South African boys of unknown tribal affiliation. Although their ages were not recorded, the youngest appears to have been no more than six or seven years old, while the oldest appears to have been a teenager. The group toured with pianist Elsie Clark, who was billed as a white native of South Africa and the daughter of "pioneer missionaries."[22] Balmer sang bass for the group, and he and Clark lectured about South African culture in between songs and staged scenes of African life such as a "Kaffir wedding scene" and various battle scenarios.

Advertisements claim that the songs were performed "mainly in English, although reviews of performances mention songs performed in English, Dutch, Kaffir, and Hottentot."[23] A promotional brochure for the group stated that "it is a novelty that [is] united to the highest type of musical art.... Their countenances are beaming with delight as though they are glad to get into the light of civilization."[24] Although the Coit Bureau emphasized the effect of bringing the Kaffir Boys "into the light of civilization," much of the rhetoric of the chautauqua and lyceum bureaus focused on using groups like the Kaffir Boys to bring "culture" to chautauqua audiences.

An Ellison-White Chautauquas advertisement from 1921 depicted various Native Americans (and one Maori, a reference to Ellison-White's brief attempt to run chautauquas in New Zealand) telling of the lengths to which the chautauqua agents had gone to sell them tickets. The final lines of the advertisement read, "What chance has a poor native today? Of his future, he has nothing to say. 'Uplift' is in the air, Ellison-White everywhere. They'll get you some sort of way."[25]

The presentation of music from remote lands to a predominantly rural American audience typifies the escapist strategy employed by circuit chautauqua bureaus. Eckman argued that this escapism was a defining component of the circuit chautauqua movement, one that was largely absent from the Chautauqua Institution and the independent assemblies.[26] Eckman's assertion, while true of the Chautauqua Institution, does not take into account the fact that many independent chautauquas were rebadged circuit chautauquas, and the majority of the independent assemblies booked talent through commercial circuit bureaus. Musical acts, especially, made virtually no distinction between circuit and independent assemblies and generally performed at both, making it unlikely that the escapism found in acts like the Kaffir Boys was absent from the independent assemblies.

The view of the audience as starved of culture, education, and even entertainment was prevalent within the chautauqua industry. Lyceum and chautauqua trade publications contain many unflattering characterizations of chautauqua audiences. They are often depicted as borderline illiterate and uncultured, with references to being dragged to the "Chee-Tau-Quay" by a sole enlightened family member or neighbor. One example of such characterization is Charles Grilley's short story, "The Chee-Tau-Quay," which appeared in the December 1907 issue of *Lyceumite and Talent*. The text, which takes up an entire page of the magazine (including an illustration) reads in part:

> Well, 'beout ten o'clock they rung a bell an' the band begun to play,
> An' folks commenced to crowd the tent, mor'n er thousand, I should say.
> They played a piece called "Susie's March"—' twould lift you off the seat.
> A preacher jest in front uv me hed ter fairly hold his feet.
> I felt jest like a two-year-old, seemed like I walked on air,
> Haint herd sech all-round music sence the Red Rock County Fair.
> Then four fellers took the rostrum an' sung a song about ther sea, —
> Fer vocal satisfaction, they jest suited to a T.
> They wuz really so extray-fine we hed to hev them back.
> An' they responded by singin' 'beout a "Teacher and a Tack."
> Funny? Jeekus-Pokus! It seemed as if I'd split,
> An' Willum J. jest hollered, we thought he'd hev a fit!

Similar portrayals of chautauqua audiences, some with accompanying unflattering cartoons, appear in other industry publications. Exposure to other cultures, even in the form of stylized, sanitized, commercialized, and often highly idealized musical performances was seen as bringing the world to people who would have no chance of learning about it otherwise.

This same rationale was often employed to justify the educational value of art music on the chautauqua circuits. In many ways, urban "high culture" was presented to audiences as something exotic, and the audience was assumed to have no more connection to or familiarity with European art music than it did with the music and culture of the Kaffir Boys. Art music performers' connections—however tenuous—with famous institutions and urban centers were emphasized in promotional materials. Performers from New York and Boston were often billed as if their city of origin was itself a musical credential. Musical group names were often chosen to invoke urban or European culture, even if the group had no discernible ties to the famous city, institution, or person implied in the name. For instance, nineteen different musical groups with names including the word "Chicago" are documented to have performed in chautauquas.[27] These included groups with potentially deceptive names likely intended to be confused with established major art music ensembles, such as the Chicago Symphonic Orchestra, which performed in Iowa in 1923, and the Chicago Operatic Company, which toured extensively on the circuits in the early years of circuit chautauqua. Seven groups invoked Boston in their names; one called itself the Manhattan Opera Company; and twelve groups' names began with "New York."

Several groups invoked the names of well-known art music composers. Three "Mozart" groups had sample programs on file with Redpath. Interestingly, only one of these programs lists any composition by Mozart. There were also several "Schubert" groups, including one named "The Schuberts" in which none of the members was named "Schubert" and none of the works on the sample program were Schubert compositions.[28] Another "Schubert" group, the Schubert Serenaders, explained their use of the Schubert name thusly: "The name 'Schubert Serenaders' denotes appropriate regard for the incomparable Franz Schubert, whose works, ranging from the simplicity of folk songs to the height of symphonic power, form the basis of all programs.[29] However, compositions representative of the masters of many lands are presented by this company."[30]

This presentation of urban culture as an arbiter of artistic merit occurred alongside chautauqua's presentation of American rural culture as morally superior. Brochures of the years prior to 1913, years in which the circuit chautauqua movement was largely confined to the Midwest, especially emphasized the role of the American small town as defender of moral values.[31] The idea that the small town was morally superior and that rural adolescents should be shielded from the lure of the city was thoroughly ingrained in the Midwest and can be seen clearly in the McGuffey Readers used by Midwestern schoolchildren (and some adults) during the nineteenth century. McGuffey's stories of upstanding rural Americans being corrupted by travel to urban centers shaped many Midwesterners' perception of the city.[32] The chautauqua was advertised as a way to bring enough of the urban experience to a community's youth that those youth would not be tempted to leave home in search of urban opportunities.

Beyond the presumed moral superiority of rural America, trade publications intended for those within the chautauqua movement sometimes presented the chautauqua and lyceum as culturally superior to the offerings of urban competitors. A cartoon in *The Lyceum Magazine* from February of 1920 proclaimed, "City folks have their theaters, and country folks the lyceum bureau." In the cartoon, the urban theater orchestra accompanies a dancing chorus line, while on the lyceum stage musicians in formal wear give every indication of performing classical music.

Charles Horner spoke of the uneasy relationship between chautauqua audiences and urban culture in his 1913 address to his assembled employees: "The big city to which the small city has ever looked for its standards of life, overrun with cheap shows and blasé with burlesque, gave it no help, and in fact is just beginning to understand what a powerful thing the chautauqua really is."[33] Edna Wilson, in an essay apparently intended to promote White and Myers Chautauquas, clearly articulated the "us vs. them" attitude often expressed by chautauqua proponents in regard to America's urban centers and the entertainments emanating from them: "Mr. George M. Cohan knows what a New York audience like in its hours off. So does the manager of Steeplechase Park. But the crowds that fill the theaters around Forty-Second Street or that flock to Coney Island on a sultry July Sunday are not typical American audiences. And Mr. Moreland Brown, of the White and Myers Chautauquas, with circuits visiting four hundred towns in fourteen states, has a clearer insight into the amusement tastes of the American citizen as he exists in his native habitat than any Broadway manager alive."[34]

Moreover, urban audiences, accustomed to a variety of readily available educational and entertainment opportunities, never embraced the chautauqua. Henry Pringle recalled a disastrous attempt at promoting a circuit chautauqua in New York City, where the star attraction, William Howard Taft, drew roughly fifty spectators in a tent designed to hold fifteen hundred.[35] Despite the cities' lack of interest in the chautauqua phenomenon, chautauqua audiences continued to look to urban centers as a source for art and culture, and bureaus capitalized on this fascination with urban "high culture."

The idea of chautauqua as a vehicle for "culture" was frequently invoked in advertising, in the rhetoric surrounding the debate over the validity of the chautauqua movement, and in the memoirs of those involved in it. The *Denton* (MD) *Journal* lauded the chautauqua movement as the flagship of humanistic education in the face of utilitarianism in the universities. The article also opined that a chautauqua "cannot be rendered in a community for a week without having some cultural effects hostile to the uncensored motion-picture show and peripatetic vaudeville company."[36] Circuit chautauqua was one of many outlets for the phenomenon Unitarian theologian William Ellery Channing dubbed "self-culture" in early twentieth-century America. Channing stressed that self-culture was not about acquisition of knowledge as much as the cultivation of an inquisitive and critical mind. This idea, also espoused by the "New Haven scholars" around Yale in the late nineteenth century, stressed the acquisition of culture as a means of thwarting materialism and creating a better person.[37] Perhaps the most crucial role of music in defining chautauqua was its ability to define the movement as a vehicle for "culture," however one might define the term.

The assumption that exposure to art music was an inherently educational experience reflects chautauqua industry perceptions of a lack of musical and cultural education among Americans. Charles Dixon, writing for *The Lyceumite and Talent*, stated that "Americans as a rule are fond of music, but it has not been a part of their general education, consequently many are able to enjoy only the simpler forms. Their tastes have not been developed, but stultified and degraded by cheap vaudeville singing, rag-time records, and by the dilettante sister who refuses to study except for her own amusement, but from whom morning till night tears from the old piano some mysterious rag, or beats out some wild Indian tom-tom."[38]

Proponents of the chautauqua movement and of inclusion of the arts in the chautauqua contended that it served to elevate the tastes of the audience. An editorial in *The Lyceumite* stated, "The platform is cultivating an upward taste in music in the towns throughout the country just as the big orchestras are doing in the big cities."[39] Harry Hibschman contended that "there is ample evidence that thousands of young people have been inspired to emulation by hearing some great artist on a chautauqua programme."[40] Whether or not Hibschman's assertion that thousands were inspired to actually emulate chautauqua performers is accurate, inspiring audiences to consume better art was certainly a selling point for circuit chautauqua. The idea that brief exposure to reasonably well executed, carefully selected art music would pique an interest in art music, and possibly inspire citizens to expand their listening habits beyond the popular and folk styles to which they were accustomed, bolstered chautauqua's image as both an educational and cultural institution. In at least one case, it seems a chautauqua performance did inspire a community to embrace art music. A young woman in attendance at the Lyndonville, Vermont, chautauqua of 1915 (a Redpath chautauqua, though the author does not mention this) remarked on Mr. Harry Barnhart, a vocal soloist and community chorus leader who traveled with Quintano's Italian Band, saying, "He left with us the idea of having a community chorus and having fine music without great expense to the town."[41]

The success of the chautauqua movement was seen as evidence that the American public had evolved, demanding enlightenment and uplift even in

V. Music Defines Chautauqua ... Cultural Institution 137

Swat That Fly!

Cartoon published in the July 1913 edition of *The Lyceum Magazine*.

entertainment and rejecting the cheap amusements of the traveling shows.[42] Those within the movement were quick to differentiate between the quality of their musical offerings and those of the traveling amusements. Hugh Orchard wrote, "Every time the lyceum [bureau] sends a Kellogg-Haines Singing Party or Schildkret's Orchestra into a community it grows a little more difficult for cheap musical talent to amuse the people."[43] While chautauqua managers and promoters were adamant about distancing themselves from vaudeville, several acknowledged that the distinction was, in some cases, not entirely clear. The best vaudeville musicians were, they argued, generally of higher quality than the worst chautauqua musicians. There were successful chautauqua acts (magicians were often invoked as an example) more suited for the vaudeville stage. In fact, many of Ralph Dunbar's musicians, including his famous Hussars, began as vaudeville acts.

Some opined that the real difference between circuit chautauqua and vaudeville was a matter of proportion and intent.[44] Chautauqua might involve popular music, but not as much as vaudeville. Vaudeville might be educational

Cartoon by Ned Woodman

The Lyceum and Chautauqua   Their Imitations

The lyceum and chautauqua as compared to "their imitators" (*The Lyceum Magazine,* April 1917).

and uplifting, but that was not the intent of its promoters. This idea is exemplified by a cartoon published in *The Lyceum Magazine* in 1919. In it, "the lyceum and chautauqua" are contrasted with "their imitators." The primary concerns of lyceum and chautauqua, including art, education, inspiration, religion, and reform, are personified by five (female) muses, while lesser concerns, including pecuniary success and entertainment, are personified by children in the foreground. The "imitators'" scene is nearly reversed, with pecuniary success, entertainment, and amusement joined by a drummer labeled "sensation" and a businessman wearing a sash reading "quantity not quality," portrayed as (male) adults, with the concerns formerly personified by the chautauqua muses represented by children cowering in the background.

The presentation of chautauqua as an educational and cultural outlet and the differentiation of the movement from traveling entertainments were necessary to justify community support for chautauqua. Communities supported it not only out of genuine interest in providing educational and entertainment opportunities to citizens, but also because community leaders felt that supporting a chautauqua reflected well on the community. An article in *The Salt Lake Tribune* of 1907 argued that the sponsoring of a chautauqua brought religious harmony to a community, as leaders of various religious groups worked together to support the chautauqua, and that the increased interest in reading spurred by the event would increase support for the free public library.[45] *The Mansfield* (OH) *News* made the unusual assertion that the chautauqua would indirectly benefit the community economically. The article stated, "It is impossible to better a community intellectually and morally and not at the same time better that community commercially."[46] The article then asserts that people who learn to take more pride in themselves will strive for better possessions and a better quality of life, thus boosting the local economy.

The *Thomson* (IL) *Review* ran a full-page advertisement urging the community to support the local chautauqua, a circuit event produced by the Cadmean bureau of Topeka, Kansas. The Cadmean bureau was one of several chautauqua bureaus owned or managed by C. Benjamin Franklin, an important figure in the later years of the movement. The advertisement contained photographs of chautauquas and articles about the movement in general as well as specific acts that would be appearing on the 1925 circuit. The page also contains a short article entitled "Why Boston Signs a Guarantee," comparing municipal funding of opera companies in Boston and Chicago with the need for community support of the local chautauqua. The article argued that if the opera was worthy of support in urban centers despite its nearly perpetual financial insolvency, smaller communities owed the same support to the chautauqua. Furthermore, the community should be prepared to absorb a financial loss in order to bring "the sort of chautauqua that will be a credit to the town." The article closes by asserting that "Boston is not satisfied with the sort of an opera season they would have if only the actual receipts were put into the program."[47]

Appealing to a community's civic pride was not unique to chautauqua, and the concept that a community's investment in its cultural life could be measured monetarily was present in discourse surrounding rural opera houses as well. Newspapers in towns without such a venue, or in which an existing opera house was financially failing, would implore readers to contribute to the construction (or support) of the opera house as a matter of civic pride and as an indicator of their dedication to attracting a "better class" of amusements for their town.[48]

Conclusion

Music was important to chautauqua's public image as an institution worthy of community support. Chautauqua asked a great deal of host communities in terms of advertising, financial guarantees, attendance, and infrastructure. These communities were often not in a position to absorb the financial loss they were risking by signing the guarantee. In order to convince communities to take the extraordinary measures required to secure a chautauqua, the circuit bureaus had to sell it as a worthwhile — even necessary —

educational and cultural endeavor. Although chautauqua was often promoted as an educational outlet, few musical acts were promoted as educational. The majority of musical acts did not involve a lecture component and made no reference to education. Instead of explicitly arguing for the educational merit of music in circuit chautauqua, promoters relied on the implicit educational value of "good" music and advertised music as such. Music served as a means of exposing chautauqua audiences to other cultures, including foreign cultures and urban American "high" culture, a recurrent theme in industry literature and a primary facet of circuit chautauqua's educational strategy.

Music also helped define chautauqua as an important cultural outlet, an important factor in distancing it from vaudeville and other traveling amusements. The quality of music offered by the circuit chautauqua was cited as an indicator of not only its superiority over competing amusements, but also of its legitimacy as a cultural institution. While legitimacy as an educational and cultural outlet was most often linked to the performance of art and exotic music in circuit chautauqua, popular music was carefully programmed to reinforce specific — usually older — values associated with the movement.

Although music was an important part of circuit chautauqua's image, it was rarely explicitly promoted as either educational or as a vehicle for high culture. Instead, promoters of musical acts relied on implied associations and iconography associated with these traits. This was due in part to internal bias within the chautauqua movement, inherited from the lyceum movement, against non-lecture acts. The fear of damaging chautauqua's image as educational by emphasizing non-lecture elements caused promoters to rely on audience perceptions of the educational and cultural value of music. While promotional materials are largely silent regarding the redeeming value of music on the circuits, there was considerable discussion of this value in internal publications, especially citing high-quality musical offerings as a distinction between chautauqua and traveling shows. All of these factors contributed to chautauqua's appeal for community support and are reflected in local newspaper reports and advertisements.

VI

Music Defines Chautauqua as American

The chautauqua movement was unquestionably an American phenomenon. The Chautauqua Institution included many references to American identity and patriotism in its official publications. Daniel Howell, an official with the institution, wrote in his guidelines for independent assemblies wishing to emulate the Chautauqua Institution that "the genuine chautauqua should stand squarely and always for three things: a true patriotism, a consistent Christianity, and an improved intellect."[1]

Patriotic sentiment was amplified in the years leading up to World War I, which coincide with the rise to prominence of the commercial circuit chautauqua movement. Circuit and independent chautauqua promoters embraced the American identity inherited from the Chautauqua Institution and, especially during the years surrounding the war, worked to brand their chautauquas as essential American institutions. A program from the 1917 chautauqua in Kimball, Nebraska, called the chautauqua "one of the greatest forces for patriotism among American institutions today" and stated that "to hold chautauqua this summer is patriotic."[2] The same bureau responsible for the Kimball chautauqua included in its 1918 programs a quote from Woodrow Wilson calling the movement a "patriotic institution that may be said to be an integral part of the national defense."[3]

Chautauqua Goes to War

Bureaus and independent communities used music to reinforce chautauqua's American identity through nationalistic musical programming and through musical acts that perpetuated a nostalgic image of American culture. Overtly nationalistic themes are common in chautauqua programming and advertising from the years around World War I. Tapia refers to this phase of circuit chautauqua promotion as the "righteous patriotic fantasy vision," which was prevalent in advertisements and program brochures from 1917–1918.[4] At that time, bureaus were also employing militaristic and nationalistic musical acts and promoting existing acts as "patriotic" and "American."

Lewis Atherton asserted that chautauqua "reached a ridiculous peak in explaining world affairs during the actual fighting of World War I."[5] Chautauqua, in Atherton's view, actively sought to reinforce the audience's perception of the war, rather than to spur meaningful contemplation or discussion on world events and America's place in global society. While it is difficult to judge, in the absence of detailed programs for World War I-era musical acts, whether these acts did in fact contribute to chautauqua's superficial (if not disingenuous) presentation of the war, chautauqua's replacement of long-favored ensemble types such as single-sex vocal quartets who doubled on instruments with similar, yet military-themed groups, points to chautauqua's depiction of World War I as more of an attempt to capitalize on popular patriotic sentiment than an honest attempt at engagement in international affairs.

Chautauqua bureaus emphasized political neutrality, even (perhaps especially) during the war. A 1918 advertisement in *The Lyceum Magazine* for Community Chautauquas listed the bureau's official platform regarding several issues pertinent to the chautauqua movement at the time, among them the place of political material in chautauqua: "Chautauquas, of course, are non-political.... Chautauquas were created to help the people to THINK, not to tell them how to vote." It is clear, though, that the ideal of political neutrality did not infringe on bureaus' engagement of World War I on the platform.

An advertisement for M. Witmark and Sons in *The Lyceum Magazine* in 1917 announced a new arrangement of chautauqua favorite "There's a Long, Long Trail" by Alonzo Elliott. This arrangement, according to the publisher, was created in response to the song's popularity among the American military. The advertisement's headline reads, "The Song of the Chautauquas Is Now the Song of the Soldiers!" and describes the addition of a "specially-arranged march-time refrain used by regimental bands in the United States." The advertisement goes on to exhort performers to keep "There's a Long, Long Trail" in heavy rotation due to "the peculiar conditions that the circumstances of the past few months have brought about." While Witmark stopped short of telling performers that performing "There's a Long, Long Trail" was their patriotic duty, the implication is clear.

In 1918 Midland Chautauquas, a commercial bureau based in Iowa with territory primarily in the Midwest, featured the Overseas Military Quartet. Advertised as "back from hell with a song," the group consisted of four soldiers discharged for their injuries. The four members sang and one member

VI. Music Defines Chautauqua as American 143

told stories based on their war experiences. The group was billed as "the real thing, both musically and as valiant soldiers."[6] In 1918, the Junior Chautauqua on the Midland circuit also performed a patriotic pageant entitled "Liberty's Torch."[7] Other patriotic or nationalistic musical groups appearing in circuit chautauqua at that time included the American Girls and the Military Girls. The Military Girls performed musical sketches depicting both military life and Midwestern culture. An article about the Military Girls claimed that they "revived frontier life." Furthermore, they would "appear as a fife and drum corps in military drills, they appear with lariats, and they do a killing 'feminist' travesty."[8]

Although the article does not provide any detail regarding the "feminist travesty," it is safe to assume that the Military Girls' performance did not portray the feminist movement positively. That the first mention of this particular act came in 1914 is interesting. Mead points to 1914 as a pivotal year in the relationship between the chautauqua movement and American society.[9] He contends that the goals and culture of the movement remained largely static throughout the existence of the movement, while American culture changed dramatically in those same years. Mead contends, therefore, that after 1914 many of the previously progressive tenets of the circuit chautauqua movement, especially the religious and social ideals inherited from the nineteenth-century Chautauqua Institution, seemed outdated or conservative.

It is true that, especially during the 1910s, many chautauqua acts reinforced older societal norms and romanticized America's past. Managers preferred to program older popular songs which they deemed less likely to cause offense, and they avoided newer and dance-based musical forms — especially jazz — almost entirely. Although nostalgia for the past may have been implied by such programming choices, promoters were rarely explicit about the movement's preferences for older, "safer" forms of popular music. By the 1910s, however, managers and promoters began to form "purpose groups" — musical and dramatic companies charged with advancing a particular cause or conveying a specific message. Purpose groups often presented musical narratives of the people or time they represented. Common themes included various ethnic groups and historical figures (American and English history were especially popular).

The Old Home Singers were a purpose group created by Charles Horner to perform an act consisting of a short concert and a two-act play. Horner wrote the play and Thurlow Lieurance, a composer and impresario heavily involved in the chautauqua movement, wrote original music and arranged older popular songs for the program. Horner called the act "pretty much Mother, Home, and Heaven."[10] "Mother, Home and Heaven" was a term used within the chautauqua movement, usually in reference to lectures, applied to acts that focused on "uplift" to the detriment (some argued exclusion) of substance. Harry Harrison called it "chautauqua's version of 'God, home and mother,'" rhetoric of the early twentieth century.[11] William Jennings Bryan's famous "Prince of Peace" lecture is considered an archetype of this genre, as was Russell Conwell's "Acres of Diamonds," an amazingly long-lived and popular lecture delivered over 5,000 times between 1900 and Conwell's death in 1925. "Mother, Home and Heaven" was often used derisively by chautauqua's critics to highlight particularly shallow aspects of the movement, and it subsequently was used by those affiliated with chautauqua to describe acts that fit that negative stereotype of empty "uplift."

The theme of the Old Home Singers was nostalgia for antebellum America, though the songs of the concert half of the program were occasionally drawn from later in the nineteenth century. The play, which Horner admitted was primarily a vehicle for the music, was set in the early twentieth century and featured a group of friends (the singers—usually a mixed group of four or five) returning home after an evening of musical theater. The composer of the work they have just seen is among the group, and as they congratulate him on his success, he condemns the "so-called popular music and ragtime." The composer, usually named Harwood, laments the popularity of music he considers vulgar and encourages his friends to instead sing older songs such as "The Old Oaken Bucket." Speaking of the old songs, Harwood exclaims, "This is the music that will live, while the popular and rag time stuff is the music of the midnight revelers and will die."[12] No less than twenty incarnations of the Old Home Singers were sanctioned by Horner for Redpath, and several imitators performed similar acts on other circuits. Similar themes appeared in American melodrama of the early twentieth century, in productions whose theme often revolved around conflict between the traditional values of "plain" Americans and the temptations of modern society.[13]

For the 1917–1918 lyceum season, Redpath-Horner managed the five-person Plymouth Singing Party in a production labeled "typically American." The program began with singers dressed as colonists singing "some of the ancient songs which these religious people brought across the seas" and music from the light operas *The Captain of Plymouth* and *The Quaker Girl*. Then, "the Indian appears in his native costume and sings the wonderfully wild and plaintive songs of his fathers. These songs are not artificial tunes of some romantic musician. They have a great historical value and have been collected from the tribes first-hand and set to music by one of America's best known composers." The composer is not named, but it seems likely, due to his connections with Redpath-Horner, that it was Thurlow Lieurance. After the colonial scenes, the Plymouth Singing Party immediately changed into evening dress and performed thirty minutes of operatic selections, ballads, and "heart songs."[14]

Chautauqua and lyceum trade publications in the years surrounding World War I indicate that decision-makers within chautauqua were keenly aware of their ability to shape public sentiment regarding the war. While I have found no evidence indicating opposition to overt patriotism on the platform, there is considerable discussion in trade magazines of the need for — and implementation of — musical expressions of patriotism in chautauqua and lyceum. In a 1918 edition of *The Lyceum Magazine*, editor Ralph Parlette reprinted an editorial by Charles Watt, editor of *Chicago Music News*, in which Watt outlined his journal's stance on musical patriotism during the war:

> We believe, in this time of war, that America should be first in the minds of everybody in this country. We believe that music is not a thing apart from life in general, and that musicians should show the same patriotism as all other citizens. We believe that all pro-Germans should be excluded from our concert and operatic stages until the war is over — and afterward, for that matter. We believe that the classic German music — such as that of Bach, Mozart, and Beethoven — is the property now of the whole world of art, and that we have as much right to it as the present day Germans — but We believe that the present day German composers should be taboo in our concert rooms until after the war. We believe that German text songs should not be used at present. We believe that, thruout [*sic*] the continuance of the war, at least, every choral and orchestral concert should begin or end with "The Star Spangled Banner" or "America," and that whenever requested by any one in the audience, every recital giver should stand ready to sing or play one of these songs at some point of his or her program. We believe that we should use the music of all our Allies freely, and thereby help to cultivate international good feeling with them. But — We believe, more than anything else, that American music and American artists should come first of all. And, not only now, but After the war and forevermore.

While Parlette stopped short of adopting these statements as an official platform — either his journal or the chautauqua and lyceum industry — it is clear that he shared Watt's beliefs. Parlette prefaced Watt's statement with this: "It would be a good stand for our platform musicians to take, wouldn't it?"[15]

In 1917, Alfred Liefeld, director of the perennial chautauqua favorite Pittsburgh Ladies' Orchestra, composed new music for Samuel Francis Smith's text of "America." Liefeld, apparently offended that one of America's favorite patriotic texts was being sung to the decidedly English tune of "God Save the King," published his new setting in *The Lyceum Magazine* along with an endorsement of the new melody by the director of the United States Marine Band (it is unclear whether that band ever actually performed Liefeld's version of "America"). Liefeld also announced that his new "America" would feature

New setting of "America," published by Alfred Liefeld.

prominently on all seventy of the Pittsburgh Ladies' Orchestra's upcoming chautauqua engagements.

There is also indication that chautauqua performers were encouraged to use the platform to boost morale, and in doing so to avoid more sedate musical styles. A cartoon originally published in the *Columbus* (OH) *Dispatch* and reprinted in *The Lyceum Magazine* shows a character labeled "Old Man Ohio" telling an elderly organist to "soft pedal the dirge, brother. I'm in the war tooth and toenail but I fight better to band music." Whether such appeals resulted in any real change in musical programming on the platform is unclear, as the majority of chautauqua musical acts avoided dirge-like music long before the war.

VI. Music Defines Chautauqua as American   147

Cut Out the Melodeon and Strike Up the Band!

"Cut Out the Melodion and Strike Up the Band!" (*Lyceum*, August 1918).

The end of World War I did not signal the end of patriotic references in chautauqua programming. In fact, the first post-armistice chautauqua season (1919) saw a flood of military acts, both musical and lecture. The Coit-Alber bureau labeled its 1919 circuit the "Victory Chautauqua" and featured the Fighting Yanks Quartet, a lecturer said to be favored by "millions of doughboys," and a junior pageant entitled "Democracy Triumphant." Despite the blatant patriotism of the program, the promotional material for the Fighting Yanks downplayed their military connection. It emphasizes that the singers were performers before the war, that their performance is worthy of the platform on musical merits, and that "more than half the program has no reference to the war." Perhaps most telling, the flyer says, "the fact [that] they saw service at the front will not be used *against* them."[16] This seems especially incongruous with a program in which members of a nonmilitary musical act, the American Girls Sextette, are pictured in Red Cross costumes and pseudo-military poses. Coit's simultaneous exaggeration and downplaying of the patriotic credentials of its musical acts is difficult to understand, but may speak to America's discomfort with the reality of war, as exemplified by the veterans comprising the Fighting Yanks.

An article in *The Lyceum Magazine* attacked the use of the German language by chautauqua singers, even after the war: "If Americans ever stood by anything they should now stand by American music and musicians. Oh, I can hear some of you 'easy-going-road-of-least-resistance' boobs saying: 'Why shouldn't we sing in German? The war is all over and the goose hangs aloft.' Let me give you the one big reason. You cannot go into Germany and sing in our language or any foreign language for that matter." Clay then asserted that chautauqua acts were singing all-German programs, and the only reason audiences were not walking out was a desire to see the following act. Later Clay states, "Every red-blooded lyceum and chautauqua act should put his shoulder to the wheel to stamp out this insidious propaganda."[17]

Music Defines Chautauqua as Non-Foreign

While chautauqua managers did employ overtly patriotic and nostalgic acts to bolster the movement's American identity, bureaus also worked on a more subtle level to ensure that audiences associated chautauqua with appropriate American attributes. In the wake of rising anti-foreign (and particularly anti–German) sentiment among American audiences in the years surrounding World War I, promoters seized on the commonly held belief that "truly American" music could be found among African Americans and Native Americans, promoting black and Native American musical groups in opposition to foreign art music.

African American Music

An article by A.L. Curtis in *Talent*, one of several periodicals dedicated to the lyceum and chautauqua movements, began as follows: "It has been said that the only truly national music in the United States is that given us by the Negro race during their dark days of bondage and despair."[18] Of course, this idea was not original to A.L. Curtis or to the lyceum or chautauqua movements. Dvořák had famously stated, thirteen years previously, "In the Negro melodies of America I discover all that is needed for a great and noble school of music."[19] Chautauqua managers seized upon the idea that African American music, especially spirituals, represented something uniquely and truly American.

Chautauqua bureaus sought to incorporate African American music into programs in a way that was respectful of the black performers and in keeping

VI. Music Defines Chautauqua as American

with the spirit of the movement. The nature of circuit chautauqua made it impossible for individual communities to refuse an act, although some tried. One community threatened to cancel its contract with Swarthmore Chautauqua, a Philadelphia-based bureau operating circuits in the northeastern U.S., if a black group, the Tuskegee Singers, appeared as scheduled. Paul Pearson, founder and manager of Swarthmore Chautauqua, refused to cancel the Tuskegee Singers, and the group performed in front of a larger than average crowd for the community, a phenomenon Pearson attributed to curiosity generated by the controversy surrounding the performance.[20] Similarly, the Redpath bureau struggled to find hotel accommodations for the Dixie Chorus, an all-black group touring Indiana on a chautauqua circuit.

The Tuskegee Singers and Dixie Chorus are examples of "jubilee" acts popular on the chautauqua circuits. The term "jubilee singers" was applied to many groups modeled on the Fisk Jubilee Singers, both in chautauqua and elsewhere. It usually denoted a group that performed spirituals and light classical music, were attired in formal dress, and conducted their act without comedy or drama. No less than fifteen such groups are documented to have traveled the circuits.[21] At least one incarnation of the Fisk Jubilee Singers made circuit chautauqua appearances. Walker's Famous Fisk Jubilee Singers billed themselves as "Acknowledged Lyceum and Chautauqua Favorites." The group was managed by Eliza (Walker) Crump, one of the founding members of the Fisk Jubilee Singers. According to their promotional brochure, Walker's Famous Fisk Jubilee Singers was one of "two jubilee companies in the world representing Fisk University," the other being the Fisk University Jubilee Singers, led by Professor John Work III of Fisk University.[22] Although the brochure is undated, it must have been published prior to 1916, as Work stepped down from managing the Nashville-based Fisk University Jubilee Singers in that year. While Walker's Famous Fisk Jubilee Singers were likely not Fisk students, the group did claim to raise money for the university. Another Fisk group, this one billed as "Fisk Jubilee Singers: The Original," toured under the management of the Central Lyceum Bureau prior to 1910. This group's pedigree is less clear, however, as none of their three listed managers seems to have been associated with known university-affiliated incarnations of the Fisk Jubilee Singers.

The records of the Redpath bureau contain several letters and telegrams between various Redpath managers and representatives of Fisk University. One such instance indicates that Redpath could be rather rigid in its booking practices. Professor A.M. Harris of Vanderbilt University (it is unclear how he came to represent Fisk) contacted Redpath in the fall of 1915 to inquire about the possibility of booking the Fisk Quartet for a full chautauqua circuit in 1916. Harry Harrison responded: "Just at present, we have more quartets on our hands than we will be able to route this coming summer." The Fisk Quartet was well known by 1915, having released ten records with Victor and nine Edison cylinders. They would almost certainly have been the most accomplished quartet in Redpath's lineup, yet Redpath declined to drop a lesser quartet in order to book them. In isolation, this incident could indicate a motivation to keep the Fisk quartet off the platform (racism naturally comes to mind). However, records indicate that Redpath rejected a quartet from the Metropolitan Opera for the same reason in 1916. Thus, it seems Redpath's sense of fairness outweighed both business and musical concerns when it came to hiring musical acts.

In 1916, a Redpath representative contacted the president of Fisk, Fayette McKenzie, about booking a group of singers for the 1917–18 winter lyceum season. It seems a representative of Fisk had previously contacted Redpath about booking a quartet from Fisk, but Redpath's rosters had been full at the time. An unexpected opening caused Redpath to reach out to McKenzie, offering $150 per week plus railroad fare for a company of four, with or without a speaker. McKenzie quickly responded that Redpath's terms were "far too low for us to consider."[23]

In 1912, the Redpath bureau presented a lecture-recital entitled *The Epic of the Negro*, produced by Ralph Dunbar and featuring the Dixie Chorus. This three-part event began with a series of scenes set in the year 1600 in Africa, continued to portrayals of slavery in Mississippi in 1850, and concluded with a scene entitled "Representative of the Development of the American Negro of Today." This last scene was, in essence, a recital consisting of seven short musical works and unspecified readings from the works of Paul Lawrence Dunbar. This is the only portion of the program with specific musical numbers listed, and they appear to have been chosen to showcase the breadth of the Dixie Chorus's repertoire. It is interesting to note that the second scene of part two, entitled "In the Prayer Meeting," carries a warning to the audience: "During this scene the audience is respectfully asked to refrain from applause. There may be much that will appeal to one's sense of humor, but it is presented in a reverential spirit, is not exaggerated and any portrayal of the old time darky before the war would be incomplete without a view of him during his religious devotions."

Such an admonishment seems strange, as it seems unlikely that a dramatized prayer meeting would involve "much that will appeal to one's sense of humor." It must be remembered, however, that many jubilee audience members would have been familiar with blackface productions in which farcical religious services were standard fare. Toll notes that by the late nineteenth century, black minstrel performers (a phenomenon that became increasingly common as the century progressed) used the term "jubilee" as a synonym for

VI. Music Defines Chautauqua as American

"plantation" in advertising materials. Toll also notes that these performances often did little to confront the stereotypes perpetuated by white minstrels earlier in the century and that they incorporated many blackface tropes, including unflattering depictions of black spirituality.[24] With this in mind, it is understandable that Redpath felt compelled to distinguish between the Dixie Chorus's "reverential" production and the minstrel-like plantation scene the audience might otherwise expect.

Jubilee groups were the most popular representation of African American music in chautauqua. The stated missionary aims of the jubilee singers phenomenon fit well with chautauqua's spirit of education and moral uplift. In fact, managers saw jubilee groups as a way to attract the minstrel show audience to the lyceum and chautauqua. An article in *The Lyceumite* stated that "the jubilee company will bring the single admissions, possibly help sell more course tickets, and — who knows? — may educate the 'other element.'" By "the other element" the author may have meant either poor white southerners or African Americans, as his endorsement of jubilee groups was preceded by the observation that "in the Southland, you know, there are three classes of people: the real, refined, educated lady and gentleman, the 'po' white trash' and the Negro."[25]

The use of jubilee groups as a substitute for blackface minstrelsy and to attract a "lower class" audience demographic is interesting, as these were not regularly cited motives for programming jubilee groups outside of the lyceum and chautauqua spheres. Brooks cites "northern liberals" as the Fisk Jubilee Singers' target audience,[26] a far cry from Burdette's target of southern "po' white trash" and "Negroes." Of course, it could be that outside of chautauqua and lyceum, no one involved with jubilee singers was concerned with the minstrel show audience demographic. Promoters outside of chautauqua and lyceum had no need to find a substitute for minstrelsy, while chautauqua and lyceum bureaus certainly did.

True blackface minstrelsy was virtually nonexistent in the chautauqua movement. The only documented example of a group billed as blackface minstrels performing in circuit chautauqua occurred in the 1922 Redpath-Vawter circuit. The group was billed simply as "Black-Face Minstrels" and labeled "a masterpiece of fun and frolic." No further information concerning the group is given in the program, and the Black-Face Minstrels are not mentioned elsewhere in the records of Redpath-Vawter or any other Redpath bureaus. Tapia states that the Black-Face Minstrels were a white group performing jubilee songs in blackface, rather than a true minstrel show. Tapia cites this group, which also performed as the All College Glee Club when not in blackface (in fact, they performed as the All College Glee Club for the afternoon prelude on the Vawter circuit), as "Caucasians made up in grease paint perform[ing]

Promotional photograph of the Ethiopian Serenaders (author's collection, gift of Fred Crane).

as jubilee singers."[27] Given the scarcity of other possible minstrel shows on the circuits, it does seem likely that the Black-Face Minstrels were an instance of "blackface jubilee" rather than true blackface minstrelsy. There is no indication of any African American troupe performing in blackface, or performing skits involving standard minstrel plots or characters, on the chautauqua circuits. Despite this lack of overt minstrelsy, Canning argues that the Redpath bureau relied on "racist iconography" to invoke minstrelsy when advertising some African American acts. For instance, African American performers were sometimes depicted in minstrel-like poses incongruous with their formal setting and attire, and with exaggerated facial expressions.

Despite turn-of-the-century efforts within the lyceum movement to replace blackface minstrelsy with jubilee singers and the resultant absence of minstrel shows on the chautauqua circuits, vestiges of blackface minstrelsy could be seen in circuit chautauqua musical programming. For instance, several former blackface minstrels created nostalgic acts using minstrel show material for chautauqua performance. These acts featured minstrel songs but

VI. Music Defines Chautauqua as American

The Manning Glee Club (records of the Redpath Chautauqua Collection, the University of Iowa Libraries, Iowa City).

did not incorporate drama, costumes, or blackface. Banjoist D.L. Leftwich advertised his act as "an evening with the old-time darkey. Ninety minutes of good cheer with story and song. No lecture." Billy Armstrong, billed as an "old-time minstrel," presented a humorous monologue with song (Armstrong sang and played banjo) entitled "Minstrel Reminiscences."

Minstrel songs were not relegated to nostalgic performances by former minstrels. The records of the Redpath bureau contain a score arranged by J. Bodewalt Lampe and published by Remick of Detroit entitled *The Sunny South: Selection of Southern Plantation Songs*. The medley, published for both orchestra and band in the same key so that multiple combinations of instruments could be used effectively, included "Old Folks at Home" (listed as "Way Down Upon the Swanee [sic] River"), "Listen to the Mocking Bird," "My Old Kentucky Home," "Arkansas Traveler," "Massa's in the Cold Ground," "Zip Coon," "Old Black Joe," and "Dixie's Land." It concluded with "The Star Spangled Banner." From markings on the piano score, it appears that the group performing from this particular score omitted "My Old Kentucky Home" and "Massa's in the Cold Ground" in performance. It also seems likely that the instrumental forces available for chautauqua performance were insufficient to execute the work as written, as evidenced by several indications in the piano score to play melodic material assigned to orchestra instruments.

In the declining years of the chautauqua movement, blackface was incorporated into performances by white musical groups. Scholars have attributed the emergence of blackface to fiscal problems; bureaus sought versatile musical acts so that they could hire fewer musicians, and so employed white vocal groups who could also fill the role of jubilee singers.

The Manning Glee Club presented the closest approximation of a minstrel show to appear on a major chautauqua platform. Managed by Redpath and led by Boston-based Ulmer H. Manning, the group of ten men was billed as "gentlemen [who] were commended at every place visited last season for their perfect deportment."[28] The group also included an unspecified number of women who performed "a burlesque in costume of the Milkmaids, from *Robin Hood*." The group's program consisted of three parts. The first part was typical for a chautauqua vocal group. Billed as "solos and concerted numbers by the best composers, interspersed with gems from the comic operas and original effects," this section involved only the male members of the group. The program, as recounted by a newspaper reporter in Nashua, New Hampshire, follows:

Hark the Trumpet	Dudley Buck
Honey, I Want You Now	Coe
The Bandit's Life (bass solo)	Harper
Annie Laurie	Geibel
Winds in the Trees (tenor solo)	Goering Thomas
Part Songs	
a) What I Have	Bohm
b) Fairest Is She	Nevin
Queen of the Earth (solo)	Pensuti

The second part of the Manning Glee Club's performance was "a miniature revival of the old-time minstrels." Promotional photographs for the group show one of the female members in blackface, presumably for this portion of the program, as well as a photograph of the male singers in a classic blackface seating arrangement. Manning himself is seated in the middle of the group on a raised platform, taking the position of Interlocutor. The group, most of whom are dressed in formal concert apparel, is flanked by two men in blackface and traditional minstrel costume, taking on the roles of Tambo and Bones, the traditional "end men" of blackface minstrelsy. The program of this part consisted of the following (performers are listed to the right; no composers were given for this section):

Opening Chorus	Glee Club
Lindy Lou	Mr. Haddock
End Song, Miss Maria	Mr. Millard
End Song, Cupid's Retreat	Mr. Lawton

VI. Music Defines Chautauqua as American　　155

Camp Meeting Song	The Club
Imitation Slack Wire Balancing	Messrs. Lawton and Millard

The evening concluded with the Milk Maid scene, which consisted of four numbers:

Morning Song	De Koven
Dance, Cozy Corner	Eugene
Song of the Dove	Luders
Finale	Glee Club[29]

Native American Music

Native American music served a dual and seemingly terribly conflicted purpose within the circuit chautauqua movement. Not surprisingly, Native American society was exhibited, discussed, and imitated on the platform in the same manner (and sometimes by the same lecturers) as were the exotic cultures of Asia and Africa. By the early twentieth century, most Americans were sufficiently distanced from Native American culture that this presentation of indigenous peoples as other would have seemed appropriate to chautauqua audiences and promoters. As the twentieth century progressed and Americans tried to distance themselves from European — especially German — associations, Native American culture would be presented to chautauqua audiences as "pure" or "truly" American. This presentation occurred alongside, and sometimes in conjunction with, the depiction of Native Americans as *other*. The use of music to define Native Americans as both foreign and American is one of the more fascinating aspects of the study of music in chautauqua.

It seems fitting that "Chautauqua" is one of a slew of American place names of vaguely "Indian" origin. Many of the older histories of the chautauqua movement begin by asserting that "Chautauqua is a Native American word meaning..." and go on to assign one of a number of purported meanings and tribal linguistic origins for the word. That this obvious inconsistency between sources did not seem to trouble those early scholars of the chautauqua movement is telling; the word was "Indian" and no one disputed that generic authenticity. The specific origin and meaning of the word was not important; the image conjured by it and the broader implications of its Indian identity were. This emphasis echoes Eckman's assertion that the chautauqua movement, and circuit chautauqua in particular, served to expose the audience to other cultures with the hope of piquing curiosity, rather than to impart specific information regarding the subject culture.[30]

The Onondaga Indian Concert Band (author's collection, gift of Fred Crane).

The circuit chautauqua phenomenon came on the heels of the popular world's fairs of Chicago and St. Louis, and circuit chautauqua's presentation of Native Americans was undoubtedly influenced by these expositions. Circuit chautauqua's early years overlapped the end of the "Indianist" movement in American composition, in which the use of Native American music was seen as a rejection of or alternative to the undeniably European heritage of American art music. This movement, which reached its peak in the early twentieth century and involved composers such as Edward MacDowell, Charles Wakefield Cadman, Arthur Farwell, and Thurlow Lieurance, strove to use Native American themes within the framework of art music and parlor songs.[31] Finally, the halcyon days of circuit chautauqua coincided with World War I and the anti-German sentiment prevalent at the time. Each of these factors would significantly affect circuit chautauqua's presentation of Native American music and culture, and how Native American music was used by performers and promoters to reinforce established chautauqua ideals.

It is impossible to pinpoint the very first (independent) community chautauqua to present a Native American performance or lecture. Lectures on Native American subjects and performances on Native American themes were present in the lyceum movement and were doubtless supplied to independent assemblies by the lyceum bureaus. While I cannot state unequivocally that a certain independent chautauqua was the first to present Native American subject matter, records indicate that Keith Vawter's initial circuit of 1904 included a performance billed as, "Drama, 'Hiawatha,' Illustrated by Moving

Pictures."[32] Of course, the Hiawatha epic was immensely popular, and performances derived from it were prevalent throughout the United States, so its inclusion in Vawter's first program is not surprising. As the movement came to prominence in rural American culture, the role of Native Americans (and those presenting Native American cultural elements) in chautauqua would extend far beyond *Hiawatha* and its derivatives.

Chautauqua programs and promotional materials chronicle a variety of Native American performers and lecturers, including bands, chamber ensembles, dramatic companies, straight lectures, lecture-recitals, motion pictures, and acts that defy categorization. Performers include Native Americans, European Americans, Europeans, and those whose ethnicity is either unclear or intentionally obscured through "adoptive" tribal affiliations. Performances ranged from all-Indian groups in military-style uniforms reminiscent of the Sousa band performing sets of European art music to groups of classically trained white people performing stylized "Indian" songs and dances in full ceremonial regalia.

Promotional photograph of David Russell Hill (author's collection, gift of Fred Crane).

Three concert bands composed of Native Americans were popular on the chautauqua circuits in the early twentieth century. The oldest of these was the Onondaga Indian Concert Band, conducted by David R. Hill. Hill was billed as a "fullblooded [sic] Onondaga chief, of long and noted family" and a graduate of the Hampton Normal School in Virginia. The band advertised that it had been organized in 1840, and emphasized that it was not affiliated with the government or with any school. For this reason, the band billed itself as "the only real professional Indian band in the world." The band's promotional flyer also stated, "This Indian band comes with no apologies for the character and quality of its concerts, either on account of blood or age of its members, but is willing to be judged on its merits as a musical organization."[33]

The Onondaga Indian Concert Band was composed of fifteen musicians representing several tribes. Unlike other Indian bands on the chautauqua circuits, the Onondaga Indian Concert Band performed in traditional Onondaga clothing. Although no program listing specific musical pieces has been located, the promotional flyer for the band describes a typical program as consisting of three distinct sets. The first set consisted "principally of classical numbers." The second set began with "the descriptive life of the American people, especially that of the Indian" and concluded with a solo or small ensemble performance of an art music transcription. Finally, the third set consisted of an Indian war dance.

The program promised the audience that they would "see just as the dance really was when the band plays the weird, death-like, sullen strains and gradually fades away only to be retreated and enlightened by the grand old number of the Star Spangled Banner."[34] "The Star Spangled Banner" was a staple of many bands across the United States during the early twentieth century and was used as either an opening or closing number by several Native American groups on the chautauqua circuits. The gradual transition from the "death-like" war dance to the "enlightened" anthem echoes a theme of evolution often present when Native American groups performed art music on the chautauqua circuits.

The Government Official World's Fair Indian Band was formed as part of the Indian exhibit at the 1904 Louisiana Purchase Exposition in St. Louis. After the exposition, the band contracted with the Central Lyceum Bureau of Chicago. The band was led by N.S. Nelson, who is listed in promotional materials as an "old employee of the Indian service."[35] It is unclear whether Nelson was himself Native American. It seems likely that he was not, since the band's promotional brochure lists the tribal affiliation of every member except Nelson and the band's assistant manager, Ray McCowan. The band advertised its membership as drawn from tribes across the United States and included a short biography of each member in its promotional materials.

The band, including conductor, appeared in green military-style uniforms and relied primarily on brass instruments augmented by clarinets, saxophones, and percussion. In the illustration in its promotional brochure, the band is seated as if for a performance. While the band's appearance is typical of any community or military band of the era, the stage on which the band is seated is draped in bright Native American tapestries. On either side of the band are placed teepees occupied by long-haired Native American women. One of the women appears to be embroidering a tapestry, the other weaving a basket.

This juxtaposition of stereotypical "Indian" imagery with the standard turn-of-the-century American appearance of the band echoes the proposed presentation of another Native American band, the Carlisle Indian Band, at the 1904 exposition. Commissioner Thomas Morgan wanted the Carlisle Band to be preceded in the opening day procession by a large group of Native Americans dressed in "native costumes, feathers, paint, moccasins, etc." Morgan reasoned that the procession of Native Americans in traditional dress followed by the Carlisle Band would represent the "conversion" of Native Americans into American citizens.[36]

The Carlisle Band also toured under commercial management after its world's fair commitments had been met. It is unclear whether the band remained affiliated with the Carlisle Indian School, but it was known as the U.S. Indian Band during its commercial tours. The band was led by Lt. J. Riley Wheelock, an Oneida Indian, and consisted of 45 members of various tribal affiliations. Princess Tsianina, the celebrated Cherokee-Creek mezzo-soprano, also joined the band for its commercial tour. The band billed itself as "the only Indian concert band in classical and popular programs," and its promotional flyer stated that "people who went to hear the Indian musicians chiefly to see the Indians do the war dance and satisfy their curiosity about Indians being wild, were disappointed, but agreeably surprised to hear high-class music rendered in an artistic manner by the Indian Band."[37]

The band's promoters seem to have been torn between emphasizing the exotic appeal of an all-Indian band and downplaying that difference in order to stress the group's musical skill and training. Promotional materials include a quote from the *Philadelphia Ledger*: "The music furnished by these red musicians is in a class by itself in that you cannot describe the quality — you like it, you enjoy their selections, and you keep going back to hear them, but why, you can't tell, their rendition is not any different probably than what any other good band plays, but there is something attractive about the Indians."[38] The sample program provided, taken from the U.S. Indian Band's performance at Carnegie Hall, would not have been out of the ordinary for any community or military band of the time. The only "Indian" pieces on the program are the "Carlisle March" and a piece entitled "Indian War," both composed by Lt. Wheelock.

Although the U.S. Indian Band certainly was not ashamed of its Indianness, its promotional materials seem to emphasize the band's musical and (American) cultural normalcy. On the cover page of the band's promotional brochure, immediately below the words "U.S. Indian Band," are the phrases "fifty American musicians" and "members of A.F. of M."[39] The band's American identity and union affiliation are placed above any other information. They appeared in red military-style uniforms for a posed photograph in front of an unidentified building. The only indication in the photo of a Native American identity is the bass drum, which reads "U.S. Indian School—Carlisle."[40]

These three bands shared several characteristics. Each used a conventional instrumentation and presented concerts in typical turn-of-the-century format. Most important, the bands' performances consisted primarily of pieces from the standard American band repertoire of the time, including orchestral transcriptions and marches. A study of the bands' promotional materials, however, exposes key differences in the way the bands and their management dealt with issues of Indian identity. The Government Official World's Fair Indian Band surrounded itself with Native American imagery while performing from the standard American band repertoire. The Onondaga band dressed in Native American costume while performing "without the characteristic of Indian music."[41] The U.S. Indian (Carlisle) Band treated its Native American identity as a novelty to attract an audience, who would then be impressed by the group's musical abilities.

Carlisle Indian School alumnus Fred Cardin was a popular attraction on the chautauqua circuits during the peak years of the movement. Cardin, a member of the Quapaw tribe, graduated from the Carlisle School in 1912 and studied the violin at Dana's Musical Conservatory in Ohio. Cardin later became a member of the orchestra at the Chautauqua Institution, but he was forced by illness to resign. In 1916 he joined the Indian String Quartet as first violin. The quartet had been formed by Ruthyn Turney, a composer on the faculty at the Chemawa School in Oregon. Turney wrote primarily "Indianist" compositions, and by 1917 was composing exclusively for the Indian String Quartet. Each member of the quartet held a different tribal affiliation. Cardin, as previously mentioned, belonged to the Quapaw tribe of Oklahoma. Alex Melodivov, second violin, was an Aleut from Alaska. The violist, William Palin, was from the Flathead tribe of Montana, and William Reddie, the cellist, was a member of the Hydah tribe of Alaska.[42]

The quartet toured the chautauqua and lyceum circuits under the management of the Redpath bureau. They were accompanied by lecturer Richard Kennedy, who spoke on a variety of Native American subjects. Kennedy seems to have given lectures on Tennyson's *Idylls of the King* and Hugo's *Les Misérables* during performances with the Indian String Quartet. While such lectures might seem incongruous with the accompanying musical performance, they shed light on the chautauqua bureaus' idea of mission. Managers felt an obligation to bring "culture" in many forms to the (primarily rural) chautauqua audience. If managers and performers believed that Tennyson was just as foreign to the average audience member as the Indian String Quartet would be, it is understandable that those in charge of programming would have no qualms about combining the two. The quartet would typically play a program divided into halves. One half would consist of standard string quartet repertoire with the musicians dressed in tuxedos. The other half was performed in Native American dress and consisted of "Indianist" compositions by Turney and others, memorized for a more "authentic Indian" effect. Kennedy would often introduce the set of Indianist music by explaining that Native American music was the only music that had not been "Germanized."[43]

After the dissolution of the Indian String Quartet, Cardin formed another musical group, The Indian Art and Musical Company. The group's instrumentation was flexible and its personnel roster unstable. William Reddie (billed as Reddy) played cello for the group, Cardin played violin, and Wanita Cardin played piano. Vocalists Sansa Carey and Te Ata were, at times, members.[44]

The Indian Art and Musical Company offered a program consisting of "songs with orchestra," "primitive songs with drums," "Pueblo songs," "modern harmonized songs," and a piano solo. The "songs with orchestra" consisted primarily of Indianist compositions by Lieurance, Kreisler, and Cadman. The group also performed compositions by Rachmaninoff, MacDowell, and Brahms during this portion of the program. The "primitive songs with drums" and "Pueblo songs" are listed by individual titles, with no composer given. The "modern harmonized songs" are all Indianist compositions by Thurlow Lieurance, and the piano solo is listed as "Indian Rhapsody" with no further information. While it is not specified, it seems likely that this was Lieurance's *Indian Rhapsody*.

The Indian Art and Musical Company differed from Cardin's previous venture in its emphasis on Native American attributes. The performers wore Native American clothing in all promotional photographs and likely during all performances. In contrast, most promotional photographs of the Indian String Quartet show them in tuxedos. Promotional materials refer to Reddie as "a typical story book Indian." The group's promotional brochure features on its cover a large profile photograph of Cardin, in headdress and holding a violin. Under the picture is the caption, "Do you know that Indians are natural-born musicians?"[45] The text on the cover is printed in a script invoking a "primitive" hand.

Solo vocalists—especially women—were also popular Native American acts on the chautauqua circuits. These women toured with larger groups like the U.S. Indian Band, as part of smaller companies like the Indian Art and Musical Company, and often with white Indianist composers and lecturers.

Unlike their male counterparts, who were nearly always known by Anglo (or Russian, in the case of some Native Alaskans) names, female musicians on the circuits were billed by Native American names, sometimes accompanied by loose English translations. Also, it was common to use the title of "princess" for female performers, although Native Americans had no such concept. The "Indian princess" myth, however, was so firmly entrenched in American society by the early twentieth century that it is not at all surprising to find it on the chautauqua platform.

Two "Indian princesses" were especially popular on the chautauqua circuits. Tsianina Redfeather Blackstone was born December 13, 1882, in Eufaula, Oklahoma. She was of Cherokee and Creek descent, although newspapers often identified her as Choctaw or Omaha. Although she used the title "princess," there is no indication that Tsianina's father held any leadership role in their community. She attended the Oklahoma Government Indian School, in Eufala, where she learned to play the piano. School officials took note of her musical talent and suggested that Tsianina move away from the reservation to pur-

Cover of a promotional brochure for the Indian Art and Musical Company (records of the Redpath Chautauqua Collection, the University of Iowa Libraries, Iowa City).

sue further study. A local family was moving to Denver, and Tsianina was sent with them to study piano with Edward Fleck. Soon after beginning studies with Fleck, Tsianina was introduced to voice teacher John Wilcox, who introduced her to composer Charles Wakefield Cadman. Wilcox believed that the teenaged Tsianina was the perfect performer and "interpreter" of Cadman's Indianist compositions, and he convinced Cadman to audition her for a national tour.[46]

This was the beginning of a long and fruitful collaboration between the Indianist composer and the Indian "princess."

Tsianina Redfeather Blackstone (Library of Congress, Prints and Photographs Division, LC-DIG-ggbain-30380).

Tsianina and Cadman toured under the management of several bureaus, performing at chautauquas, expositions, and in independent concerts. During World War I, Tsianina traveled to Europe to entertain the American army. Back in the U.S., she was billed as part of an "All-American program" in which, "in her native costume, she makes a picture." Tsianina toured the chautauqua circuits with Cadman, performing his compositions, and also with the U.S. Indian Band.

Cadman's opera *Shanewis*, or *The Robin Woman*, was loosely based on Tsianina's life. *Shanewis* was performed at the Metropolitan Opera during the 1918 and 1919 seasons. Tsianina was in the audience at the Metropolitan premiere and sang the role of Shanewis in her operatic debut at a performance in Denver.

(Princess) Watahwaso was born Lucy Nicolar on June 22, 1882, on Indian Island, Maine. Her parents were prominent figures in the Penobscot community, and several of her ancestors were famous Penobscot chiefs. Her father, Joseph Nicolar, was tribal representative to the state legislature and was considered highly intelligent by his peers.[47] As a child, Lucy often accompanied her father as he gave lectures on Native American customs, songs, and dances.[48] She attended the local Catholic primary school as a child and had ambitions to attend public high school on the mainland. After the death of her father in 1894, Lucy and her sisters helped their mother craft baskets for sale to tourists. Lucy also performed in seasonal productions designed to promote "rustic" Maine vacations and to sell outdoor equipment. These events gave her the opportunity to interact with a variety of travelers, and at one such event Lucy came to the attention of Harvard administrator Montague Chamberlain. Chamberlain would become Lucy's patron, hiring her to be his assistant, welcoming her into his household, and providing her with musical and educational experiences in Boston and New York. It was during her time in Boston and New York that Lucy began using the name "Watahwaso," capitalizing on the novelty of her heritage in those social circles.[49]

In 1913, Watahwaso moved to Chicago to study the piano at a conservatory for lyceum and chautauqua performers, identified in her biography as the Music School of Chautauqua. I have found no other reference to this particular school, although there were several conservatories in Chicago dedicated to training chautauqua and lyceum performers. She gave her first public performance in Chicago in 1916, and in 1917 signed with the Redpath bureau, with whom she would remain until 1919. By this time, she was using the stage name "Princess Watahwaso." She often toured with Indianist composer Thurlow Lieurance, and his songs were featured on her programs. Her 1917 program consisted of two sets: the first half of the program was a mix of Indianist pieces by Cadman and opera arias, and the second half included Indianist pieces by Lieurance and Cadman as well as Native American pieces arranged by Troyer. The program notes emphasized that Watahwaso would tell the stories behind the pieces of the second half, and would sing them in costume while doing traditional dances.[50] It is unclear whether the first half was performed in native dress, or if Watahwaso, like the Indian String Quartet, changed clothes at intermission to delineate between the "classical" and "Indian" portions of the program.

After her tours with Redpath, Watahwaso performed regularly in New York. In 1927 she joined a troupe of Native American performers on the Keith Vaudeville Circuit, with whom she travelled until 1929. It was on this tour that she met Kiowa performer Bruce Poolaw, who would become her third (and last) husband. Watahwaso and Poolaw would eventually return to Indian Island, where they were active in the Penobscot community and ran a successful tourist attraction until her death in 1969.[51]

Despite the "fullblooded" Native American status of the most prominent Chautauqua performers of Native American music, the repertory consisted

VI. Music Defines Chautauqua as American

primarily of Indianist pieces by white composers. Of twenty-one pieces of music with acknowledged composers performed by Native Americans on the chautauqua circuits, twelve were composed by Thurlow Lieurance and five were composed by Charles Cadman. The remainder included compositions by MacDowell, Bergen, Wheelock, and Kreisler, whose Sonata in G Major, Op. 100: II was performed by Fred Cardin with the Indian Art and Musical Company under the title "Indian Lament." The Lieurance compositions performed on the circuits were primarily short songs for voice and piano with an obbligato part most often performed on the flute or violin.

It was not uncommon for Native American groups to perform works from the standard art music concert repertory of the era. Some groups, such as the Indian String Quartet, featured art music prominently. Others, like the Indian Art and Musical Company, seem to have performed art music as a way to legitimize themselves as musicians. The program notes from one Indian Art and Musical Company performance state, "To prove their versatility, the Indians will play the Rachmaninoff prelude. This Russian composition is one of the most difficult ever written.... You'll be surprised at the remarkable talent of the quartet who play this piece."[52]

Most Native American chautauqua acts avoided implications of novelty or comedy in their advertising. Although some promotional materials did mention the novelty of an all-Indian group, that novelty was usually limited to the ethnicity of the performers, and did not extend to the musical material. The Official Government World's Fair Indian Band advertised as follows: "To committees looking for 'something new,' the novelty of this band will commend itself. To thoughtful men and women, interested in development and advancement of the Indians, the wonderful results obtained will be an encouragement and a triumph."[53]

The majority of music performed by Native American musicians on the circuits was serious in nature. In fact, the proportion of novelty music performed by Native Americans seems to have been smaller than in chautauqua as a whole. This serious tone did not always extend to "Native American" performances by non-Indians. The Musical Maids, a six-member, all-white, orchestra, vocal group, and novelty act managed by the Redpath bureau, performed popular songs as well as "Indian songs and legends and stories of the woods" and also gave archery and fencing demonstrations. The group dressed for their "Indian" segments in buckskin smocks and single-feathered headbands, outfits very similar to those worn by the Campfire Girls organization at that time. The Musical Maids' performance seems to have had more in common with the Campfire Girls and other popular forms of "playing Indian" than with the Native American performances discussed previously.

Chautauqua depictions—musical and otherwise—of Native Americans differed in several key aspects from Wild West shows, medicine shows, and other popular venues in which Native American culture was portrayed. First, there is no indication that so-called Indian intermezzi popular during the early twentieth century were performed in circuit chautauqua. These works, generally crafted by popular songwriters, were billed as "translations" of the Indianist art music works of composers such as Farwell, Cadman, and MacDowell. In reality, these "intermezzi" bore no musical relation to the Indianist works, and were in fact based on popular song forms of the time with the addition of stereotypical "Indian" melodic, harmonic, and rhythmic devices.[54] Circuit chautauqua was certainly not above using stereotypical depictions of other cultures couched in popular songs, but "Indian intermezzi" were apparently absent from the major chautauqua circuits.

Another striking difference between chautauqua and other venues presenting Native American subjects relates to the performers involved. Medicine show acts were often populated by whites masquerading as Native Americans, or by Native Americans misrepresenting their tribal affiliations. McNamara asserts that the Kickapoo Medicine Show, which claimed to have employed almost eight hundred Indians, involved no members of the Kickapoo tribe. Rather, the show employed Iroquois, Pawnees, Creeks, Blackfeet, and even native Peruvians.[55] Chautauqua performers were generally forthcoming with their biographical information. White performers of Native American music did not present themselves as Native Americans, but rather emphasized their work in Indian territories or adopted affiliation with specific tribes. Native American performers most often listed their actual tribal affiliation, although these sometimes conflicted with the affiliations listed in non-chautauqua promotional materials.[56]

Also absent from the chautauqua circuits was the popular depiction of Native Americans at war with white settlers. This scenario, the foundation of the Wild West show and popular in medicine shows as well, appears in chautauqua only through musical allusions (musical works based on "war dance" themes being the most common). Chautauqua's depiction of the Native American was more akin to the Victorian image of the Indian struggling to find and maintain a place in the drastically altered North American landscape.

Finally, it should be noted that, while some who lectured on Native American music also studied the music of other cultures and Native American music was occasionally presented alongside Western art music or other European art forms, chautauqua programmers did not group Native American and African American performances together, as did Wild West and medicine shows. Accounts of such shows frequently mention banjo solos, minstrelsy, spirituals, and ragtime performed alongside Native American acts, sometimes performed by the Native Americans (or those claiming to be Native Americans). One observer of an Indian medicine show described the climactic sales pitch as follows: "The Indians kept chanting monotonously and beating their tom-toms, the doctor himself roaring like a bull, while the minstrels kept up a furious ragtime dancing until the sweat rolled down their black faces."[57] There is no evidence of such conflation of Native American and African American themes on the chautauqua circuits.

The emphasis on an assimilationist portrayal of Native American culture by the majority of chautauqua performers is evidenced by the preponderance and popularity of lectures devoted to Native American topics. Many of these lectures addressed Native American music, whether as the focus of discussion or as part of a larger performance including folklore, art, dance, and song. Lecturers on Native American subjects ranged from ethnographers to Native Americans to professional lecturers with limited knowledge of the topic beyond the script of the lecture. This gamut of backgrounds and qualifications is seen in lectures focusing on Native American music, as well. Prominent Native American musicians such as Princess Watahwaso lectured in conjunction with Indianist composers and ethnographers: white lecturers and art music performers presented "musical travelogues" of their experiences among Native Americans; and more eclectic lecturers presented Native American music as one item in a large collection of exotic musical artifacts.

Of all the lecturers who traveled the chautauqua circuits discussing Native American music, none was more active or more invested in the chautauqua movement than Thurlow Lieurance. Lieurance was born in Iowa, raised in Kansas, and attended the Cincinnati College of Music before embarking on a career as a music teacher and band leader. In 1911 he traveled to Montana to visit his brother, who was employed in the Indian Service. There he became interested in Native American music and made the first of many field recordings of Native American songs. This experience in Montana changed the course of Lieurance's career. He began to compose Indianist music, became an advocate for recording and study of Native American music, and formed or managed several groups dedicated to the performance of Native American music. Lieurance also created, managed, and performed in other musical groups ranging from brass ensembles to small string orchestras. These groups toured on both the chautauqua and lyceum circuits. Through this activity, Lieurance built relationships with many prominent Native American musicians. It was also through his chautauqua activities that he met his wife, Edna Wooley.[58] Wooley was a veteran chautauqua performer and appeared with her husband as "Nah Mee — soprano and interpreter." Lieurance composed many Indianist pieces, primarily for voice and piano, which were published by Theodore Presser. The most popular of these, "By the Waters of

Minnetonka," was recorded by several prominent musicians, including Glenn Miller and Ernestine Schuman-Heink, and was a staple of circuit chautauqua performances.

Although his name was attached to several chautauqua and lyceum acts, Lieurance's greatest personal investment was in his own lecture tour. Lieurance toured for several years with his wife and a flutist (either George Tack or Hubert Small, depending on the season), giving lectures with titles such as "Songs, Stories and Legends of the American Indian." Mrs. Lieurance was billed as Edna Lieurance, Edna Wooley, Mrs. Thurlow Lieurance, and Nah Mee on various programs. One promotional brochure explained that "Nah Mee" meant "little sister" and was the name given her when she was "christened and adopted into the [Chippewa] tribe in March, 1915."[59]

The program of a Lieurance lecture consisted entirely of pieces composed by the lecturer, interspersed with "analyses of Indian themes" and explanations of the stories that inspired the compositions. Lieurance played piano, Nah Mee sang and told stories, and every lecture involved a demonstration of Native American flutes and often a flute solo (also one of Lieurance's compositions). Each program ended with a selection "from the Fire Dance." Within a program, songs were usually grouped by either theme or geography.

There is no indication of novelty in the Lieurance lecture ephemera, nor in Lieurance's several articles published in *Etude* or his self-published newsletters. Lieurance was deeply invested in Native American music, and his reputation as a composer and scholar was tied directly to public perception of his chautauqua activities. It is clear from his writings and promotional publications that Lieurance was concerned with issues of educational value and authenticity. Like many chautauqua performers, he reprinted complimentary articles and correspondence in his promotional materials. Unlike many of his contemporaries, however, he focused on praise from educators and government officials, using the more standard newspaper reviews and personal correspondence only when they praised the lecture's educational value or authenticity. The most telling correspondence reprinted in Lieurance's programs read as follows:

> To Our Best Friend:
> We, the undersigned, want to thank you for the great work you are doing in preserving the songs of our people. You are the musical mouthpiece of the American Indian. You are the one good and BIG MEDICINE and friend to our people. We owe all to you. We want the world to know that you are genuine and we Indians want this fact known.[60]

The letter was signed by Fred and Wanita Cardin, Sensa Cary, William Reddie, Princess Te Ata, Elizabeth Thompson, J.B. Shunatona, and Princess Oyapela.

Albert and Martha Gale, veteran chautauqua lecturers who also lectured on the music of Japan, were careful to distance their lecture from the novelty performances present on the circuits, and also from medicine and Wild West shows. Gale was billed as "the ethnologist of music," and his lecture, entitled "Songs and Stories of the Red Man," focused on the performance of songs recorded by Gale and others, as well as short lectures on Native American mythology and art. The Gales advertised their lecture as "instructive," "full of life and action without resort to claptrap," and "not the usual 'Wild West' type of Indian entertainment." Promotional materials feature the Gales in elaborate Native American costumes with photographs of "old Indians who have assisted Mr. Gale in his research work" and the Gales on their research expeditions.

Lecture recitals such as those presented by Lieurance and the Gales were in many ways similar to Arthur Farwell's lecture recitals on Native American music, which he first presented in 1903 as a means of promoting his primary Indianist endeavor, the Wa-Wan Press.[61] Farwell's lectures, like those presented on the chautauqua circuit, included a combination of Native American music and Indianist compositions (usually his own). Farwell designed his lectures for an audience of musicians, however, and thus focused more on music theory and methods of incorporating Native American music into both art and popular musical compositions.[62] Chautauqua lecture recitals involving Native American music, in deference to the broad scope of musical abilities present in the audience, tended to avoid musical details and focused more on cultural significance of the music discussed.

That most performers and lecturers involved in Native American music, especially the most visible and popular among them, presented the subject in a serious manner speaks to the important function of Native American music within the chautauqua movement. Chautauqua needed to be perceived as educational in order to maintain its edge over competing forms of entertainment. Presenting Native American topics in a lecture-recital setting and allowing Native American musicians to perform in ways that challenged popular stereotypes set circuit chautauqua apart from Wild West shows, medicine shows, and other venues where Native Americans were represented musically.

Native American music, especially when used as the basis of or inspiration for art music, filled another important need for chautauqua: it was perceived as purely American in a way that most of the art music—and many of the classically trained performers of the time—could not be. The peak of the chautauqua movement coincided with the anti–German sentiment of the years surrounding World War I. Even decades prior to the war, American composers struggled with issues of musical identity. Arthur Farwell, having had his Indianist music rejected by publishers, claimed that the American art music public "saw everything through German glasses."[63] Others, such as Walter Spalding, believed that America lacked a folk music tradition, and that Americans could not produce art music until they had a folk music tradition on which to base it. Spalding wrote in *Musical Quarterly* that the absence of American folk songs was "a severe indictment that the people have so long relied upon music made for them by others that their natural emotional and expressive powers have become seriously impaired."[64]

It is clear that at least one important musical figure within the chautauqua movement viewed Native American music not merely as an exotic alternative to German (and Germanic) music, but as the folk music needed for the foundation of an American art music tradition. Charles Wakefield Cadman, whose Indianist compositions were popular on the chautauqua circuits and who toured as a lecturer with Princess Tsianina, wrote the following:

> It is true, as I have pointed out in times past, that the brief span of years so far allotted our nation, with the struggle for survival and physical development, has not permitted any sudden outburst of folk song.... However, the folk song we have attempted to idealize has sprung into existence *on American soil!* ... Indian themes, at least, are as much the heritage of American music and the musicians of America, as the music of the barbaric hordes of Russia is the heritage of cultured Russians and Russian composers.[65]

Whether they railed against German influence or upheld it as the only option for a new nation somehow devoid of its own folk culture, everyone involved in art music in America recognized that German music was a large part of American musical life. As World War I approached, most recognized this as a delicate situation, if not a problem. Many musical organizations, including those on the chautauqua circuits, shied away from or downplayed the importance German music in their programs. Even in the realm of orchestral music, which was inextricably tied to German musical culture, performance of music by German composers declined dramatically after 1917. For instance, Barbara Tischler determined that during the 1916–17 season, the Boston Symphony Orchestra's repertoire was 62 percent German. The following season it dropped to 42.6 percent, and in the 1918–19 season only 29.7 percent of pieces performed were by German composers. Tischler noted a similar trend in the programming of the New York Philharmonic during those years.[66]

The scope of the chautauqua movement and the lack of complete program records make it impossible to conduct such a precise study of chautauqua programming. Furthermore, the smaller size of touring ensembles created an aversion to programming many of the larger German works throughout the chautauqua era that had nothing to do with politics. For these reasons and others, it is impossible to quantify anti–German sentiment in chautauqua the movement by clear percentages. One can, however, point to sentiments such as Kennedy's aversion to "Germanized" music and the U.S. Indian Band's billing as "Fifty American Musicians" as assertions of the "100 percent Americanism" philosophy prevalent during the Wilson administration.

Chautauqua audiences did not want to be reminded of American music's debt to Europe and to Germany in particular. Their thirst for the exotic was in direct conflict with their distrust of the foreign, and Native American music was the perfect resolution to this problem. Native Americans were different and romantic, but American. Native American performances were a way for chautauqua audiences to experience another culture without feeling unpatriotic, and their American identity garnered Native American acts a respect not consistently afforded to other "exotic" chautauqua acts.

Chautauqua's American Identity in the 1920s and 1930s

After the patriotic fervor surrounding World War I, circuit chautauqua bureaus dramatically altered their promotional strategies. Their focus shifted from portraying the United States in a struggle against foreign forces to a narrative in which the individual American confronted local and domestic issues. Germany ceased to be portrayed as the primary threat and was replaced by Bolshevism. Tapia labeled this the "conspiratorial fantasy vision."[67] During this phase of chautauqua's history, which lasted from 1919 until the mid–1920s, international issues were once again relegated to a few lectures by specialists in foreign affairs. Furthermore, promoters did not draw correlations between Bolshevism and Slavic culture as they had between German culture and the German government during World War I. Thus, there was no significant anti–Slavic sentiment in chautauqua musical programming during the postwar period. In the absence of a looming German threat, it was no longer necessary to bill musical acts as "American" or to have them perform patriotic music in order to ensure that the audience would accept the act.

The declining years of the movement (1926–1934) saw yet another promotional reinvention of the chautauqua movement. In this last incarnation of circuit and independent chautauqua, technology and new value systems were embraced as "progress."[68] Circuit chautauqua — its music in particular — was promoted as a healthy diversion from the pursuit of business success, which replaced overt patriotism as the defining American ethos. In circuit chautauqua's quest to remain relevant in the face of competition from technological advances, musical acts were increasingly billed as "entertaining" and "fun." The idea that music could be used to convey any message — patriotic or not — was largely abandoned in order to meet audience expectations of entertainment in an attempt to keep the movement alive. Furthermore, the embrace of "progress" forced circuit chautauqua to accept newer forms of popular music, formerly avoided whenever possible, which were largely devoid of patriotic and nostalgic references. Thus, in the final years of the circuit chautauqua movement we see very little assertion of American identity, musical or otherwise, other than the promotion of circuit chautauqua as part of the ambiguous zeitgeist of "progress."

Conclusion

It should be remembered that chautauqua's identity as an American institution was never questioned. Assertions of its American identity, therefore, were not reactions to external challenges or criticism leveled directly at the movement, but rather represented attempts by bureaus to maintain chautauqua's connection with its audience in a changing social and political climate. Initially, the circuit and independent chautauquas' ideas regarding patriotism and expression of American identity were inherited from the Chautauqua Institution, and music was used positively to assert that identity in much the way it had been in the early years at Chautauqua Lake.

Chautauqua incorporated both African American and Native American musical acts during a period in which these cultures were represented musically to white audiences primarily as novelties. While musical representations of African American and Native American cultures outside of chautauqua focused on cultural differences and perpetuated the idea of these groups as *other*, circuit chautauqua, following the model of the Indianist musical movement of the turn of the century and of late nineteenth-century efforts to codify and construct an American musical identity, presented African American and Native American music not as *other*, but as American, and eventually as essentially American, in opposition to European art music.

World War I served as a catalyst for change in circuit chautauqua's expression of nationalism. During the war, patriotic expression became a near necessity for all chautauqua acts, including music, and music was used to define chautauqua's American identity negatively, setting "truly American" music against German or German-influenced art music. Rather than capitalizing on the (by then waning) novelty of African American and Native American cultures, chautauqua managers promoted the idea central to Farwell's early lectures that the advancement of the music of "Negroes, Indians, and cowboys" was necessary for the United States to attain the musical independence he dubbed "the margin of the Un-German."[69]

VI. Music Defines Chautauqua as American

Finally, the end of the chautauqua era saw entertainment become paramount in a quest for a new American ideal rooted in technology and financial success. During these last years of circuit and independent chautauquas, less consideration was given to the message conveyed by musical acts, and subsequently music became less important to the maintenance of chautauqua's American identity.

VII
Music in Chautauqua's Decline

Eduard Lindeman, writing for the *Bookman* in 1927, declared, "Lyceums and chautauquas belong to our pioneering days and those days are over."[1] That statement reveals much about the prevailing sentiment among American cultural critics of the late 1920s. The chautauqua movement, long considered by rural Americans to be a conduit for high culture and progressive thought, was by that time frequently derided in the national press as "banal," "empty," and "conservative." Sinclair Lewis' *Main Street* (1920) depicted the Gopher Prairie chautauqua as "a combination of vaudeville performance, Y.M.C.A. lecture, and the graduation exercises of an elocution class." Many in the national press saw the movement's growing distance from its turn-of-the-century progressive ethos as the result of capitalistic catering to the rural audience. Allen Albert, himself a circuit chautauqua lecturer, wrote of it in 1922: "The very foundation of the home guard, which musters under chautauqua tents, is the most old-fashioned conservatism and morality. If ever you wonder what counterweight America has to the growing volume of radicalism, think of the chautauqua." He went on to declare that the chautauqua was "the most monotonously moral agent I have ever observed among men."[2] It should be noted that Albert, writing from inside the movement, did not seem to view this conservatism as entirely negative, and he spoke approvingly of circuit chautauqua bureaus' policing of lecture content and offstage performer behavior.

In retrospect, it appears that the chautauqua movement did not actually become more conservative as the twentieth century progressed, but rather it remained relatively static both in terms of prevailing morality and of aesthetic and literary tastes, despite gradual shifts in these areas among much of the American public.[3] This phenomenon can be seen in circuit chautauqua's opposition to jazz. Early in the movement, many American cultural institutions rejected jazz and its "lowbrow" connotations. Circuit chautauqua persisted in this attitude into the 1930s, as jazz was gaining acceptance in many mainstream American venues, as evidenced by the proliferation of jazz in places such as dance halls and concert settings, as well as a marked rise in radio airplay. Thus, chautauqua's attitude concerning jazz — much like its perceived moral and political conservatism — was more a result of stagnation than influence by the predominantly rural audience.

Although criticism of the chautauqua movement was common in the national press during the movement's declining years, chautauqua did not fail — either as a cultural movement or as a commercial enterprise — due to criticism from outside the movement. The chautauqua movement, and circuit chautauqua in particular, had faced criticism from urban progressives and educators since its inception. That these voices became louder as the movement waned speaks more to changes in the American social climate than it does to the decline of chautauqua. Nevertheless, the increasing prominence of these dissenting voices, and the public's increasing access to these viewpoints through increased availability of national print media and radio, likely contributed to a decrease in civic support for circuit chautauqua. It did not necessarily affect ticket sales; but as community leaders became disillusioned with the chautauqua ideal, communities questioned the necessity of the chautauqua, and especially the need to guarantee its financial success with civic funds.

Other factors did in fact contribute to a decline in chautauqua ticket sales. Competing media such as radio, motion pictures, and phonographs contended with circuit chautauqua for audience attendance, and also called into question the need for chautauqua, especially concerning musical, dramatic, and other "entertainment" aspects of the movement. The lecture, considered by many to be the core of the chautauqua movement, struggled in the 1920s as well. Lindeman asserted that the chautauqua lecture was not alone in its struggle to survive the 1920s, but that lecturing as a whole was becoming less popular. Education — especially adult education — was becoming increasingly interactive. Adults, Lindeman reasoned, were more interested in dialog than in the lecture, and it would be impossible for the chautauqua lecture to adapt to this new format.[4]

Chautauqua musical programming adapted to the challenges of this new era, but in doing so fundamentally changed the function of music in the movement. In many instances, music became chautauqua's drawing card, along with magicians, dramatic acts, and other features that had been previously marginalized or forbidden by bureaus. The movement as a whole distanced itself from educational associations and references to "high culture" in the late 1920s, instead emphasizing entertainment. Music could more easily make this adaptation, whereas the lecture was more difficult to present as lighthearted or entertaining. For this reason, among others, music increased in prominence within chautauqua as the movement itself declined in popularity.

Chautauqua's decline parallels that of the rural American opera house. In his study of Appalachian opera houses, William Condee cites competition from newly constructed venues—often school auditoriums and gymnasiums—as a principal cause of the demise of the rural opera house.[5] Interestingly, the records of several independent chautauqua assemblies mention abandoning the tent in favor of a preexisting permanent structure such as a gymnasium in the declining years of the assembly. The final incarnations of the Marshalltown, Iowa, chautauqua were held in the local coliseum rather than a tent.[6] Evert Winks, a tent supervisor for Community Chautauqua in the last years of that organization, noted that several communities on his circuit had begun to use civic amphitheaters in the 1920s.[7] Winks appreciated the lightened workload afforded by preexisting structures and does not seem to have made the connection between these new civic institutions and the decreasing relevance of the tent chautauqua. Others, however, point to the physical deterioration of the tents—many of which were more than a decade old by the 1920s—as indicative of the general state of the chautauqua movement in its final years. Nineteen twenty-seven would also be the last year of tent chautauquas for Swarthmore Chautauqua. From 1928 until the collapse of Swarthmore Chautauqua in 1930, assemblies were held in indoor venues such as gymnasiums or auditoriums. These indoor facilities were becoming more common in small towns and were frequently incorporated into construction of new schools. The availability of indoor venues combined with the physical degradation of much of the chautauqua equipment (accounts from the late 1920s frequently mention heavily patched tents and unsafe platforms) caused Paul Pearson, Swarthmore's founder and manager, to move his chautauquas indoors.[8] Although the move indoors did not directly affect Swarthmore's programming, it did remove the chautauqua from its signature tent and open the possibility of off-season chautauquas that would be in direct competition with lyceums, movies, and variety theater. In fact, in the declining years of the chautauqua movement, Swarthmore did attempt a number of shorter indoor chautauquas labeled "festivals." These were not terribly successful (the greatest number ever booked in one year was five, in a year in which Swarthmore Chautauqua visited over nine hundred towns running five simultaneous circuits), although it is difficult to ascertain whether the failure was due to the indoor aspect of these festivals or to the general decline in the chautauqua movement.

1932 marked the thirtieth anniversary of the Central Iowa Chautauqua at Tama-Toledo, and was also the last year that the chautauqua would be held.[9] Although the independent status of the chautauqua was prominently

VII. Music in Chautauqua's Decline

featured in advertising, the fine print of the program indicates that the committee was by that time relying on Redpath-Loar Service of Chicago to provide talent for its assembly. James Loar had been involved in booking talent for independent chautauquas beginning in the 1910s, operating under several corporate names. As late as 1930, Loar was managing chautauquas as Loar Independent Chautauquas; the merger with Redpath must have happened in 1931 or 1932. Redpath absorbed several smaller chautauqua bureaus and talent agencies in its final years, a tactic often cited in discussions of the circuit chautauqua movement's decline.

Although the 1932 Central Iowa Chautauqua spanned six days, a respectable but not exceptionally long independent assembly, it should be noted that the first day consisted solely of a magic show. The second day featured two concerts by the same ensemble, as did the sixth day (the Eureka Jubilee Singers and the Welsh Imperial Singers, respectively). The fifth day consisted of two plays. Of the two remaining days, one featured two "entertainments" by the Brown-Meneley Entertainers, a variety act combining music and comedy, and a lecture on "Soviet Russia's Successes and Failures." Only the third day of the Central Iowa Chautauqua featured two concerts and two lectures, a format that had been standard in circuit (and many independent) chautauquas during the movement's heyday.

The 1944 Mediapolis, Iowa, independent chautauqua, one of the last surviving assemblies, embraced and invoked technological innovations throughout the program. The first afternoon lecture of the week was a travelogue by a newsreel cameraman, Jack Barnett, who gave another lecture in the evening accompanied by newsreel footage. The Sunday evening sacred concert was performed by "radio artists" from WCAZ in Carthage, Illinois. The following evening's lecture featured motion pictures of Mexico, and the final lecture of the chautauqua was a travelogue of the South Seas, accompanied by motion pictures.

Excessive expansion is often cited as a primary reason for chautauqua's decline. With bureaus adding more circuits and music occupying more platform time, expansion meant an overall increase in the number of musical acts on the circuits. As bureaus reached farther into the talent pool to find musicians to fill rosters, a decline in overall ability of chautauqua acts was nearly inevitable. Shrinking profit margins and attempts to appeal to popular tastes meant bureaus avoided the expensive "highbrow" musical acts that had previously headlined chautauquas in favor of smaller, more versatile, less expensive acts. Thus, the declining years of chautauqua saw a higher quantity of music, but expansion came at the expense of quality.

Swarthmore Chautauqua, considered by some to be the gold standard of circuit chautauqua quality, also presented perhaps the clearest example of overexpansion hastening decline. In 1925, Swarthmore had five circuits reaching 987 communities. While this was certainly the largest number of chautauqua events Swarthmore produced in one year, in the absence of complete attendance records, it is unclear whether 1925 was also Swarthmore's peak for attendance. The 1925 season did turn a profit of over $25,000, the first profitable season in three years. The success was not enough, however, to offset the large deficits of the 1923 and 1924 seasons, failures that Swarthmore's creator and manager, Paul Pearson, blamed on rapid expansion. Pearson's strategy of expanding in the face of deficits created by expansion seemed to work in 1925, but that would be the last year of profits for Swarthmore. Whether Pearson's strategy would have worked in a static economic and cultural environment is impossible to know. American culture moved away from chautauqua so quickly and completely that none of Pearson's efforts (he also made drastic cuts to expenses in 1926) could save Swarthmore. After a few seasons of declining public interest and plummeting ticket sales, Swarthmore Chautauqua closed permanently in 1930.[10]

As early as 1920, those within the chautauqua movement were beginning to doubt that the movement could sustain its impressive trajectory. In that year, Redpath-Horner used advertising space in *The Lyceum Magazine* to address the rapid expansion of the movement and express concern regarding the subsequent dilution of the talent pool: "So great an expansion in the future is not possible.... Program standards must be raised. A reduction in the number of chautauquas is preferable to a reduction of program standard[s]." Later that year, Charles Horner wrote an article in which he declared, "We must very decidedly improve our programs at whatever cost — even at the cost of reducing the number of chautauquas if necessary, at the cost of reducing the number of bureaus if necessary. I also believe that, while our profits may not be so large for a single year, they will be sufficient in the long run if all chautauqua managers will better their programs to a sufficient degree. Some cannot put out good programs while others are putting out bad ones, unless all suffer because of the bad ones."[11] Of course Horner, head of one of the largest and most respected chautauqua bureaus in the industry, could make such pronouncements secure in the knowledge that a reduction in the number of bureaus was unlikely to affect him.

Atherton postulated that chautauqua's decline, while undeniably fast, seemed even sharper because community leaders hid the movement's deterioration from the public until collapse was imminent, at which point it could no longer be denied. As discussed previously, support of chautauqua was a signifier of culture and progressive thought for many rural communities, and to admit that the community no longer attended the chautauqua in numbers great enough to cover the financial guarantee was embarrassing to community

A small set of organ chimes (author's collection, gift of Fred Crane).

leaders. Newspapers, continuing a long tradition of avoiding negativity when discussing chautauqua, focused on successful aspects of a faltering event, such as one sold-out performance amid several days of paltry attendance.[12] Even some within the movement were surprised by chautauqua's seemingly rapid demise. Winks wrote, "To the best of my recollection we were not aware at the time that we were working with a fading business. The crowds were large, the required guarantee usually was over-subscribed, and we all worked harder than any dying job could have asked. Only in my last year with the chautauqua was I aware of a decline, and this most of us credited to the recession of the early twenties rather than to a permanent disability."[13]

Chautauqua bureaus and independent communities employed several strategies to adapt musical programming to a changing society. These included the programming of more musical novelties and comedies, embracing competing forces such as the automobile and motion pictures, and shrinking the chautauqua program to reflect chautauqua's waning importance on rural communities' calendars.

While novelty acts were nothing new to chautauqua, they proliferated in the movement's declining years. In 1927, Swarthmore Chautauqua featured the Jacksonville Boys Brass Band. Billed as "a band that cannot hear itself play," the Jacksonville Boys Brass Band consisted of 21 students from the Illinois School for the Deaf. The band was touted as having "mastered the difficulty by 'feeling' the vibrations."[14] The 1924 Radcliffe Chautauqua, billed as a "canvas covered temple of joy and inspiration," featured the Clarke Novelty Company in "unusual programs of readings, soprano and cello solos, xylophone selections and the fascinating Musical Lyre."[15]

Novelty instruments also increased in popularity as the chautauqua movement declined. Organ chimes and musical glasses were especially popular, as was the marimbaphone, a now-obsolete keyboard percussion instrument whose bars could be rotated into a vertical position for ease of bowing. Vocal groups, even those who featured primarily art music, would often perform on such novelty instruments. The Boston Lyrics, a vocal duo with piano accompaniment, also performed on the marimbaphone and the bowena, an instrument described as "an ideal instrument of entrancing sweetness, new to the Lyceum platform, which they have recently had constructed especially for their use."

A study of the promotional brochures collected by the Redpath bureau indicates that musical acts in the 1920s embraced the term "novelty" and were thus willing to accept the label, while not necessarily presenting substantially different music than had appeared on the platform in prior years. Groups such as the Petrie Novelty Quintet, the Novelty Four, and the Arcadia Novelty Company proliferated on the chautauqua circuits in the late 1920s, but promotional materials indicate instrumentation, personnel, and presentation not perceptibly different from earlier groups that were billed as "high class" and would have wholeheartedly rejected the "novelty" label. The Chicago Novelty Quartet, a creation of Bohumir Kryl, featured seasoned chautauqua performers playing classical instruments in standard configurations of solos with piano accompaniment, duets, and trios. Furthermore, it appears the Novelty Four, a quartet active during the last decade of the circuit chautauqua movement, was a pared-down incarnation of the Musical Guardsmen, a group that had performed at chautauquas since at least 1917.

While the move to embrace novelty — in music as well as other facets of chautauqua — is well documented, it is possible that advertising made the shift appear more drastic than it really was. Bell ringers, for instance, had been a part of chautauqua from the very earliest years of the movement, as were vocal quartets doubling on an array of strange instruments and (somewhat later) exotic acts of dubious authenticity and educational merit. The previously discussed scarcity of detailed programs for musical novelty groups makes it impossible to trace programming trends within the novelty faction of chautauqua, but it is clear that what came to be branded as "novelty" in the declining years of the movement had always existed in chautauqua, albeit in lower concentration and certainly lower profile. By the second half of the 1920s, in an effort to remain relevant in a changing American culture, chautauqua bureaus embraced terms such as "novelty" and "entertainment" along with "pep" and other terms that would previously have been avoided for fear of appearing frivolous. Thus, novelty musical acts — and in fact, musical acts in general — were pushed to the fore in later chautauqua advertisements and given more time in steadily shrinking programs in an effort to keep the chautauqua movement alive in an environment of intense competition.

Jazz in Chautauqua's Decline

It appears the chautauqua audience would embrace novelty before it accepted jazz. A review of Leake's Orchestral Entertainers from the *Atlanta Constitution*, reprinted in a promotional brochure for the group, reads, "Announced as a 'novelty' number, some may have feared that the music would be of the trashy, jazz type, but the novelty lay in the instruments used." Those instruments were later identified as "two big marimbaphones."

The critic was not alone in his fear that jazz's increasing mainstream popularity would lead to its acceptance on the chautauqua platform. In fact, the fear was so pervasive that some chautauqua acts specifically advertised their avoidance of — and sometimes outright opposition to — jazz. An undated advertising flyer for the Chicago Orchestral Club states that the group is an "artist company," and as such "do not tell a lot of humorous stories ... nor do they depend for applause upon the rendition of jazz music." A 1929 brochure for the Shumate Brothers states that they perform as "a brass quartet composed of two trumpets and two trombones. With these instruments they produce clean, velvety tones, devoid of the blast and blare of jazz, and cause a genuine feeling of respect and admiration for these lately abused instruments." It goes on to praise their unaffected singing voices, stating, "They have not permitted themselves to have big, robust, voices, but they have instilled into their singing that sweet, appealing quality that is a reflection of their clean living and brotherly dispositions."

George Laird, a popular chautauqua lecturer and humorist, advertised a lecture-recital entitled "The Fiddle and the Bow": "humorous and yet philosophical, it illustrates the power of music, especially of the old-time music, to charm the savage soul. And we're all savages, you know, says Laird, who has joined hands with Henry Ford and others to restore old-fashioned music and to war on jazz. Himself an old-time fiddler, Laird, in this lecture, is ably assisted by his wife — Phigenia Laird — a talented pianist and graduate of the Detroit Conservatory of Music — who not only accompanies her husband but plays several splendid Masterpieces from the Old Masters." The evocation of Ford is interesting, as Ford's opposition to jazz (and the broader popular music industry) was largely rooted in anti–Semitism.[16] There is nothing to indicate, however, that Laird espoused anti–Semitism in his "war on jazz," and it is unlikely that such sentiment would have been tolerated by the chautauqua industry.

Jazz was even invoked negatively by nonmusical acts. An undated promotional flyer for Lincoln and Roosevelt impersonator James Henry McLaren reads, "In these days of jazz and mediocre vaudeville acts it does one good to hear an offering such as Dr. McLaren presented last evening." Similarly, a promotional brochure for lecturer Lewis Horton stated, "The American Lyceum Bureau believes that there are pastimes other than automobiles, picture shows, and jazz, and therefore offers you Mr. Horton on Books." Opposition to jazz in chautauqua was not universal. Some chautauqua acts embraced jazz and touted their musical modernism. An annotated list of attractions available for the 1926 chautauqua season published by Ralph Dunbar explains the evolution of his most famous and long-lived act, the White Hussars:

> Time and circumstance have influenced their instrumentation and programs somewhat. Banjos, Saxophones and the Spirit of Classic Jazz are somewhat dominant in their Hussaring now, but this is 1925 — the Spirit of Irving Berlin has chased the shades of the old masters from even the center poles of the Chautauqua tent, the old folks have fallen for it, the young folks demand it, the Hussars must be up to date, so what'll they do if they don't give the public what they want?

Some musical acts justified their incorporation of jazz by claiming to elevate it. The Shannon Quartet, managed by the Redpath Lyceum Bureau, advertised their superior technique and musicality: "Every available minute finds them working together on some new idea or perfecting a passage in an old number. As a result their work has become finished, and even their rendition of so called jazz numbers can be termed artistic." This particular rationale reflected prevailing sentiment within the broader art music community regarding vernacular music in the early twentieth century. John Philip Sousa, for instance, acknowledged the importance of ragtime in the musical culture of the era and performed rags himself, remaining ever-conscious of his responsibility to guide, rather than pander to, popular taste.[17]

It appears that chautauqua audiences were less conflicted about jazz than the chautauqua industry was. A newspaper review of a performance by Maupin's Band on the 1925 Ellison-White circuit reveals contradiction on the platform regarding the place of jazz in chautauqua: "Less than a week after [former baseball player and evangelist] Billy Sunday told a Boise chautauqua audience that America was trying to jazz its way to the bow-wows, a Boise chautauqua audience in the same tent applauded a jazz program till its hands were sore." It is interesting, and perhaps an indicator of a lack of oversight by the bureau, that Ellison-White booked an anti-jazz speaker and a jazz act on the same circuit.

Chautauqua vs. Radio

Reynold Wik postulated that "chautauqua died in the mid-twenties because radio could provide these opportunities [music and lectures] and do the job in much better fashion."[18] Although Wik did not explain how radio's delivery was superior to chautauqua's, he did go on to discuss that radio made current events available even to children. This could be interpreted to mean that radio, broadcast directly into the home, provided a more child-friendly means of delivering programming than the chautauqua, which required sitting on hard benches in (often sweltering) tents. Wik could also be referencing the widely held belief that radio broadcasts were of higher musical quality than chautauqua performances. It is true that the musical groups broadcast on the radio in the late 1920s were often world class, while the vast majority of chautauqua musicians were young and relatively untrained. It could be argued that the superior musical ability of groups such as the New York Philharmonic was offset by the inferior quality of broadcast technology at the time, and that the inherent value of live performance offset the musical inferiority of chautauqua musicians. But whether or not radio did in fact "do the job in much better fashion," it is undeniable that radio broadcasts drastically affected the chautauqua movement.

Beyond strictly musical performances, some radio broadcasts included a lecture component supplemented by or concerning music. For instance, the long-running *Music and the Spoken Word* began broadcasting from Salt Lake City in 1929. This program featured the Mormon Tabernacle Choir in performances of sacred and secular music, as well as spoken messages, often on themes familiar to chautauqua patrons such as uplift or patriotism, by announcer Richard Evans. The success of *Music and the Spoken Word*, conceived just as chautauqua was dying, indicates that it might not have been the content of chautauqua that audiences had tired of, but rather the medium.

Invocation of the radio not as a competitor but as an allied force of entertainment can be seen in later circuit chautauqua advertising. Radcliffe Chautauquas advertised "a big new deal in outdoor chautauqua entertainment," a three-day event comprising only six acts, of which only one was a lecture. The primary draw of the chautauqua was "an entire radio broadcasting unit that will broadcast radio programs right before your eyes."[19] Not only does this brochure heavily tout radio, it also invokes vaudeville and minstrelsy, and the cover of the brochure features two white performers in blackface.

It seems radio and blackface minstrelsy were linked in the minds of the chautauqua managers, and possibly those of their audience, in a way twenty-first century readers might not readily expect or comprehend. It could be coincidental that the rise of radio references in later chautauqua programs corresponded with an increase in both actual blackface minstrelsy and minstrel-like performances on the chautauqua platform, but it should be noted that a disproportionate number of late chautauqua acts with "radio" in their names or advertising language also involved or invoked minstrelsy. The Deep River Plantation Singers Radio Quartette, an all-black group performing on the depression-era Canadian Chautauquas circuit, performed "jubilee chants, plantation melodies, religious hymns, voodoo songs, old tribal melodies and spirituals."[20] Most notably, the group's typical performance was divided into two sets, the second being devoted to plantation songs and entertainments. This was a format common to blackface minstrel shows beginning in the nineteenth century. Similarly, Marguerite Austin and her Dixie Broadcasters, an all-white female group whose name simultaneously invoked minstrelsy and radio, split their program between "favorite classical airs" and songs from or about the South.[21] The Dixie Broadcasters are especially noteworthy because Austin was a longtime chautauqua performer, having played violin with the Jess Pugh Concert Company as early as 1911. Her 1929 advertising material with the Dixie Broadcasters marks the first use of southern or radio connotations in her long chautauqua career.

In 1926, Swarthmore featured Uncle Eli and his Down Home Entertainers. The last event of that circuit, this act featured old-time songs and dancing, and culminated in a fiddling contest open to local fiddlers, judged by Uncle Eli himself. Such an event appears unparalleled in chautauqua history and was likely an attempt to capitalize on the popularity of radio barn dances such as the National Barn Dance (first aired in 1924) and the Grand Ole Opry (first aired in 1925).

Even as chautauqua tried to embrace radio, it could not replicate the ability of national radio broadcasts to bring stars to the audience, nor could it counter the expectation of star power that radio had implanted in the rural audience. By the late 1920s, chautauqua was competing with radio not only for audience, but also for talent. Radio personalities largely rejected attempts to book them on chautauqua tours, due to adverse working conditions and relatively low pay on the circuits.[22] First-rate musicians, already avoided by struggling chautauqua bureaus due to their high cost, were further tempted away from chautauqua by the lure of a relatively stationary career in radio or recordings. Overexpansion meant that more chautauquas of lower quality traveled the circuits, and thus it was, in many cases, an inferior chautauqua product that faced competition from radio in the 1920s.

Chautauqua vs. Motion Pictures

Charles Horner made his feelings about motion pictures clear in a 1920 article for *The Lyceum Magazine*:

> In my opinion, those who are seeking causes for the present social and industrial unrest will find one of the chief causes in the moving picture house. Many of the dramas depicted are elevating, instructing, and inspirational. Maybe a little of the worst of them will not do any harm, but the great quantity that the average citizen is absorbing is too much for anybody. Domestic standards and fidelity are very frequently made light of. The so-called "triangle" is a favored theme in dramatic interest. The sacred subject of love is made callow, bold, and is unadorned. It is deprived of the saving grace of imagination, and is made so common that it is very easily made a thing, in the minds of some people, to be taken on today and put off tomorrow.... At the very worst, the lyceum and chautauqua has been fairly sincere and has been quite true to sound human instincts and to honest, if primitive, ideals. May the Lord forgive those institutions and those men who have done so much to shatter by ridicule the very sound instincts and ideals of the ordinary neighborhood, especially the rural neighborhood.[23]

While motion pictures are often implicated in chautauqua's decline, moving picture attractions occasionally appeared on chautauqua programs. The C.J. Hite Company, based out of Chicago and managed by the Mutual Lyceum Bureau, offered a "chautauqua moving picture attraction" accompanied by "a musical program arranged with excellent taste." Hite's 1908 brochure offered a variety of programs, the most elaborate of which required the use of a chronophone, a device that synchronized a phonograph and a film projector. Hite advertised that the chronophone reproduced "everything from popular songs to grand opera, such as scenes from *Faust, Cavaleria Rusticana, Carmen* and *The Mikado*; songs of sterling worth such as the Psalms, 'Bedouin Love Song,' 'Good Bye,' etc." Hite stressed the limited availability and considerable expense of the chronophone (which was likely true, as it was a relatively new invention at the time) and offered many programs requiring less cutting-edge technology. It is unclear how the music for these programs was produced. Reviews mention realistic sound effects, but do not state whether those effects were mechanical or if live musicians provided the soundtrack for the films.

While it is obvious that motion pictures competed with chautauqua for a finite amount of discretionary income and leisure time among rural audiences, it should be noted that movies more directly challenged other indoor amusements, such as vaudeville and the lyceum. Condee notes that motion picture distributors often demanded exclusive use of venues, effectively pushing vaudeville and local events out of community opera houses.[24] These opera houses had long been the preferred venue for lyceums, and the shift from live events to motion pictures in opera houses coincides with an increase in lyceum bookings at high school and church venues. High schools and churches were not ideal replacements for dedicated community auditoriums, and the stability offered by a string of professionally managed theater venues working with one lyceum booking agency was shattered. This contributed to a lack of stable winter employment for performers in lyceums, which must have been detrimental to a chautauqua movement on the verge of collapse due to other factors.

Chautauqua vs. Urbanization

Much has been made of the impact of national media such as radio and motion pictures on chautauqua's decline. While direct competition from these entertainments was certainly a major nail in chautauqua's coffin, it is also important to consider the effect that national media, coming as it did from urban centers, had on rural audiences' perception of chautauqua. Chautauqua had never been successful in large cities, and there is ample evidence that urban culture bearers were dismissive and often disdainful of the chautauqua movement. This was part of a larger cynicism from urbanites — many of Midwestern extraction — toward Midwestern culture. Atherton labeled this sentiment a "debunking crusade" and pointed to Sinclair Lewis as its primary — but not sole — crusader.[25]

VII. Music in Chautauqua's Decline   187

Rieser states that "the shrillest attacks [against the chautauqua movement] came from intellectuals uncomfortable with their own Midwestern upbringing."[26] While some of chautauqua's critics may have intentionally distanced themselves from Midwestern culture, that distance also existed between those involved in the production of circuit chautauqua and those in the audience. Most of the key administrators in the movement were either from, or had spent considerable time in, the Midwest. The bureaus, however, were headquartered in Midwestern urban centers, and most of the upper-level administrators had some college education. Many leaders in the circuit chautauqua movement harbored genuine concern and respect for Midwestern culture, while simultaneously endeavoring to "elevate" Midwestern tastes to align with those of early twentieth-century East Coast American urbanites.

Charles Seeger viewed the chautauqua movement and the "missionary" efforts of the Northeastern musical elite (exemplified by the creation of large permanent orchestras and choral societies) as two sides of the same coin, a movement he referred to as "make-America-musical." Seeger saw the conflict between chautauqua and the urban northeast as emanating from musical ignorance on the part of chautauqua organizers and supporters. While he believed their hearts were in the right place, Seeger saw the Midwest faction of "make-America-musical" as "comparatively ignorant of the fine art, they fostered mainly the only other they knew—the popular art that had taken firm root among the middle and lower classes of the cities. To the urban missionaries this was anathema." Seeger went on to compare chautauqua to shape-note singing and the urban revulsion spawned by that (highly popular, much like chautauqua) movement.[27]

As the urban sphere of influence spread through radio and increasingly inexpensive print media, rural Americans may have questioned their loyalty to the chautauqua movement. Several studies of chautauqua cite Sinclair Lewis' *Main Street* as a prime example of urban backlash against chautauqua—and it is—but no studies have addressed the nearly contemporary play *The Brightville Indoor Chautauqua*. Published in 1921 by Eldridge Entertainment House of Denver, the play seems to have been a parody of a chautauqua course. It is divided into five parts, each representing a day of the chautauqua. The cast includes a platform manager, a concert company, twelve actors to portray "living pictures" (this was more common in variety theater than in chautauqua), a flexible number of musical entertainers, four farmers, and several actors to portray the Coonville Jubilee Singers.

Part I of the play, representing the first night of the fictional chautauqua, was a concert by the Chautauqua Concert Company. The script does not dictate an exact makeup for the group, but does suggest "a pianist, a reader and a mixed quartet ... appearing in evening dress if possible." Nor does the script list specific pieces to be played, but it does suggest a rough program order (quartet, duet, reading, solo, quartet) and suggests that musical selections can be purchased through the Eldridge Entertainment House catalog. The script does give the opening speech to be made by a member of the Chautauqua Concert Company, in which is mentioned "intellectual uplift and inspirational entertainment." The speaker tells the audience "very few cities of this size are given such a wonderful privilege as you are having."

Part three of the play was a performance by the Musical Entertainers, an orchestra whose repertoire is dictated by "available musical talent." As with the Chautauqua Concert Company, the playwright does not specify works for the Musical Entertainers to perform, but rather suggests the following: orchestra number, violin and clarinet solo, cornet solo, orchestra number, trombone solo, orchestra number. This seems to indicate an ideal instrumentation very similar to chautauqua orchestras. Before the performance, an actor playing the manager of the Musical Entertainers was to give a speech encouraging the audience to attend Friday's performance of the Coonville Jubilee singers, ending with, "Don't fail to invite your colored friends particularly."

The Coonville Jubilee Singers act, comprising the fifth part of the play representing the last day of the fictional chautauqua, is certainly the most offensive by 21st-century standards (although the preceding "Farmers' Night" is not much better) and goes farthest in demonstrating the playwright's contempt for the chautauqua phenomenon. It is important to note that the Coonville Jubilee Singers are instructed to appear in blackface and garish minstrel costumes. In contrast, jubilee groups on the chautauqua circuits nearly always performed in formal attire and were composed of African American singers, rather than white performers in blackface. The manager of the Coonville Jubilee Singers speaks in a thick "Negro" dialect and misuses many words. For instance, his opening statement reads, "De Coonville Jubilee Singers are completely flabbergasted wid dis omniverous audience and de obstreperous welcome you hab gibben us." Blocking instructions given in the script call for the performers to sit in a semicircle with the manager on a platform in the center of the arc of performers. This is reminiscent of the typical stage setup for the opening of a blackface minstrel performance, a similarity that cannot be coincidental.

After fifteen lines of such dialog, the manager announces their first number, "Swing Low, Sweet Chariot." It is interesting that the playwright chose this song, as it was a staple of jubilee groups. This is perhaps the first element of this fictional performance that reflected the reality of chautauqua. The manager of the Coonville Jubilee Singers announces that "Swing Low, Sweet Chariot" will be performed by "our salugribus baritone, Mr. Garfield Meechum White," to be followed by a dramatic reading by "Miss Euphonia

Black." An unnamed choral number and lullaby followed by "Quit Dat Ticklin' Me," a popular song commercially recorded in 1901 by Silas Leachman. An unspecified tenor solo followed, and the show closed with "Dixie." While "Dixie" is certainly a strong nod to the blackface minstrel tradition, it was not uncommon in chautauqua performances. Performers such as banjoist D.L. Leftwich and others who presented "minstrel remembrances" would likely have performed "Dixie" as part of their chautauqua programs. In fact, Harry Harrison of the Redpath bureau admonished Bohumir Kryl to limit his playing of "Dixie" to once per chautauqua engagement and quoted an unnamed audience member who had written to complain to Redpath: "I believe if Kryl were playing at a funeral, he would weave in 'Dixie.' Of course, we like 'Dixie,' but we don't want to be insulted by having it thrown in our faces every other piece."[28] It seems the way the Coonville Jubilee Singers inclusion of "Dixie," then, is one of the more accurate aspects of what was, by and large, a gross caricature of a chautauqua.

The Automobile

The proliferation of the automobile in the United States in the early twentieth century was, in general, harmful to the chautauqua movement. Rural Americans could use their cars to drive to a chautauqua, of course, but they could also drive to any number of competing amusements, including permanent amusements such as theaters, museums, and concert venues in urban centers. Chautauqua bureaus, aware of the inevitability of the automobile age, attempted to embrace the new technology by designating "Automobile Day" at a chautauqua. In an undated promotional mailer, Redpath-Vawter advertised its automobile day, featuring Bohumir Kryl and his band, as "A Sure Enough Joy Ride":

> Here is a chance to prove what a glorious thing it is to own an automobile. You have pointed that beloved machine of yours down many a road bent on pure pleasure. But you never consumed gasoline in pursuit of so great a musical event as the sublime festivals of harmony, to be produced by Kryl and his Bohemian Band, within easy driving distance of you, at the town and date mentioned on the front cover of this announcement. It will be automobile day at the Chautauqua. Such another collection as will come whirling in has seldom been seen. Slick her up and bring all the folks along.[29]

The brochure alternately describes the day of Kryl's performance as "Music Day," a designation commonly used in chautauqua programming to indicate the day on which the headlining musical act was to perform. The designation of a "music day" did not mean that music would not be presented on other days, nor did it signify a lack of nonmusical attractions on that day. In general,

Advertisement for 1918 Ellison-White Chautauquas invoking the automobile (*The Lyceum Magazine,* June 1918).

there was no difference in the programming formula for a designated music day compared to any other, aside from the appearance of the most popular musical act.

Whether this attempt to appeal to automobile owners helped stem the tide of competing amusements is uncertain. Several chautauqua bureaus made similar efforts, however, and later chautauqua advertising is peppered with references to — and pictures of — the automobile. An Ellison-White chautauqua advertisement from 1918, touted as the first chautauqua advertisement designed for national publication in general (not chautauqua-specific) magazines, features an automobile prominently. An undated Redpath-Vawter advertisement, couched as a letter from Keith Vawter to "Mr. Automobile Driver," reads, in part, "The Chautauqua and the Automobile are twin sisters when it comes to putting pep into human life. They both take you into the big out-of-doors. They go hand in hand increasing the joy of living, by ironing furrows from the brow of care." Vawter then described the Ben Greet Players, a theater company producing *The Comedy of Errors,* as "a six cylinder, 90-horsepower organization of unusual merit."[30] The Ben Greet Players were perennial chautauqua favorites, having been the first theatrical troupe to perform on a Redpath circuit, and the evocation of the automobile in reference

VII. Music in Chautauqua's Decline

to their performance of Shakespeare seems forced, even compared to other efforts to link chautauqua with America's automotive obsession.

Musicians After Chautauqua

Since many chautauqua musicians, especially in the movement's final years, were young with relatively little investment in their musical careers, it is not surprising that some left chautauqua for non-musical pursuits. Others took their acts, largely unchanged, from chautauqua to the school assembly circuit. Winks indicated that several of the performers he had known on the Community Chautauqua circuit went on to work for the National Association for Schools, a booking agency focusing on providing educational entertainment for primary and secondary schools.[31] The remaining chautauqua bureaus followed a similar course, shifting focus from chautauquas and lyceums to school assemblies, churches, and civic organizations.

Many of the more prominent musicians associated with the chautauqua movement had divested from chautauqua before the decline began. A.F. Thaviu, whose band completed seven seasons of circuit chautauqua and performed at many independent assemblies in the 1910s and early 1920s, seems to have been wholly unaffected by the demise of the chautauqua movement. Thaviu's band had used chautauqua as a springboard to more profitable engagements such as state fairs, and in the heyday of chautauqua the band used the summer chautauquas as a stable source of income early in its traveling season, almost a warm-up for the fall fair season. Thaviu parted ways with chautauqua for economic reasons; his band was big, unionized, and expensive compared to other chautauqua acts. Chautauqua bureaus were increasingly reluctant to book large ensembles like Thaviu's, although larger independent chautauquas booked him until at least 1929. In 1928, the demand for Thaviu's band was so great that he formed a smaller band led by his son Samuel to play for smaller venues such as county fairs.

In its post-chautauqua years, the Thaviu band played extended engagements at the Steel Pier in Atlantic City, the Cincinnati Zoo, and dozens of state fairs and other expositions. Thaviu's band was one of the early featured ensembles in the Grant Park Concerts in Chicago, begun in 1935.[32] Thaviu remained active as a conductor and teacher until his death in 1945. Thaviu's exit from chautauqua in many ways paralleled that of Bohumir Kryl. Kryl used the reputation he had established as a chautauqua performer and impresario to craft a career in Chicago as a conductor and manager of several ensembles. He also exercised his considerable business acumen, evidenced by his dealings with circuit bureaus during his chautauqua career, to enter into the financial industry later in life. When he died in 1961, he left a sizable estate.

The Weatherwax Brothers, like many platform musicians, did not pursue musical careers once they left chautauqua. Asa ran a restaurant in Charles City, Iowa. Lester worked in the insurance industry and radio in Wichita, Kansas. Tom briefly ran a music store in Charles City before moving to Des Moines to become a grain broker. Will, the only brother to continue a performing career after chautauqua, toured part-time as a lecturer for schools and civic societies to supplement his income as a farmer and administrator for the YMCA.

Epilogue

In hindsight, chautauqua's quick decline and ultimate demise is not surprising and likely was not avoidable. It seems music may have prolonged chautauqua's life slightly, but at the expense of quality (both musical and in context of the chautauqua program as a whole). The story is familiar; a century before, critics were debating whether music had saved or destroyed the lyceum movement. This time, however, music could not save chautauqua, and destruction came from without.

There was, of course, one important survivor of chautauqua's collapse: the Chautauqua Institution still exists, and is arguably a larger force in America's musical life than it was during the chautauqua movement's heyday. The "Mother Chautauqua" survived by adapting, and is today an important summer festival for young classical musicians. It also boasts a professional symphony orchestra and opera company and hosts many other events, musical and otherwise. The Institution had chartered its course towards art music and away from its independent and circuit namesakes (and also, as I have argued, away from its own roots in religious and even popular music) before the broader chautauqua movement was seriously threatened by radio and automobiles. As such, the Institution was sufficiently distanced from the rest of the movement that it survived the late 1920s unscathed, and in fact marked several of its most important musical milestones during that period. For instance, the first radio broadcast from the Chautauqua Institution took place in 1927, and 1929 saw the formation of both the Chautauqua Symphony Orchestra and the Chautauqua Opera Association.

The Chautauqua Literary and Scientific Circle still exists, though it too has seen considerable transformation since its founding in 1878. The CLSC is in many ways tied more closely to the Chautauqua Institution today than in its early years; authors of books chosen for the CLSC now speak at the institution during the summer, for instance (books of deceased, or otherwise unavailable, authors are still selected, with scholars presenting on those works at the institution). It is still possible to graduate from the CLSC, but it is no longer a clear-cut distance education curriculum. The last book on a musical topic chosen for the CLSC reading list was Deena Rosenberg's *Fascinating Rhythm: The Collaboration of George and Ira Gershwin*, in 1993.

Several scholars have discussed the legacy of the chautauqua movement as a whole and its impact on American society, especially on education. Likewise, in-depth analyses of the various aspects of chautauqua, including the circuit chautauqua movement, lyceums, the CLSC, and of course the Chautauqua Institution have been published. Music's place in chautauqua's legacy, however, is difficult to discuss. While music was important — probably essential — to the chautauqua movement, the music itself was, in general, unremarkable. Very few musical works were premiered on the chautauqua circuits, and most of the musicians appearing on the platform had limited careers beyond the chautauqua movement. Perhaps it is not appropriate to apply these criteria, more suited for permanent, stationary musical institutions, to chautauqua. After all, chautauqua thrived in geographic areas and demographic circles where permanent orchestras, conservatories, and opera companies did not exist. Why, then, judge chautauqua's musical legacy by standards it never attempted to meet?

It is more useful to judge chautauqua by its stated goals of community edification and cultural evangelism. Just as many of the larger independent assemblies left behind a physical legacy of parks and amphitheaters bearing the chautauqua name, chautauqua musicians left a legacy of increased support and appreciation of music in rural communities. While it is difficult at times to cut through the lofty prose of chautauqua organizers and the flowery reviews of chautauqua performances in local newspapers in order to discover the true effect of chautauqua on small towns, there are numerous records of community choruses and recital series being founded after a chautauqua performance inspired the community. And without a doubt, many rural Americans heard music through chautauqua that would have been inaccessible to them otherwise. While the quality and educational merit of many chautauqua performances is debatable, music gave the chautauqua movement the momentum to succeed beyond expectations for decades, and chautauqua gave art music the vehicle to reach far beyond its traditionally urban audience.

Chautauqua music certainly was not perfect. Evidence shows that some of it was not even adequate. But music was unquestionably important to the chautauqua movement, as chautauqua was to rural America. Chautauqua helped define its audience as curious, engaged, and community-minded, and music helped define chautauqua as educational, entertaining, and worthwhile.

Appendices

A. Itinerary: Standard Chautauqua Bureau, 1904*

Marshalltown, Iowa
MacGregor Heights, Iowa
Des Moines, Iowa
Iowa Falls, Iowa
Sioux City, Iowa
Albert Lea, Minnesota
Chariton, Iowa

Bedford, Iowa
Glenwood, Iowa
Fremont, Nebraska
Fullerton, Nebraska
Lexington, Nebraska
Auburn, Nebraska

*This circuit began on July 1, 1904. The itinerary above was derived from accounts in Harry Harrison, *Culture Under Canvas: The Story of Tent Chautauqua* (New York: Hastings House, 1958). Due to the considerable distance between chautauquas on this circuit, it is safe to assume that most chautauquas did not begin on consecutive days. The exact dates for this circuit are unknown, although the circuit order listed above is accurate, according to Harrison.

B. Redpath–New York–New England Itinerary, 1925

Niagara Falls, NY
Ransomville, NY
Attica, NY
Perry, NY
Arcade, NY
Dunkirk, NY
Batavia, NY
Akron, NY
Williamsville, NY
North Tonwanda, NY
Lockport, NY
Olcott, NY
Lyndonville, NY

Albion, NY
Brockport, NY
East Rochester, NY
Honeoye Falls, NY
Geneseo, NY
Canandiagua, NY
Naples, NY
Williamson, NY
Newark, NY
Clifton Springs, NY
Ovid, NY
Waterloo, NY
Moravia, NY

Cortland, NY
Cazenovia, NY
Hamilton, NY
Norwich, NY
Walton, NY
Oneonta, NY
Cobleskill, NY
Cooperstown, NY
Herkimer, NY
Dolgeville, NY
Fort Plain, NY
Oneida, NY
Fulton, NY

Wolcott, NY	Tupper Lake, NY	Lancaster, NH
Oswego, NY	Saranac, NY	North Conway, NH
Camden, NY	Plattsburg, NY	Laconia, NH
Adams, NY	Burlington, VT	Portsmouth, NH
Carthage, NY	Hardwick, VT	Kennebunk, ME
Theresa, NY	Montpelier, VT	Auburn, ME
Ogdensburg, NY	Lyndonville, VT	Rumford, ME
Gouverneur, NY	Newport, VT	Farmington, ME
Potsdam, NY	Woodsville, NH	Skowhegan, ME
Massena, NY	Berlin, NH	Waterville, ME

Paul M. Pearson Papers, 1890–1969, Friends Historical Library of Swarthmore College (Swarthmore, Pennsylvania).

C. List of Known Chautauqua Musical Acts

Abernathy Concert Company
Aborn Opera Company
Accordion Novelty Company
Ackley K. of P. Band
Adams, Crawford
Adams, Edith
Adams Sisters Orchestra
Adanac Male Quartet
Adriatic Orchestra
Aida Quartet
Alabama Blossoms
Alamo Quintet
Alarcon Family
Alexander Novelty Four
Alexander Trio
Alford, Harry L.
All Brothers Quintet
Allerton Band, The
Alpine Singers and Yodelers
Alpine Tyrolean Yodelers
Althea Concert Company
Althea Players
Amato, Paravale
American Entertainers
American Girls
American Glee Club
American Ladies Band
American Ladies Grand Concert Band
American Ladies Quartette
American Opera Company
American Quartet
American Symphony Orchestra
Amphion Four
Amlden Concert Company
Anderson Brogan Duo
Anderson, Hugh
Anderson, Wilma
Andreev, W.W.
Angebilt Trio
Anitas, The
Apollo Duo
Apollo Musical Club
Apollo Quintette and Bell Ringers
Arcadia Concert Company
Arcadia Novelty Company
Arcadians
Arden Entertainers
Ardmore Entertainers
Arion Male Quartet
Arlington Male Quartet
Artist Concert
Artist Entertainers
Artist Quartet
Artists Company, The
Artist's Trio
Australian Duo
Australian Trio
Bachman's Band
Batunos Band
Batwam

Appendix C

Bailey, Celilia Effinghauser
Bailte-Stoeber Trio
Baker, Elsie
Balmer, Elizabeth
Balmer, J.H.
Barbara Orchestra
Barber of Seville Co.
Barborka, Vaclay
Barnaby Entertainers
Barnard Orchestra, The
Barton Family Orchestra
Bates, Ruth
Batting-Mahler Trio
Beethoven Musical Co.
Beethoven Trio
Beggar Opera Company
Beilharz Entertainers (Noah and Jane)
Bell Ringers, The
Bell Ringer Orchestra
Bellino Concert Co.
Berlino, Sam, and Theressa Shehan
Bern's Little Symphony
Beatley Trio
Birmingham-Southern Glee Club
Bispham, David
Bland, H.L.
Bland's Orchestra (Bland's Boys)
Bland's Wesleyan Quartet
Blue Danube Singers
Bohemian Girl Co.
Bohemian Orchestra
Boland Orchestra
Bostock's Novelty Co.
Boston Concert and Carnival Co.
Boston Lyrics
Boston Musical Art Co.
Boston Opera Singers
Bostonia Orchestra-Band
Bostonia Sextette Club
Bostonians, The
Boy Scout Band
Boy Choir of Christ's Episcopal Church
Boyds, The
Brahms Quartet
Bratton Concert Four
Brewer Concert Co.
Brollier's Band

Brook, Ellis
Brown-Meneley Co.
Bryant Sisters
Bryant, Tone
Budapest Hungarian Orchestra
Buddies, The
Burlington Choral Society and Burlington Symphony Orchestra
Burus Sisters
Burt, Evelyn
Burt, Grace Sylvia
Buschlea, Maud
Bush, Hattie
Butler, Helen May
Buzza, Frank
Byron('s) Troubadours
Cadman, C.W.
Cambrea Artists
Cambridge Players
Cameron Quartette
Campanari, G.
Capitol Serenaders
Cap's Orchestra
Capps Male Quartet
Carkeek, W.J.
Carmelini
Carmelimy's Colonial Band
Carrie Jacobs Band
Carroll Glees
Carroll Quartet
Cartwright Brothers Quartet
Casals, Pablo
Casford Concert Co.
Casford Trio
Cass, Harriet A.
Cartellucci's Neapolitans
Cartillian Orchestra Club
Castle Square Entertainers
Cates Musical Co.
Cathedral Choir
Cathedral Trumpeters
Cavaliers, The
Cavanwelsh Co.
Cello Ensemble
Cello Ensemble and Little Symphony
Chamberlin Trio
Chapel Singers
Charleston Choral Club
Chatham Concert Co.

Chautauqua Concert Party
Chautauqua Ladies' Orchestra
Chenette, Edward Stephen
Cheney Concert Co.
Cherniavsky Brothers
Chesney Sisters
Chicago Artists Quartet
Chicago Concert Co.
Chicago Ensemble Trio
Chicago Festival Quintet
Chicago Grand Opera Company
Chicago Ladies Orchestra
Chicago Ladies Singing Party
Chicago Ladies Symphony
Chicago Lady Entertainers
Chicago Lyceum Lady Quartette
Chicago Lyric Quartet
Chicago Male Quartet
Chicago Melody Trio
Chicago Musical College
Chicago Novelty Quartet
Chicago Operatic Company
Chicago Orchestral Choir
Chicago String Quartet
Chicago Symphonic Orchestra
Chimers of Britanny Company
Chocolate Soldier Company
Christie-Gjerdrum Concert Company
Christy Girls, The
Cilley Company
Cimera, Jaroslav
Cincinnati Conservatory Ensemble
Circicillo, Salvatore
Clark Concert Company
Clark, Edward
Clark, May
Clark-Bowers Co.
Clark-French Co.
Cleveland Ladies Orchestra
Close, Anna S.
Clough, Alice
Coates, Francis
Coats Sax Band
Colangelo's Italian Band and Orchestra
Cola Santo Concert Band
Colby, Martha Reynolds
Colleens, The

Collegians, The
Collette-Rhode-Hedges Singers
Collidge, Irene
Colonial Harp Ensemble
Colonial Quartet
Columbia Girls Quartet
Columbian Quartet
Columbians, The
Columbus Entertainers
Columbus Junction Band, The
Commercial Club Band (of Mediapolis)
Commonwealth Orchestra
Concert Entertainers
Concordia Concert Company
Conway, Patrick
Cook's Orchestra
Cornell Glee Club
Cosmopolitan Quartet
Cox, Henry G.
Cramer Trio
Craven Family Orchestra
Creatore, Fred Williams
Crooks, Richard
Crosland-Moor United Handbell Ringers
Culp, Mme. Julia
Cutler-Griffin Company
Cymbalom Orchestral Quartet
Daily News Band
Dalin Company
Davenny Quintet
Davies, Harry
Davies Opera Company
Davis Sisters
Dayne Trio
DeArmond Concert Company
Decca Opera(tic) Company
DeGrasz's Band
DeKoven Male Quartette
DeLuxe Singers and Artists
DeMoss Entertainers
Deak, Mme. Fyvie
DeSure Orchestra
Devault Entertainment Company
De Willo Concert Company
Di Giorgio Orchestra
Dixie Duo, The
Dixie Glee Club

Dixie Quintet
Dixie Trio, The
Dixie Vagabond Quartet
Doering Orchestral Quartet
Don Phillippini's Symphony Band
Dorothy Haines Company
Dudley Buck Choir
DuMond Company
DuMond Male Quartet
Dunbar, Ralph
Dunbar Singing Bell Ringers
Dunbar Quintette and Bell Ringers
Dunbar Singing Orchestra
Duval-Baldi Company
Duvall Brothers
Eastern Glee Quartet
El Dorado Grand Opera Company, The
Elias Tamuritza Serenaders, The
Elite Sextette
Elks Quartet of Concert Brass
Ellert, Clem A
Ellert's Band
Elliots, The
Ellsworth and His Metropolitan Singers
Elman, Mischa
Elesian Trio
Empyrean Male Quartette
English Opera Company
Ensmeyer, Grace
Entertainment Duo
Erdoedy
Ettinger, Alice
Ettinger, Mabel
Ettinger, Victor
Euphonium Glee Club
Eureka Glee Club
Eureka Male Quartet
European Quartette
Ewing's Ladies Band
Ewing's Overseas Military Band
Ewing's Zovave Band
Fairchild Company
Fairfield Iowa Band
Fairfield Knights of Pythius Band
Falk, Louis
Farnum Trio
Faubels, The

Faust Company
Feathertone, Floyd
Ferranti's Hungarian Orchestra
Ferullo Band, The
Ferranta's Concert Band
Fetterman's Band
Fidelio Opera Company
Fifty-fifth Iowa Infantry Band
Fifty-third Regiment Band
Filipino Collegians
Filipino Players
Filipino Quintette
Filipino Serenaders
Fine Arts Quartet
Fink's Hussars
Fioravante and His Band
Fischer Exposition Orchestra
Fischer Quartet
Fischer's Band
Fitzgerald's Band
Five Violin Girls
Fleischman Hungarian Orchestra
Florentine Trio
Florida Concert Promotion
Fornia, Rita
Forter Concert Company
Fourth Regimental Band
Fox Sisters Quartette
Francean, Edward
Fraternity Glee Club
Fraunfelder Swiss Yodelers
Fries, Burke, Wilson
Fuller, The Misses
Gall, Ruby
Galli-Curie, Amelita
Galt Band
Galt Kiltie Band
Gamble, Ernest
Garay Sisters
Gorden, Mary
Georgetown Glee Club
Giant Concert Company, The
Gibsonian Orchestra and Fisher Shipp
Gilbert Quartet
Goforth's Black and Gold Band
Goforth, George
Golden Gate Concert Company
Gondoliers Company
Gordman, Elenor

Gordon Quartet
Gordon Trio
Gorman, Dora
Grabel's Band
Grand Opera Singers
Grand Opera Stars
Grangier, Percy
Granville Accordianists
Gray-Llievinne Company
Great Lakes String Quartet
Great Welsh Choir
Green, Marion
Green, Frese
Greeenfield Orchestra
Greenfield Symphonic Quintet
Grenadiers, The
Griffin, _____
Griswold Duo
Grosiean Company
Grosien Trio
Grossman's Orchestra
Guatemalan Marimba Band
Guitar and Mandolin Club
Gwalis Lady Glee Singers
Gypsies
Hall, Stanley
Hampton Court Singers
Hand Band
Hanson, Howard
Happy Harmony Girls
Hardie, Hope
Harding String Quartet
Hardy Family Orchestra
Harlan's Musquattie Indians
Harmony Concert Co.
Harmony Glee Club
Harmony Singers
Harp Ensemble
Harp Novelty
Harp Symphony
Harper, Earl
Harrison, Charles
Hartland Quartet
Harvesters, The
Hawaiians Company
Hazeltine Opera Company
Herrons Sisters Concert Company
Heimerdinger Entertainers
Hemphill, Prof. J.W.

Hernande Brothers
Herrick Company
Herrick Duo
Herrick Male Quartet
Hewling's Rainbow Orchestra
Highland Ladies Orchestra
Hinshaw (Grand) Opera Company
Hinton-Mordelia Company
Hipple Concert Company.
Holt, Vivian
Holton's Concert Band
Homeland Quartet
Honolulu Students, The
Hoosier Male Quartette
Horbury Hand-Bell Ringers
Hougen's Chicago Orchestra
Houstons, The
Howard Orchestral Quintette
Hoyt, Katherine
Hruby Bohemian Orchestra
Hruby Brothers Quartette
Hruby Brothers Quintet
Hruby Company
Hudson Male Quartet
Huff and Music Matters
Huguelet Instrumental Trio
Hull Concert Co.
Hull Family Quartet
Humphrey's Orchestra
Hungarian Orchestra
Hussar Company
Illinois Glee Club
Immanuel Male Quartet
Imperial Hand Bell Ringers
Imperial Russian Balalaika Court
    Orchestra
Imperial Russian Balalaika Orchestra
    Troupe
Imperial Russian Quartet
Indianapolis Newsboys Band
Indian Quartet
Indian String Quartet, The
In Harpland Company
Innes Band
Iinternational Operatic Company
Iowa Euterpean Quartette
Iowa State Band
Iris Concert Company, The
Irish Colleens, The

Ithaca Concert Company
Irogun, Maria
Jackson, Howard F
James, Bertha
Jamesworth Marimba Band
Johnston Company (Lillian Johnston)
Jones, Dr. Lester B.
Jordan Musical Entertainers
Jost and Wunderle
Joymakers Male Quartette
Joymakers Quartet, The
Jugo Slav Tamburica Orchestra
Juvenile Court Band
K&K Concert Orchestra
Kachel's Metropolitan Singers
Kalteborn Quartet
Sherman Kamps Recital Company
Karl's Band
Kedreff Wuartet
Kelchver Trio
Kellog-Haines Singing Party
Killarney Girls
Kilties Orchestra, The
King Male Quartet
Kirksmiths Orchestra
Kiser Sisters
Knapp's Military Band and Orchestra
Knapp's Parlor Orchestra
Kneisle Quartet
Knights of Pythias Band
Knights of Pythias Glee Club
Theodore Knox Concert Party
Knoxville College Singers
Kohl
Krautz Family Concert Company
Kremlin Art Quintet
Kringsberg Company
Hans Kronold Concert Company
Kryl, Bohumir
Kryl, Frank
Kryl, Marie
Kublick, Heari
Kuehn Concert Company
L.A.C. Orchestra
Ladies' Apollo Club of Mediapolis
Ladies String Quartet
Ladies Welch Choir
Lady Entertainers Quartette
Lady Washington Quartette
Lahissa
Lamont's Birds
Landers, Major
Landis Singing Orchestra
Larcher, Bessie
LaRue's Band of Waterloo
La Sheck, Katherine
Latvian Singers
Laurant and Concert Party
LaValle Grand Opera Company
LaVerdi, Pietro
Lawrence Conservatory
Lay, Georgiella
Lea-Bel Company
LeBrum Grand Opera Company
Lee Band
Lee-Lathrop Fullenwider Concert
Lee's Concert Band
Lenska, Mme. Augusta
Liberati, Allesandro
Liberati's Band and Grand Opera Co.
Liberati Concert Band
Lievrance, T.
Light Opera Mirror
Light Opera Revue
Lindsay, Charles K.
Ling and Long
Link's Orchestra
Lions Quartet
Listemann, Virginia
Liszt Concert Company
Litchfield Trio
Little Symphony Orchestra
Lockhart Concert Company
Loftus, Ceclia
Lomax, John
Lombard Entertainers
London Symphony Quartet
Lone Star Band
Longfellow Juvenile Symphony Orchestra
Lorelei Ladies Quartet
Lot's Pacific Serenaders
Lotus Company
Lotus Ladies Quartette
Loveless Quartet
Lutheran a Cappela Choir
Lyceum Entertainers

Lyceum Singers Quartet
Lyon Brothers Quartet
Lyric Glee Club
Lyric Ladies Quartette
Lyric Male Chorus
Lyric Quintet
Mac Donald Concert Company
Mac Donald Highlanders
Mac Dowell Concert Company
Macey, Eva
MacFarren Symphony Quartet
MacGregor, Knight
MacRae, Tolbert
Mac's Band
Mandell and Corbley
Madrigal Concert Party
Maitland Trio
Majestic Quartet
Male Instrumental and Singing Quartet
Mallebay, Germanic
Malleby Company
Mallory and Company
Manhattan Opera Company
Manktelow Brothers
Manning Sisters
Mansfield, Clara
Manuel and Williamson
Marchetti's Swiss Yodelers
Maresealchi Quartette
Marigold Quartette
Marion Quartet
Marsh, Lucy
Marsh, Mabel
Martha Company
Mascot Orchestra
Mason, Edith
Masque Musicians
Master Singers
Mat's Band
Mathesen Concert Pasrty
Matt and His 22nd Regiment Band
Matteson Studio Ensemble
Matyas, Maria
Maurer Sisters Orchestra
Mayflower Company
McCords, The
McGrath Brothers, The
McGregor, Knight
McKenzie Highlander Band
Mead, Olive
Mediapolis Band, The
Meistersingers Male Quartette and Organ Chimes
Melody Singers
Melody Trio
Melton, James
Mendelssohn Male Quartet
Mendelssohn Trio
Mercedes Melody Quartette
Mercer Concert Orchestra
Merrilees Ladies Quartet
Merry Musical Maids
Merrymakers, The
Metropolitan Concert Company
Metropolitan Glee Club
Metropolitan Orchestra
Metropolitan Singers
Metropolitan String Quintet
Metropolitan Symphony Orchestra
Mexican Serenaders
Middleton, Arthur
Middletons, The
Mikado Company
Military Girls
Mills and His Band
Minneapolis Ladies
Minneapolis Municipal Band
Minnesota Ladies Quartet
Minnesota Symphony Players
Minor-Schubert Quartet
Miraurba Band
Miserendino, Illuminato
Mitchell Brothers
Mitchell Family Orchestra
Molino Grand Opera Company
Mollenhauer Trio
Momense Hawaiian Ensemble
Montague Light Opera Company
Montavore Entertainers
Montan Sisters
Morphets, The
Morrow Brothers Quartet
Moscow Artists Ensemble
Mount Vernon Singing Party
Mozart Company
Mozart Male Quartet
Mozart Trio

Murray Family Orchestra
Murray Variety Company
Music Makers
Musical Entertainers
Musical Favorites
Musical Four, The
Musical Guardsmen
Musical MacDonalds
Musical Maids
Musical Silver Sleigh Bells
Muscateers
Muzio, Claudia
Myre's Orchestra
Nacoomee, Princess
Nadonis, Princess
Natiello Band
National Bureau for the Advancement of Music
National Dramatic and Opera Company
National Light Opera Company
National Male Quartet
National Music League
Navy Band
Navy Girls
Neapolitan Serenaders
Neapolitan Trio, The
Nevia Concert Company
Newell, Fenwick
New England Male Quartet
New England Trio
Newlan's Concert Band
New Schumann Quintet
New York Brass Choir
New York City Band
New York City Marine Band
New York Festival Trio
New York Glee Club
New York Grand Opera Company
New York Ladies Trio
New York Lyric Singers
New York Madrigal Singers
New York Marine Band
New York Opera Singers
Nielsen, Alice
Nolan, Bob
Normal Ladies Band
Norton, W.W.
Noruo, Red
Novelty Entertainers
Novelty Four
Novelty Trio
Oakley Concert Company
Oberlin Sextet
Occidental Band and Orchestra
Oceanic Concert Company
Oceanic Quintet
O'Connor, James
Ohio Male Quartet
Ojibway Hiawatha Indians
Old Glory Quartet
Old Home Singers
Olsen Sisters
Olson Trio
Olympia Ladies Quartette
168th Iowa Band and Regiment Quartet
Opera and Drama Society of San Francisco
Opera Clippings
Opera Festival
Opera Revue
Opollo Quartet
Oratorio Artists
Orchestra Comique and Dolly Randolph, Violin
Orchestral Entertainers
Orchestral Quartet
Orchestral Troubadours
Oriels, The
Orpheum Concert Company
Orpheum Concert Orchestra
Orpheum Musical Club
Orpheus Concert Trio
Osborn, Jenny
Otterbein Male Quartet
Ottumwa Male Quartette
Overseas Military Quartette
Oxford Company
Oxford Operatic Quartet
Paderewski, Ignace
Page Concert Company
Page-Stone Ballet
Paine, Helen
Palleria's Band
Palmer's Lyceum Quintette
Pampamgo Players and Singers

Panama Quartet
Paramount Entertainers
Parisian "Red Heads" Orchestra
Park Sisters Quartette
Parker Concert Company
Parkinson Ensemble
Parks, Florence
Parland-Newhall Male Company
Parnells
Passeri Band
Patterson Ladies' Quartette
Peerless Quartet, The
Peoples Grand Opera Association
Petri, Egon
Petrie Novelty Quintet
Petschnikoff, Madame
Petty John Concert Party
Philadelphia Male Quartet
Philharmonic Ensemble
Phillippe, Dora de
Philipine Orchestra
Phillipine Quartet
Philipinos, The
Phillips Sisters
Picard's Chinese Synocopaters
Pierce Company
Pilgrim Girls
Pinafore Company
Pittsburgh Ladies Orchestra
Planson, C. Pol
Ploner, Alois
Plymouth Male Quartet
Plymouth Singers
Poepping's Band
Poluhni and Company
Ponselle, Rora
Powell, Maud
Powelson, Mary
Power, Jessie
Premier Artist Quintette
Premier Concert Party
Pryor's Band
Pugh, Jess
Pugh-Riner Co.
Pupillo, Luigi
Quaglia, Luigi
Quaker Quartette
Qualen Company
Quick, Robert

Quintino's Band
Rainbow Saxophone Band
Ramon Mexican Orchestra
Ramos Spanish Orchestra
Randall Entertainers
Rappold, Marie
Raweis, The
Recital Artists Company
Redpath Grand Opera Company
Redpath Grand Quartet
Reeves, A.W.
Regimental Quartet, The
Regniers
Reilhofer's Tyrolean Yodelers and
    Concert Company
Remnant Quartet
Reohs, Ruth
Retz-Reichard Recitals
Rhondda Welsh Male Quartet
Ricardi Orchestra
Rich, Rita
Richards and His Band
Richmond's Little Symphony
Riggs Musical Agency
Rigoletto Opera Company
Riheldaffer, Grace Hall
Riner Sisters
Ring, Anderson
Ripon College Glee Club
Rivers Sisters
Roach, Ada
Robby Male Quartet
Robertson's Cleveland Band
Robin Hood Company
Robinson Sisters
Rob Roy Quartet
Rocky Mountain Quartette
Rocky Mountain Warblers
Rodney Boys
Rogers-Grilley Company
Romanian Orchestra
Roney's Boys Concert Company
Rose Garden Four
Romanian Orchestra, The
Roumd's Ladies Orchestra
Rouse Sisters
Royal Austro-Hungarian Orchestra
Royal Black Huzzar Band
Royal Dragons, The

Royal English Hand Bell Orchestra
Royal Grenadiers
Royal Gwent Welsh Male Singers
Royal Gypsy Concert Company
Royal Hawaiians
Royal Hungarian Orchestra
Royal Italian Guard Band
Royal Male Quartet
Royal Russian Company
Royal Scotch Entertainers
Royal Scotch Highlanders
Royal Troubadours
Royal Welch Quartet
Royal Welsh Ladies
Rude, Theodore C.
Runner, Charles
Russell, Howard
Russell's Scottish Revue
Russian Balalaika Orchestra
Russian Cathedral Choir
Russian Cathedral Quartet
Russian Cossack Chorus
Russian Royal Balalaika Band
Russian Sextette
Russian Symphony Orchestra
Sacco's Band
Saint Clair Sisters
Sammis, Sybil
Samuel Brothers
San Carlo Opera Company
Sands, W.A.
Sapho Quartette
Saxonians
Scheerer, Maude
Schildkret's Hungarian Orchestra of Chicago
Schramm Orchestra of Burlington
Schroder Quartet
Schubert Quartet
Schubert Orchestral Sextet
Schubert Serenaders
Schubert Trio
Schumann Concert Company
Schumann Ladies Quartette
Schumann Quartet
Schumann Quintet
Schumann-Heink, Ernestine
Schuster Family
Schutz, G. Magnus

Scotch Ballad Singers
Scotch Highlanders
Scotch-Irish Male Quartet
Scotch Singers
Scott-Denny Company
Scott, Henri
Seaburg-Baldi Company
Serenaders, The
Seven Liberty Bells
Shamrock Trio
Shannon Quartet
Shaw Trio
Shawn, Ted
Sheets Concert Company
Shields, Edith
Shields Trio
Shining Star Company
Shipp, Fisher
Sholle's Family Orchestra
Shorter, Gilbert
Shubert Quartet
Schubert's Ladies Orchestra
Shumate Brothers Quartet
Shumway Male Quartet
Silvertone Quartet
Simon, Zelda
Sindler Band
Singer's Midget Band
Singer's Royal Midget Jazz Band
Singing Cadets, The
Sissle, Noble
Six Royal Holland Bell Ringers
Skibinsky, Alexander
Smith, Katherine
Smith, Mrs. Myron
Soldiers' Quartet
Solis' Band
Soellander and Her Band
Sorority Girls Sextette
Sousa's Band
Spafford, L.P.
Spanish Ladies Orchestra
Spanish Orchestra
Spanish Revelers
Spaulding, Nina
Spring, Coyla
Speaks, Oley
Standard Entertainers
Starck's Musical Comedy

Star Male Quartet
Stearns Trio
Steely Company
Steininger Trio
Sterling Varieties
Stire, Francis
Stolofsky Company
Stolofsky Trio
Studenmyer Orchestra
Stratford Comedy Four
Stratford Male Quartet
Stratford Operatic Company
Stratfords, The
Strayer Sisters
Striegel, _____
Strollers Male Quartet
Strout Military Band
Stuckman Novelty Trio
Sunday, William A
Sundelius, Marie
Suntano Band
Swarthout, Gladys
Swedish Ladies Quartet
Sweet, Al
Sweethearts Operetta Company
Swiss Bell Ringers
Sylkov Orchestra
Taggert's Fiddlers
Tamburitza Players
Tangerine Company Musical Comedy
Taylor, Bob
Te Ata, Princess
Temple Quartette
Thatcher's Orchestra and Mrs. Beach
Thaviu's Band
Theobaldi and His Concert Company
Thomas, Edward
Thomas, John Charles
Three Musketeers
Tiffany, Marie
Tiffany Male Quartet and Bell Ringers
Tobias, Jay
Toenniges Quartet
Tollefsen, Carl
Toller, Warren
Tomaro, Salvatore
Tom Brown's Highlanders
Tommy Company

Tooley Opera Company
Toronto Male Chorus
Toronto Male Quartette
Troubador Quartet
Twin City Preachers Quartette
Twin City Singing Party
Tyrolean Concert Troupe
Tyrolean Troubadour Combination
Tyrolean Yodelers
United States Indian School Band
University Girls, The
University of Alabama Glee Club
University of Illinois Glee and Mandolin Club
University of Michigan Glee and Mandolin Club
Unkrich's Bly's Band
Updegraff, Grace
U.S. Indian Band
Valley, Olof
Van Browne Trio
Vanden Bosch Brothers Male Quartet
Van Grove Opera Company
Vanney's Orchestra
VanVeachton-Rogers Harp Duo
Varallo Gross Company
Variety Club, The
Varsity Male Quartet
Vaudeville Artists Company
Venetian Trio
Verdi Mixed Quartet
Vernon Concert Ensemble
Ver Hoar Concert Company
Vessey, Bernard
Victor, Leonard
Victorian Serenaders, The
Vierra's Royal Hawaiians
Violin Maker of Cremona Company
Vitale Band
Wabash Entertainers
Wagner-Shank Grand Opera Company
Wallenstein, Alfred
Walter, Marie
Walters Company
Ward-Waters Company
Washburn, Charles
Washington High School Band
Watahwaso

Appendix C

Waterloo Conservatory Orchestra
Waterloo Glee Club
Waterloo Ladies Orchestra
Waterloo Ministers Quartette
Waterloo Orchestra
Waters Concert Band
Waverly Company
Weatherwax Family
Weber Male Quartette
Weber's Quartette
Weber's Band
Wehrmann Quartet
Welch Choir
Welch Quartet
Wells Company
Wells Entertainers
Wells Four
Welsh Imperial Singers
Welsh Quartet
Welsh Quintette
Werno Company
Werrenrath, Reinald
Wesleyan Male Quartette
Waybelle Concert Company
Wheelock and Band
White, Frank
White Hussars, The
White Rose Orchestra
Whitehall, Clarence
Whitney Brothers Quartet
Whittemore Trio
Wilcox Entertainers
Willard, Perry
Williams, Burt
Williamson Sisters Quartet
Willis Band
Wills, Glen
Wimberly, F.W.
Winter, Julius
Wood, Jack
Wood-Watkins, Clara
Woodland Quartet
Woodman Brass Band
Woods Quartet
Woods Symphonie Band
Wright Entertainers
Y's Men's Glee Club
Yaw, Ellen Beach
Ye Olde New England Choir
Ye Olde Time Village Quartet
Yodeling Troubadours
Youna Company
Youna-Baldi Company
Zahradka Concert Band
Zandorff Entertainers
Zedler Company
Zeisler, Fannie
Ziegler-Howe Orchestra
Zimmerman Swiss Yodelers

Chapter Notes

Introduction

1. J.D. Reed, "Program: Elmwood Chautauqua" (Elmwood, NE: 1912).
2. LeRoy Ashby, *With Amusement for All: A History of American Popular Culture Since 1830* (Lexington: University Press of Kentucky, 2006), 253.
3. Sumiko Higashi, *Cecil B. Demille and America Culture: The Silent Era* (Berkeley: University of California Press, 1994), 203.
4. James Eckman, "Regeneration Through Culture: Chautauqua in Nebraska, 1882–1925" (PhD diss., University of Nebraska, 1989), 203–43.

Chapter I

1. Carl Bode, *The American Lyceum: Town Meeting of the Mind* (New York: Oxford University Press, 1956), 8–14. An expanded version of this document was printed as a pamphlet in 1829 under the title *American Lyceum, or Society for the Improvement of Schools and Diffusion of Useful Knowledge*. See bibliography.
2. John Noffsinger, *Correspondence Schools, Lyceums, Chautauquas*, Studies in Adult Education (New York: MacMillan, 1926), 102.
3. Malcolm Knowles, *The Adult Education Movement in the United States* (New York: Holt, Rinehart and Winston, 1962), 17.
4. Carl Bode, *The American Lyceum: Town Meeting of the Mind* (New York: Oxford University Press, 1956), 190–91.
5. Quoted in Bode, *The American Lyceum*, 12.
6. Carl Bode, *The American Lyceum: Town Meeting of the Mind* (New York: Oxford University Press, 1956), 188.
7. Vern Wagner, "The Lecture Lyceum and the Problem of Controversy," *Journal of the History of Ideas* 15, no. 1 (January 1, 1954): 125–126.
8. John E. Tapia, *Circuit Chautauqua: From Rural Education to Popular Entertainment in Early Twentieth Century America* (Jefferson, NC: McFarland, 1997), 13.
9. Josiah Holbrook, *American Lyceum, or Society for the Improvement of Schools and Diffusion of Useful Knowledge* (Boston: Perkins and Marvin, 1829), 3.
10. Marjorie Eubank, "The Redpath Lyceum Bureau from 1868–1901" (PhD diss., University of Michigan, 1968), 3.
11. Ibid., 90.
12. John E. Tapia, *Circuit Chautauqua: From Rural Education to Popular Entertainment in Early Twentieth Century America* (Jefferson, NC: McFarland, 1997), 14–15.
13. Marjorie Eubank, "The Redpath Lyceum Bureau from 1868–1901" (PhD diss., University of Michigan, 1968), 107–09.
14. John E. Tapia, *Circuit Chautauqua: From Rural Education to Popular Entertainment in Early Twentieth Century America* (Jefferson, NC: McFarland, 1997), 15.
15. Jeanette Wells, "A History of the Music Festival at Chautauqua Institution from 1874 to 1957" (PhD diss., Catholic University of America, 1958), 8.
16. Joseph Gould, *The Chautauqua Movement: An Episode in the Continuing American Revolution* (Albany: State University of New York Press, 1961).
17. Jeanette Wells, "A History of the Music Festival at Chautauqua Institution from 1874

to 1957" (PhD diss., Catholic University of America, 1958), 10–12.

18. John Scott, "The Chautauqua Movement: Revolution in Popular Higher Education," *Journal of Higher Education* 70, no. 4 (1999): 394.

19. John E. Tapia, *Circuit Chautauqua: From Rural Education to Popular Entertainment in Early Twentieth Century America* (Jefferson, NC: McFarland, 1997), 22.

20. John Vincent, *The Chautauqua Movement* (Boston: Chatauqua Press, 1886), 267, quoted in Jeanette Wells, "A History of the Music Festival at Chautauqua Institution from 1874 to 1957" (PhD diss., Catholic University of America, 1958).

21. Sandra Manderson, "The Redpath Lyceum Bureau: An American Critic; Decision-Making and Programming Methods for Circuit Chautauquas, Circa 1912 to 1930" (PhD diss., University of Iowa, 1981), 216.

22. "George C. Rheinfrank: Popular Lecturer" (Chicago, IL: Lyceumite Press, 1909); Redpath Chautauqua Collection, University of Iowa.

23. See John E. Tapia, *Circuit Chautauqua: From Rural Education to Popular Entertainment in Early Twentieth Century America* (Jefferson, NC: McFarland, 1997), 26.

24. Twelfth Annual Assembly, Ames Chautauqua Association (1915).

25. Ames Chautauqua Program (1909), http://www.ameshistoricalsociety.org/exhibits/events/chautauqua.htm.

26. Twelfth Annual Assembly, Ames Chautauqua Association (1915), http://www.ameshistoricalsociety.org/exhibits/events/1913chautauqua1a.htm.

27. "Chautauqua Era Ends, No Show This Summer," *Ames (IA) Tribune*, March 9, 1927.

28. "Klantauqua Goes Over Despite Bad Weather," *McLeansboro (IL) Times*, May 29, 1924.

29. Harry Harrison, *Culture Under Canvas: The Story of Tent Chautauqua* (New York: Hastings House, 1958), 52.

30. John E. Tapia, *Circuit Chautauqua: From Rural Education to Popular Entertainment in Early Twentieth Century America* (Jefferson, NC: McFarland, 1997), 28.

31. Harry Harrison, *Culture Under Canvas: The Story of Tent Chautauqua* (New York: Hastings House 1958), 60.

32. Henry Clay Work, 1876.

33. Matt Damon, 1826.

34. Anna Curtis, "A Quartet with a History," *Talent*, November 1903, 10.

35. Charlotte Canning, *The Most American Thing in America: Circuit Chautauqua as Performance*, ed. Thomas Postlewait, Studies in Theatre History and Culture (Iowa City: University of Iowa Press 2005), 9.

36. Ibid., 9.

37. Program, Redpath-Horner, 1920.

38. John Tapia, "Circuit Chautauqua's Promotional Visions: A Study of Program Brochures, Circa 1904 to 1932" (PhD diss., University of Arizona, 1978), 35.

39. Donald Graham, "Circuit Chautauqua: A Middle Western Institution" (PhD diss., University of Iowa, 1953), 37.

40. John E. Tapia, *Circuit Chautauqua: From Rural Education to Popular Entertainment in Early Twentieth Century America* (Jefferson, NC: McFarland, 1997), 178.

41. A circuit persisted in Canada until 1934.

42. R.B. Tozier, "A Short Life-History of the Chautauqua," *American Journal of Sociology* 40, no. 1 (1934): 71.

43. For a brief discussion of the depression's effect on circuit chautauqua, see Patricia Wardrop, "Chautauqua," in *Encyclopedia of Music in Canada*, ed. Giles Potvin Helmut Kallmann, Kenneth Winters (Toronto, ON: Historica Foundation, 2008).

44. Keith Vawter, January 17 1929.

45. Harry Harrison, *Culture Under Canvas: The Story of Tent Chautauqua* (New York: Hastings House, 1958), 248.

46. Russell Johnson, "'Dancing Mothers': The Chautauqua Movement in Twentieth-Century American Popular Culture," *American Studies International* 39, no. 2 (2001): 63.

47. Program, Sidney, IL, 1923.

48. "A Lyceum and Chautauqua Platform," *The Lyceum Magazine* 26, no. 2 (1916): 1.

49. John Tapia, "Circuit Chautauqua's Promotional Visions: A Study of Program Brochures, Circa 1904 to 1932" (PhD diss., University of Arizona, 1978), 51.

50. James R Schultz, *The Romance of Small-Town Chautauquas* (Columbia: University of Missouri Press 2002), 150.

51. Ibid., 151.

CHAPTER II

1. Sandra Manderson, "The Redpath Lyceum Bureau, an American Critic:

Decision-Making and Programming Methods for Circuit Chautauquas, Circa 1912 to 1930" (PhD diss., University of Iowa, 1981), 115.

2. R.B. Tozier, "A Short Life-History of the Chautauqua," *American Journal of Sociology* 40, no. 1 (1934): 70.

3. Charles Horner, *Strike the Tents: The Story of Chautauqua* (Philadelphia: Dorrance, 1954), 174.

4. See Russell Wilson, "100 Years of Leadership: University of Missouri-Kansas City Conservatory of Music," http://conservatory.umkc.edu/100/leadership.asp, for a detailed history of the Horner Institute/UMKC Conservatory and its leaders.

5. Brochure archived online at "Horner Institute of Fine Arts," Vintage Kansas City, http://www.vintagekansascity.com/education/hornerinstituteofarts/.

6. Wilson, "100 Years of Leadership: University of Missouri-Kansas City Conservatory of Music."

7. "The Elias Day School of Lyceum Art" (Chicago: Shirley, 1913).

8. Esther Williams interview by Beverly Agee, May 1977.

9. "The Lyceum Arts Conservatory," *The Lyceum Magazine*, April 1915, p. 49.

10. "Boston Lyceum School," *Lyceum*, February 1916.

11. Harry Dunbar, "The Dunbar Chautauqua Bureau" (Chicago). This document appears to have been intended to be the cover or preface to a brochure (it refers to "the sixteen following pages"). However, no such document seems to have survived.

12. Charles L. Wagner, *Seeing Stars* (New York: Arno, 1977), 80.

13. Gay MacLaren, *Morally We Roll Along* (Boston,: Little, Brown, 1938), 227.

14. Ralph Dunbar, "Ralph Dunbar Attractions: Available for Chautauquas of 1926 and Lyceum Season of 1926–27" (Chicago, 1926).

15. La Sheck's contracts and other papers are housed at the Iowa Women's Archives, University of Iowa Libraries (Iowa City).

16. Horner, *Strike the Tents: The Story of Chautauqua*, 175.

17. "From Our Viewpoint," *Lyceum*, July 1913, p. 1.

18. "Lyceum: The Lyndon-Gordon Co.," 1.

19. Contract between Harry Harrison, representing the Redpath Musical Bureaus and B. Csillag, representing the Royal Gypsy Orchestra, fated January 9, 1926, Redpath Chautauqua Collection, Special Collections Department, University of Iowa Libraries (Iowa City)

20. Claussen's Redpath contracts are located in the Julia Claussen file, Redpath Chautauqua Collection, Special Collections Department, University of Iowa Libraries (Iowa City)

21. Season ticket sales were guaranteed by the sponsoring community and were used to recoup the community's investment and pay the bureau's expenses. It was not uncommon for headlining attractions to negotiate a portion of single-ticket admission receipts as part of a contract.

22. Contract between Harry Harrison, representing the Redpath Musical Bureau, and Julia Claussen. Dated January 22, 1916, Redpath Chautauqua Collection, Special Collections Department, University of Iowa Libraries (Iowa City)

23. This correspondence can be found in the Lexington, Kentucky, file in the Redpath Chautauqua Collection at the University of Iowa. They are dated between December 16, 1926 and January 3, 1927.

24. Similar rules for performer appearance and behavior existed in vaudeville. See Arthur Wertheim, *Vaudeville Wars* (New York: Palgrave MacMillan, 2006).

25. Manderson, "The Redpath Lyceum Bureau: An American Critic; Decision-Making and Programming Methods for Circuit Chautauquas, Circa 1912 to 1930," 118.

26. Ibid., 119–20.

27. Similar rules existed for vaudeville performers on the major circuits. See Wertheim, *Vaudeville Wars*.

28. Manderson, "The Redpath Lyceum Bureau," 116–17.

29. A complete week of Platform Superintendent's Daily Reports (from 1926) is housed in the Lexington, Kentucky, box at the Redpath Chautauqua Collection, Special Collections Department, University of Iowa Libraries (Iowa City). Other platform reports are available in the collection, but the Lexington records are extraordinarily complete.

30. Edwin Harder, *The First Clarinet, or Chautauqua Chit-Chat* (Chicago: Mayer & Miller, 1913), 11.

31. Ibid., 23.

32. Ibid., 61.

33. These records are located in the Redpath Chuatauqua collection in the "Dixie Chorus" folder.

34. "The Lyceumiteman Talks," *Lyceumite* 4, no. 9 (1906): 275.
35. Clay Smith, "Canning Old Stuff, See the New Coming!," *The Lyceum Magazine*, November 1919, p. 30.
36. Harry Harrison, *Culture Under Canvas: The Story of Tent Chautauqua* (New York: Hastings House, 1958), 114.
37. Ernestine Schumann-Heink to Harry Harrison, July 21, 1919. Located in Redpath Chautauqua Bureau Records, Special Collections Department, University of Iowa Libraries (Iowa City).
38. These letters and telegrams are housed at Iowa in the "Schumann-Heink" folders.
39. These letters and telegrams are housed in the Redpath Chautauqua Collection, University of Iowa in a folder labeled "Sousa."
40. Harry Harrison wrote that his bureau "never was able to tie [Sousa] to a contract" (Harrison, *Culture Under Canvas*, 99.
41. Horner, *Strike the Tents: The Story of Chautauqua*, 178.
42. Dorothy Kohl interview by Frederick Crane, May 21, 1976.
43. Harold Plotts interview by Frederick Crane, July 22, 1979.
44. Unless otherwise noted, biographical details are taken from an unpublished biography by Sister Victorine Fenton, entitled "Katharine La Sheck" and housed in the Katharine La Sheck papers at the Iowa Women's Archive, University of Iowa Library (Iowa City).
45. *Des Moines Register and Leader*, "Iowa City Friends of Miss Rachel Lasheck," October 24, 1911.
46. This wire correspondence is apparently lost and is quoted in Fenton's biography.
47. Frederick Crane, "A.F. Thaviu Redux," *Journal of Band Research* 36 (2000): 1–25.
48. "Kryl and His Band" (Tarpon Springs, FL: 1927).
49. Nolbert Quayle, "The Cornet's Sole Survivor," *Music Journal* 19, no. 6 (1961).
50. Vawter to Kryl, October 2, 1919.
51. Crotty to Kryl, June 13, 1919.
52. Crawford Peffer to Bohumir Kryl, March 8, 1920.
53. Lingeman, *Sinclair Lewis*, 129.
54. Bohumir Kryl to L.B. Crotty, October 20, 1919.
55. Ibid., March 1, 1920.
56. These documents are housed in the Redpath Chautauqua Collection at the University of Iowa in the Bohumir Kryl file.
57. Obituaries and newspaper articles from later in Kryl's life often list "bank president" among his titles.
58. This offer is one of the most often repeated anecdotes about Kryl. It is mentioned in several sources, including Marie Kryl's obituary in the *New York Times* (October 27, 1987) and in both sisters' wedding announcements.
59. The incident concerning the Indianapolis date took place during Nielsen's second chautauqua tour, which focused on Ohio and the surrounding area.
60. Thomas Nielsen, March 24 1916.
61. Alice Nielsen, May 8 1915.
62. Charles Horner, March 18 1916.
63. *Musical Courier*, "Alice Nielsen, Prima Donna Soprano," March 3, 1913, p. 9.

CHAPTER III

1. See Jeanette Wells, "A History of the Music Festival at Chautauqua Institution from 1874 to 1957" (PhD diss., Catholic University of America, 1958).
2. Ibid, 10–14.
3. Ibid., 30.
4. Ibid., 30.
5. Clay Smith, "'Canning' Old Stuff: See the New Coming!," *The Lyceum Magazine*, November 1919, 30.
6. John Noffsinger, *Correspondence Schools, Lyceums, Chautauquas*, Studies in Adult Education (New York: MacMillan, 1926), 113.
7. John R McKivigan, *Forgotten Firebrand: James Redpath and the Making of Nineteenth-Century America* (Ithaca: Cornell University Press, 2008), 216.
8. Ibid., 221.
9. Charles F Horner, *The Life of James Redpath and the Development of the Modern Lyceum*, (New York; Newark: Barse & Hopkins, 1926), 213–214.
10. McKivigan, *Forgotten Firebrand*, 217–218.
11. John Noffsinger, *Correspondence Schools, Lyceums, Chautauquas*, Studies in Adult Education (New York: MacMillan, 1926), 141.
12. Edward Ott, "Some Practical Needs of the Lyceum," *Lyceumite*, August 1906, p. 315.
13. "CLSC Historic Book List."
14. John Heyl Vincent, "Chautauqua: A Popular University," 10.

15. *Chautauqua Hymnal and Liturgy* (New York Novello, Ewer, 1903).
16. "An International Musical Success: The Dunbar Company" (Chicago: Manz).
17. Sister Victorine Fenton, "Katharine La Sheck," 15–16. This unpublished biography is housed in the Katharine La Sheck papers at the Iowa Women's Archive, University of Iowa.
18. Clay Smith, "Music Reviews," *The Lyceum Magazine*, May 1920, 14.
19. See Belle Squire, "The Unpopularity of a Popular Instrument," *Lyceumite*, October 1904, pp. 340–41.
20. Charles Hiroshi Garrett, "Chinatown: Whose Chinatown? Defining America's Borders with Musical Orientalism," *Journal of the American Musicological Society* 57, no. 1 (2004): 131.
21. For a thorough discussion of dehumanizing and emasculating stereotypes in popular depictions of Chinese men, see Judy Tsou, "Gendering Race: Stereotypes of Chinese Americans in Popular Sheet Music," *Repercussions* 6, no. 2 (1997).
22. Garrett and Tsou discuss frequent allusions to opium, both in lyrics and in cover art, during this period.
23. See Andrew Rieser, "Canopy of Culture: Chautauqua and the Renegotiation of Middle-Class Authority, 1874–1919" (PhD diss., University of Wisconsin, 1999), 328–31.
24. Advertisements for Witmark's "Department C" and this particular package of sample songs appeared frequently in the *Lyceum* from 1915 through 1917.
25. Louis Runner, "How the Platform Is Popularizing Music," *The Lyceum Magazine*, March 1920, p. 22.
26. "An International Musical Success: The Dunbar Company."
27. Henry Roney, "The Masses Don't Want to Be 'Educated Up,'" *The Lyceum Magazine*, March 1920, p. 23.
28. Luella Keller, "Good Music Winning the Masses," *The Lyceum Magazine*, September 1914, p. 34.
29. B.C. Boer, "Keep Unpopular Music Off Popular Programs," *The Lyceum Magazine*, April 1914, p. 21.
30. A.A. Thornburg, "What the Lyceum May Learn from Vaudeville," *Lyceumite and Talent*, August 1912, p. 22.
31. Frank Morgan, "An Explanation," *Lyceumite*, December 1905, p.50.

32. "Art and the Musician," *Lyceumite and Talent*, May 1916, p. 8.
33. Smith, "Canning Old Stuff, See the New Coming!," 30.
34. *Waterloo (IA) Daily Times Tribune*, "Opened with Large Crowd," July 5, 1906, p. 5.
35. *Thomson (IL) Review*, "Chautauqua Revue Easy to Listen To," June 10, 1926, p. 5.
36. S.W. Sibley, "Makes Critical Estimate of the Wesleyan Singers," *Coshocton Weekly Times*, July 26, 1906, p. 8.
37. *Emmettsburg (IA) Palo Alto Reporter*, "The Chautauqua Closes," July 24, 1919, p. 1.
38. D.R. Gebhart, "On Music 'Write Ups,'" *Music Supervisors' Journal* 7, no. 1 (September 1920): 26.
39. *Terril (IA) Record*, "More Lowdown on Chautauqua," August 7, 1930, p. 8.
40. Harry Hibschman, "Chautauqua Pro and Contra," *North American Review*, no. 225 (1928): 602.
41. "The Lyceumiteman Talks," *Lyceumite* 4, no. 9 (1906): 275.

Chapter IV

1. Sandra Manderson, "The Redpath Lyceum Bureau: An American Critic; Decision-Making and Programming Methods for Circuit Chautauquas, Circa 1912 to 1930" (PhD diss., University of Iowa, 1981), 116.
2. As noted in chapter two, Crawford Peffer's Redpath–New York–New England circuit outlasted the rest of the Redpath bureaus, which had begun to fold in the late 1920s.
3. Canning discusses the role of the "Junior Girl" and the Junior Chautauqua in *The Most American Thing in America*, 42–46.
4. Harry Harrison, *Culture Under Canvas: The Story of Tent Chautauqua* (New York: Hastings House, 1958), 58.
5. Victoria Case and Robert Case, *We Called It Culture* (New York: Doubleday, 1948), 46.
6. Reproduced in Case and Case, *We Called It Culture*, 47–48.
7. Case and Case, *We Called It Culture*.
8. While the carol "Hark the Herald Angels Sing" predates Mendelssohn by nearly a century, the melody commonly used for the song today is derived from a section of a cantata by Mendelssohn, and he is often credited as the composer, with credit for the text given to Charles Wesley.
9. "The New Zealanders in Song, Story

and Picture: From Cannibalism to Culture" (Chicago: Manz Engraving, 1916).
10. Harrison, *Culture Under Canvas*, 58.
11. Ibid., 199.
12. MacLaren, *Morally We Roll Along*, 151.
13. Stark's Musical Comedy Revue and Light Opera Association, Iowa.
14. Repath Lyceum Program for Next Year Announced," 1.
15. MacLaren, *Morally We Roll Along*, 260–261.
16. Ibid.
17. "Losseff's Russian Orchestral Quartet," Redpath Chautauqua Collection, Special Collections Department, University of Iowa Libraries (Iowa City).
18. Allen Albert, "The Tents of the Conservative," *Scribner's*, July 1922, 56.
19. Jubilee Singers are discussed more thoroughly in chapter 6.
20. J.D. Reed, "Program: Elmwood Chautauqua" (Elmwood, NE: 1912).
21. "Dearborn Concert Party" (Chicago: International Lyceum Bureau).
22. "Rag pictures" likely refers to a short talk illustrated by the use of felt shapes on a board combined in novel ways.
23. "Van O. Browne Novelty Trio" (Wauwatosa, WI: Wauwatosa Playground Fund, 1920).
24. Redpath Chautauqua Collection, Special Collections Department, University of Iowa Libraries (Iowa City).
25. American Tour: Russian Balalaika Orchestra (1913).
26. "Music Makers Quartet" (Daytona Beach Lyceum).
27. State Historical Society of Iowa (Iowa City).
28. "Chautauqua: North English, Iowa" (Redpath-Vawter, 1913).
29. The texts for these songs are printed side by side, indicating that it may have been intended for one to be selected and sung, rather than both.
30. "Vesper Service as Conducted on Redpath Vawter Chautauquas" (Redpath-Vawter).
31. "Chautauqua North English Iowa" (Redpath-Vawter 1915).
32. "Midland Chautauqua: Pocahontas, Iowa" (Midland Chautauquas, 1922).
33. These records are housed in Special Collections at the University of Iowa, Iowa City. They are located alongside, but are not part of, the Redpath collection.

CHAPTER V

1. *The Lyceum Magazine*, June 1919 "Magic Educational," 16.
2. Condee, *Coal and Culture*, 14
3. Ned Woodman, "The Home Town Spirit," *Lyceum*, August 1918, p. 26.
4. Joan Rubin discusses the growth of non-traditional educational movements in the first half of the twentieth century in *The Making of Middlebrow Culture*.
5. Frank Bray, "The Educational Value of Chautauquas," *Talent*, December 1906, 19.
6. Brooks Fletcher, "Bury Your Hammer and Buy a Horn," *The Lyceum Magazine*, July 1916, p. 16.
7. Frederic Haskin, "Our Intellectual Circus," *Portsmouth (OH) Daily Times*, July 30 1921, 12.
8. "Chautauqua: Mount Pleasant, Iowa" (Redpath-Vawter, 1910), Redpath Chautauqua Collection, Special Collections Department, University of Iowa Libraries (Iowa City).
9. George Vincent, "How to Make an Assembly Truly Educational," *The Lyceumite and Talent*, November 1908, 12–13.
10. Davis Dewey, January 10 1892. Quoted in Andrew Rieser, "Canopy of Culture: Chautauqua and the Renegotiation of Middle-Class Authority, 1874–1919" (PhD diss., University of Wisconsin, 1999), 196.
11. "A Lyceum and Chautauqua Platform," *The Lyceum Magazine* 26, no. 2 (1916): 1.
12. Russell Johnson, "'Dancing Mothers': The Chautauqua Movement in Twentieth-Century American Popular Culture," *American Studies International* 39, no. 2 (2001).
13. "Heink's Famous Lecture Recital." Redpath Chautauqua Collection, Special Collections Department, University of Iowa Libraries (Iowa City).
14. "Music for Today" (Streator, IL: Anderson), Redpath Chautauqua Collection, Special Collections Department, University of Iowa Libraries (Iowa City).
15. Quoted in Edna Erle Wilson, "Canvas and Culture: When Chautauqua Comes to Town," 599.
16. "Opera Talks and Lecture Recitals: Henriette Weber" (1917), Redpath Chautauqua Collection, Special Collections Department, University of Iowa Libraries (Iowa City).
17. From the *New York Sun*, reprinted in *Lonesome Tunes: Kentucky Mountain Balladry* (New York: 1917), Redpath Chautauqua Col-

lection, Special Collections Department, University of Iowa Libraries (Iowa City).
18. *Lonesome Tunes: Kentucky Mountain Balladry.*
19. These primarily involved African American and Native American music, although there were also concerts of music of the American Southwest),
20. Jeffrey P. Green, *Black Edwardians: Black People in Britain, 1901–1914* (London ; Portland, OR: Frank Cass, 1998), 103.
21. Bernth Lindfors, *Africans on Stage: Studies in Ethnological Show Business* (Bloomington: Indiana University Press, 1999), 214.
22. "Balmer's Kaffir Boy Choir of Africa" (Cleveland, OH: Britton), Redpath Chautauqua Collection, Special Collections Department, University of Iowa Libraries (Iowa City).
23. Ibid.
24. Ibid.
25. *The Lyceum Magazine*, April 1921, 6.
26. James Eckman, "Regeneration Through Culture: Chautauqua in Nebraska, 1882–1925" (PhD diss., University of Nebraska, 1989), 204–13.
27. See Appendix C for a list of musical acts known to have performed at chautauquas.
28. "The Schuberts: Singers and Entertainers" (Cleveland, OH: Britton), Redpath Chautauqua Collection, Special Collections Department, University of Iowa Libraries (Iowa City).
29. This particular group furnished no sample programs, and no programs from performances have been found.
30. "Schubert Serenaders: Vocal and Instrumental Artists" (Kansas City: Horner, 1934), Redpath Chautauqua Collection, Special Collections Department, University of Iowa Libraries (Iowa City).
31. John Tapia, "Circuit Chautauqua's Promotional Visions: A Study of Program Brochures, Circa 1904 to 1932" (PhD diss., University of Arizona, 1978), 133.
32. Atherton, *Main Street on the Middle Border*, 66.
33. This speech was reprinted in the August 1913 issue of *The Lyceum Magazine*, p. 26.
34. Edna Erle Wilson, "Canvas and Culture: When Chautauqua Comes to Town," 598.
35. Pringle, Henry. "Chautauqua in the Jazz Age," *American Mercury* 16 (January 1929), 85–93.

36. *Denton (MD) Journal*, "Chautauqua Movement and Culture," July 3, 1915, p. 2.
37. Joan Rubin, *The Making of Middlebrow Culture* (Chapel Hill: University of North Carolina Press, 1992), 6–7.
38. Charles Dixon, "Can Music Win on Its Merit?," *Lyceumite and Talent*, April 1923, p. 17.
39. "The Lyceumiteman Talks," *Lyceumite* 4, no. 9 (1906): 275.
40. Harry Hibschman, "Chautauqua Pro and Contra," *North American Review*, no. 225 (1928): 599.
41. Dorothy Walter to Margaret Church, August 24, 1915, quoted in "Chautauqua Week in Lyndonville: A Description Written in 1915."
42. O.W. Coursey, "Chautauqua vs. Street Carnival" *The Lyceum Magazine*, May 1916, p. 14.
43. Hugh A. Orchard, "The Lyceum Course Versus the Cheap Show," *Lyceumite and Talent*, August 1912, p. 23, reprinted from *Lyceum News.*
44. Russell Bridges, "The Relation Between Lyceum and Vaudeville," *Lyceumite and Talent*, July 1912, pp. 31–33.
45. Frederic Haskin, "The Chautauqua Movement," *Salt Lake Tribune*, July 17, 1907, p. 8.
46. *Mansfield (OH) News*, "Community Improves as People Improve," June 2, 1915, p. 5.
47. *Thomson (IL) Review*, "Why Boston Signs a Guarantee," June 25, 1925, p. 5.
48. Condee, *Coal and Culture: Opera Houses in Appalachia*, 14–15.

CHAPTER VI

1. Daniel Howell, "Assembly Ideals and Practice," *Chautauquan*, July 1908, p. 251.
2. *Chautauqua Program: Kimball, Nebraska* (Lincoln, NE: Standard Chautauqua System, 1917).
3. Ibid. (1918).
4. See John Tapia, "Circuit Chautauqua's Promotional Visions: A Study of Program Brochures, Circa 1904 to 1932" (PhD diss., University of Arizona, 1978). The discussion of the righteous patriotic fantasy vision rhetoric begins on page 142.
5. Atherton, *Main Street on the Middle Border*, 282.
6. "Midland Chautauqua: Wabasha, Minnesota" (Des Moines, IA: Midland Chau-

tauquas, 1918), State Historical Society of Iowa (Iowa City).
7. Ibid.
8. "The Lyceum 'Purpose Companies,'" *Lyceum*, August 1914, p. 13.
9. David Mead, "1914: The Chautauqua and American Innocence," *Journal of Popular Culture* 1 (1968): 339–56.
10. Charles Horner, *Strike the Tents: The Story of Chautauqua* (Philadelphia: Dorrance, 1954), 176.
11. Harry Harrison, *Culture Under Canvas: The Story of Tent Chautauqua* (New York: Hastings House, 1958), 136.
12. "The Lyceum Purpose Companies," *Lyceum*, August 1914, pp. 12–14.
13. Toll, *On with the Show!*, 146–147.
14. "The Plymouth Singing Party," *Lyceum*, February 1917, p. 45.
15. Parlette, "Musical Program Patriotism."
16. The Victory Chautauqua, Iowa.
17. "Stick to English Language and American Compositions," *Lyceum*, June 1921, p. 24.
18. A.L. Curtis, "The Fisk Jubilee Singers," *Talent* 16, no. 9 (1906): 1.
19. *New York Herald*, "Real Value of Negro Melodies," May 21, 1893, quoted in Michael Beckerman, *New Worlds of Dvo_ák: Searching in America for the Composer's Inner Life* (New York: W.W. Norton, 2003).
20. Charlotte Canning, *The Most American Thing in America: Circuit Chautauqua as Performance*, ed. Thomas Postlewait, Studies in Theatre History and Culture (Iowa City: University of Iowa Press 2005), 84.
21. Ibid., 83.
22. Eliza Crump, "Walker's Famous Fisk Jubilee Singers" (Chicago: 191?), Redpath Chautauqua Collection, Special Collections Department, University of Iowa Libraries (Iowa City).
23. McKenzie to Redpath Lyceum Bureau, December 18, 1916.
24. Toll, *Blacking Up*, 243–244.
25. Robert Burdette, "Worth Trying," *Lyceumite*, February 1903, p. 51.
26. Brooks, "'Might Take One Disc of This Trash as a Novelty': Early Recordings by the Fisk Jubilee Singers and the Popularization of 'Negro Folk Music,'" 280.
27. John E. Tapia, *Circuit Chautauqua: From Rural Education to Popular Entertainment in Early Twentieth Century America* (Jefferson, NC: McFarland, 1997), 173.
28. "The Manning Glee Club."
29. "Star Course."
30. James Eckman, "Regeneration Through Culture: Chautauqua in Nebraska, 1882–1925" (PhD diss., University of Nebraska, 1989), 203–43.
31. Tara Browner, "'Breathing the Indian Spirit': Thoughts on Musical Borrowing and The 'Indianist' Movement in American Music," *American Music* 15, no. 3 (1997): 265–84.
32. Standard Chautauqua Bureau, "Program: Iowa Falls Chautauqua" (1904). Reproduced in Harrison, *Culture Under Canvas*.
33. "David Russell Hill and His Onondaga Indian Concert Band" (Syracuse, NY: Empire Lyceum Bureau), Redpath Chautauqua Collection, Special Collections Department, University of Iowa Libraries (Iowa City)
34. Ibid.
35. "The Government Official Indian Band" (Chicago: Hollister Brothers), Redpath Chautauqua Collection Special Collections Department, University of Iowa Libraries (Iowa City).
36. Robert Trennert, "Selling Indian Education at World's Fairs and Expositions, 1893–1904," *American Indian Quarterly* 11, no. 3 (1987).
37. "The U.S. Indian Band" (Philadelphia: Hammond and Harff), Redpath Chautauqua Collection, Special Collections Department, University of Iowa Libraries (Iowa City).
38. Ibid.
39. American Federation of Musicians
40. "The U.S. Indian Band."
41. "David Russell Hill and His Onondaga Indian Concert Band," Redpath Chautauqua Collection, Special Collections Department, University of Iowa Libraries (Iowa City).
42. "Indian String Quartet" (1917), Redpath Chautauqua Collection, Special Collections Department, University of Iowa Libraries (Iowa City).
43. John Troutman, "'Indian Blues': American Indians and the Politics of Music, 1890–1935" (PhD diss., University of Texas, 2004), 206.
44. Ibid., 276.
45. "Indian Art and Musical Company" [191?], Redpath Chautauqua Collection, Special Collections Department, University of Iowa Libraries (Iowa City).
46. Tsianina Redfeather Blackstone, *Where Trails Have Led Me* (Santa Fe, NM: Vergara, 1970), 20–25.

47. Bunny McBride, "Lucy Nicolar: The Artful Activism of a Penobscot Performer," in *Sifters: Native American Women's Lives*, ed. Theda Perdue (Oxford: Oxford University Press, 2001), 143.

48. John Koon, "Indian Musicians in the Modern World," *Etude* 38, no. 10 (1920): 665.

49. McBride, "Lucy Nicolar: The Artful Activism of a Penobscot Performer," 144–47.

50. "Song Recital in Costume: Princess Watahwaso" (1917), Redpath Chautauqua Collection, Special Collections Department, University of Iowa Libraries (Iowa City).

51. McBride, "Lucy Nicolar: The Artful Activism of a Penobscot Performer," 149.

52. "Indian Art and Musical Company."

53. "The Government Official Indian Band."

54. William Schafer and Johannes Riedel, "Indian Intermezzi: 'Play It One More Time, Chief!,'" *Journal of American Folklore* 86, no. 342 (1973): 382–83.

55. Brooks McNamara, "The Indian Medicine Show," *Educational Theatre Journal* 23, no. 4 (1971): 437.

56. "Princess" Tsianina is the most famous example of this phenomenon.

57. David Edstrom, "Medicine Shows of the '80s," *Reader's Digest*, June 1938, p. 78.

58. "Thurlow Lieurance Collection: Wichita State University," http://library.wichita.edu/music/thurlow_lieurance.htm.

59. "Songs, Stories and Legends of the American Indian," Redpath Chautauqua Collection, Special Collections Department, University of Iowa Libraries (Iowa City).

60. "Songs, Stories and Legends of the American Indian."

61. For a discussion of the Wa-Wan Press and its significance to the Indianist movement, see Evelyn Culbertson, "Arthur Farwell's Early Efforts on Behalf of American Music, 1889–1921," *American Music* 5, no. 2 (1987): 156–75.

62. Michael Pisani, "From Hiawatha to Wa-Wan: Musical Boston and the Uses of Native American Lore," *American Music* 19, no. 1 (2001): 48.

63. Arthur Farwell, "Introduction," *The Wa Wan Press* 2, no. 1 (1903), quoted in Culbertson, "Arthur Farwell's Early Efforts on Behalf of American Music, 1889–1921," 159.

64. Walter Spalding, "The War in Its Relation to American Music," *Musical Quarterly* 4, no. 1 (1918): 7.

65. Charles Cadman, "The American Indian's Music Idealized," *Etude* 38, no. 10 (1920): 660.

66. Tischler, "One Hundred Percent Americanism and Music in Boston During World War I," 172.

67. Tapia, "Circuit Chautauqua's Promotional Visions: A Study of Program Brochures, Circa 1904 to 1932," 149.

68. Ibid., 157.

69. Arthur Farwell, "Aspects of Indian Music," *Southern Workman* 31, no. 4 (1902): 211–17.

Chapter VII

1. Eduard Lindeman, "After Lyceums and Chautauquas, What?," in *Bookman: A Review of Books and Life* 65 (1927): 246.

2. Allen Albert, "The Tents of the Conservative," *Scribner's*, 1922, p. 55.

3. David Mead, "1914: The Chautauqua and American Innocence," *Journal of Popular Culture* 1 (1968): 339–56.

4. Lindeman, "After Lyceums and Chautauquas, What?," 248.

5. William Faricy Condee, *Coal and Culture: Opera Houses in Appalachia* (Athens: Ohio University Press, 2005), 156.

6. Ferd Riechmann, "Public or Folk Response to the Circuit Chautauqua" (University of Iowa, 1951), 50.

7. Evert Winks, "Recollections of a Dead Art: The Traveling Chautauqua," *Indiana Magazine of History*, March 1958, p. 46.

8. Dillavou, *The Life Cycle of an Adult Education Enterprise: The Swarthmore Chautauqua*, 10.

9. Programs from this assembly are housed at the State Historical Society of Iowa, Iowa City.

10. George Dillavou, *The Life Cycle of an Adult Education Enterprise: The Swarthmore Chautauqua* (U.S. Department of Health, Education, and Welfare, 1968).

11. Charles Horner, "The Future Chautauqua Program," *Lyceum*, December 1920, p. 11.

12. Atherton, *Main Street on the Middle Border*, 329.

13. Winks, "Recollections of a Dead Art: The Traveling Chautauqua," 41.

14. "Band That Can't Hear Itself Play Here on Monday," *Roanoke World News*, June 30, 1927.

15. Iowa

16. Henry Ford, "Jewish Jazz Becomes Our

National Music," in *The International Jew: The World's Foremost Problem*, vol. 3 (4 vols.) (Dearborn, MI: Dearborn, 1920).

17. Edward A. Berlin, *Ragtime: A Musical and Cultural History* (iUniverse, 2002), 49.

18. Reynold Wik, "The Radio in Rural America During the 1920s," *Agricultural History* 55, no. 4 (October 1981): 348.

19. "Radcliffe's All New Chautauqua Entertainers," Iowa.

20. "Canadian Chautauquas: Brings the World to Your Door," Iowa.

21. "Canadian Chautauquas 1929," Iowa.

22. Russell Johnson, "'Dancing Mothers': The Chautauqua Movement in Twentieth-Century American Popular Culture," *American Studies International* 39 (2001): 60.

23. Charles Horner, "The Future Chautauqua Program," *The Lyceum Magazine*, December 1920, p. 11.

24. Condee, *Coal and Culture: Opera Houses in Appalachia*, 156.

25. Atherton, *Main Street on the Middle Border*, 122.

26. Andrew Rieser, "Canopy of Culture: Chautauqua and the Renegotiation of Middle-Class Authority, 1874–1919" (University of Wisconsin, 1999), 366.

27. Charles Seeger, "Music and Class Structure in the United States," *American Quarterly* 9, no. 3 (Autumn 1957): 286.

28. Harry Harrison to Bohumir Kryl, May 9, 1919.

29. "Drive Over to Big Doings."

30. Vawter, "Mr. Automobile Driver."

31. Winks, "Recollections of a Dead Art: The Traveling Chautauqua," 48.

32. Frederick Crane, "A.F. Thaviu Redux," *Journal of Band Research* 36 (2000): 1–25.

Bibliography

PRIMARY SOURCES

Archives and Manuscript Collections

Charles Horner Papers, Special Collections Department, University of Iowa Libraries, Iowa City.

Chautauqua Collection, State Historical Society of Iowa, Iowa City.

Harrison Thornton Papers, Special Collections Department, University of Iowa Libraries, Iowa City.

Katharine La Sheck Papers, Iowa Women's Archives, University of Iowa, Iowa City.

Keith Vawter Papers, Special Collections Department, University of Iowa Libraries, Iowa City.

Keith/Albee Vaudeville Theater Collection, Special Collections Department, University of Iowa Libraries, Iowa City.

Krantz Family Papers, Special Collections Department, University of Iowa Libraries, Iowa City.

Lincoln Chautauqua Bureau Materials, Special Collections Department, University of Iowa Libraries, Iowa City.

Paul M. Pearson Papers, 1890–1969, Friends Historical Library of Swarthmore College, Swarthmore, Pennsylvania.

Redpath Chautauqua Collection, Special Collections Department, University of Iowa Libraries, Iowa City.

Rosa Kohler/Radcliffe Chautauqua Papers, Special Collections Department, University of Iowa Libraries, Iowa City.

Theatre Museum of Repertoire Americana, Mt. Pleasant, Iowa.

Thurlow Lieurance Papers, Special Collections and University Archives, Wichita State University, Wichita, Kansas.

CORRESPONDENCE

Crotty, L.B. Letter to Thomas Nielsen, 1916.

Harrison, Harry. Letter to A.M. Harris, November 6, 1916.

———. Letter to Fred Wolf, October 7, 1919.

———. Telegram to Ernestine Schumann-Heink, March 15, 1916.

McKenzie, Fayette. Letter to Redpath Lyceum Bureau, December 18, 1916.

Peffer, Crawford. Telegram to Keith Vawter, 1929.

Schumann-Heink, Ernestine. Telegram to Harry Harrison, July 21, 1919.

Vawter, Keith. Letter to Bohumir Kryl, October 2, 1919.

INTERVIEWS

Harper, Clara. 1977. Interview by Fred Crane. April 19. State Historical Society of Iowa, Iowa City.

Kohl, Dorothy. 1976. Interview by Fred Crane. May 21. State Historical Society of Iowa, Iowa City.

Mickle, Harry. 1977. Interview by Beverly Agee. State Historical Society of Iowa, Iowa City.

Plotts, Harold. 1979. Interview by Fred Crane. July 22. State Historical Society of Iowa, Iowa City.

Weatherwax, John. 1977. Interview by Fred Crane. November 25. State Historical Society of Iowa, Iowa City.

Weatherwax, Richard. 1978. Interview by Fred Crane. May 16. State Historical Society of Iowa, Iowa City.

Williams, Esther. 1977. Interview by Beverly Agee. State Historical Society of Iowa, Iowa City.

Secondary Sources

Books

Adorno, Theodor W. *Introduction to the Sociology of Music*. New York: Seabury Press, 1976.

Ahlquist, Karen. *Democracy at the Opera: Music, Theater, and Culture in New York City, 1815–60*. Urbana: University of Illinois Press, 1997.

_____. "Mrs. Potiphar at the Opera: Satire, Idealism, and Cultural Authority in Post-Civil War New York." In *Music and Culture in America, 1861–1918*. New York: Garland, 1998.

Ashby, LeRoy. *With Amusement for All: A History of American Popular Culture Since 1830*. Lexington: University Press of Kentucky, 2006.

Beckerman, Michael. *New Worlds of Dvořák: Searching in America for the Composer's Inner Life*. New York: W.W. Norton, 2003.

Berlin, Edward A. *Ragtime: A Musical and Cultural History*. iUniverse, 2002.

Blackstone, Tsianina Redfeather. *Where Trails Have Led Me*. Santa Fe, NM: Vergara, 1970.

Bledstein, Burton J., and Robert D. Johnston. *The Middling Sorts: Explorations in the History of the American Middle Class*. New York: Routledge, 2001.

Bode, Carl. *The American Lyceum: Town Meeting of the Mind*. New York: Oxford University Press, 1956.

Bordman, Gerald, and Thomas S. Hischak. *The Oxford Companion to American Theatre*. New York: Oxford University Press, 2004.

Briggs, Irene, and Raymond DaBoll. *Recollections of the Lyceum and Chautauqua Circuits*. Freeport, ME: Bond Wheelwright, 1969.

Camp Fire Girls. *The Book of the Camp Fire Girls*. New York: George H. Doran, 1913.

Brown, Richard. *The Strength of a People: The Idea of an Informed Citizenry in America, 1650–1870*. Chapel Hill: University of North Carolina Press, 1996.

Canning, Charlotte. *The Most American Thing in America: Circuit Chautauqua as Performance*. Iowa City: University of Iowa Press, 2005.

Case, Victoria, and Robert Case. *We Called It Culture*. New York: Doubleday, 1948.

Chautauqua Institution. *Chautauqua Hymnal and Liturgy*. New York: Novello, Ewer, 1903.

Condee, William Faricy. *Coal and Culture: Opera Houses in Appalachia*. Athens: Ohio University Press, 2005.

Devitis, Joseph, and John Rich. *The Success Ethic, Education and the American Dream*. Albany: State University of New York Press, 1996.

Ford, Henry. "Jewish Jazz Becomes Our National Music." In *The International Jew: The World's Foremost Problem*. Vol. 3. Dearborn, MI: Dearborn, 1920.

Gentile, John. *Cast of One: One-Person Shows from the Chautauqua Platform to the Broadway Stage*. Urbana: University of Illinois Press, 1989.

Gould, Joseph. *The Chautauqua Movement: An Episode in the Continuing American Revolution*. Albany: State University of New York Press, 1961.

Green, Jeffrey P. *Black Edwardians: Black People in Britain, 1901–1914*. Portland, OR: Frank Cass, 1998.

Harder, Edwin. *The First Clarinet, or Chautauqua Chit-Chat*. Chicago: Mayer & Miller, 1913.

Harrison, Harry. *Culture Under Canvas: The Story of Tent Chautauqua*. New York: Hastings House, 1958.

Higashi, Sumiko. *Cecil B. DeMille and America Culture: The Silent Era*. Berkeley: University of California Press, 1994.

Holbrook, Josiah. *American Lyceum, or Society for the Improvement of Schools and Diffusion of Useful Knowledge*. Boston: Perkins and Marvin, 1829.

Horner, Charles. *Strike the Tents: The Story of Chautauqua*. Philadelphia: Dorrance, 1954.

Hoyt, Harlowe. *Town Hall Tonight*. Englewood Cliffs, NJ: Prentice-Hall, 1955.

Knowles, Malcolm. *The Adult Education Movement in the United States*. New York: Holt, Rinehart and Winston, 1962.

Levine, Lawrence W. *Highbrow/Lowbrow: The Emergence of Cultural Hierarchy in America*. Cambridge, MA.: Harvard University Press, 1988.

Lewis, Sinclair. *Main Street*. New York: Harcourt, Brace, 1920.

Lindfors, Bernth. *Africans on Stage: Studies in Ethnological Show Business*. Bloomington: Indiana University Press, 1999.

Lipman, Samuel. *Arguing for Music, Arguing for Culture*. Boston: D.R. Godine, 1990.

MacLaren, Gay. *Morally We Roll Along.* Boston: Little, Brown, 1938.

McBride, Bunny. "Lucy Nicolar: The Artful Activism of a Penobscot Performer." In *Sifters: Native American Women's Lives.* Oxford: Oxford University Press, 2001.

Noffsinger, John. *Correspondence Schools, Lyceums, Chautauquas.* New York: MacMillan, 1926.

Orchard, Hugh A. *Fifty Years of Chautauqua: Its Beginnings, Its Development, Its Message and Its Life.* Cedar Rapids, IA: Torch, 1923.

Parsons Smith, Catherine. "Inventing Tradition: Symphony and Opera in Progressive-Era Los Angeles." In *Music and Culture in America, 1861–1918.* New York: Garland, 1998.

Preston, Katherine K. *Opera on the Road: Traveling Opera Troupes in the United States, 1825–60.* Urbana: University of Illinois Press, 1993.

Rieser, Andrew. *The Chautauqua Moment: Protestants, Progressives, and the Culture of Modern Liberalism.* New York: Columbia University Press, 2003.

Rubin, Joan. *The Making of Middlebrow Culture.* Chapel Hill: University of North Carolina Press, 1992.

Samuels, Charles, and Louise Samuels. *Once Upon a Stage: The Merry World of Vaudeville.* New York: Dodd, Mead, 1974.

Schultz, James R. *The Romance of Small-Town Chautauquas.* Columbia: University of Missouri Press, 2002.

Schwartz, Howard. *Bands of America.* Garden City, NY: Doubleday, 1957.

Stein, Charles W. *American Vaudeville as Seen by Its Contemporaries.* New York: Knopf, 1984.

Tapia, John E. *Circuit Chautauqua: From Rural Education to Popular Entertainment in Early Twentieth Century America.* Jefferson, NC: McFarland, 1997.

Toll, Robert C. *Blacking Up: The Minstrel Show in Nineteenth Century America.* New York: Oxford University Press, 1974.

_____. *On with the Show! The First Century of Show Business in America.* New York: Oxford University Press, 1976.

Vincent, John. *The Chautauqua Movement.* Boston: Chatauqua Press, 1886.

Wagner, Charles L. *Seeing Stars.* New York: Arno Press, 1977.

Wertheim, Arthur. *Vaudeville Wars.* New York: Palgrave MacMillan, 2006.

DISSERTATIONS AND THESES

Adler, Ayden. "Classical Music for People Who Hate Classical Music: Arthur Fiedler and the Boston Pops, 1930–1950." University of Rochester, 2007.

Berrigan, Donna. "Circuit Chautauqua Theatrical Performers: Eight Interviews." California State University-Northridge, 1981.

Eckman, James. "Regeneration Through Culture: Chautauqua in Nebraska 1882–1925." University of Nebraska, 1989.

Eubank, Marjorie. "The Redpath Lyceum Bureau from 1868–1901." University of Michigan, 1968.

Graham, Donald. "Circuit Chautauqua: A Middle Western Institution." University of Iowa, 1953.

Hedges, Alan. "Actors Under Canvas: A Study of the Theatre of Circuit Chautauqua 1910–1933." Ohio State University, 1976.

Hemingway, Abigail. "Wallace Bruce Amsbary: A Social and Intellectual Case Study of a Chautauqua and Lyceum Circuit Performer from 1886 to 1921." Northern Arizona University, 1989.

Howland, John. "Between the Muses and the Masses: Symphonic Jazz, 'Glorified' Entertainment, and the Rise of the Musical Middlebrow, 1920–1944." Stanford University, 2002.

Manderson, Sandra. "The Redpath Lyceum Bureau, an American Critic: Decision-Making and Programming Methods for Circuit Chautauquas, Circa 1912 to 1930." University of Iowa, 1981.

Mooney, Matthew. "'All Join in the Chorus': Sheet Music, Vaudeville and the Formation of the American Cinema, 1904–1914." University of California-Irvine, 2006.

Moore, Victor Ivan. "The American Circuit Chautauqua: A Social Movement." University of Texas, 1927.

Oberdeck, Kathryn. "Labor's Vicar and the Variety Show: Popular Religion, Popular Theatre, and Class Conflict in Turn-of-the-Century America." Yale University, 1991.

Riechmann, Ferd. "Public or Folk Response to the Circuit Chautauqua." University of Iowa, 1951.

Rieser, Andrew. "Canopy of Culture: Chautauqua and the Renegotiation of Middle-

Class Authority, 1874–1919." University of Wisconsin, 1999.
Tapia, John. "Circuit Chautauqua's Promotional Visions: A Study of Program Brochures, Circa 1904 to 1932." University of Arizona, 1978.
Troth, Willard. "The Teacher Training Program in Music at Chautauqua Institution, 1905–1930." University of Michigan, 1958.
Troutman, John. "'Indian Blues': American Indians and the Politics of Music, 1890–1935." University of Texas, 2004.
Wells, Jeanette. "A History of the Music Festival at Chautauqua Institution from 1874 to 1957." Catholic University of America, 1958.

ARTICLES

Albert, Allen. "The Tents of the Conservative." *Scribner's* 72 (1922): 54–59.
Ames (IA) Tribune. "Chautauqua Era Ends, No Show This Summer." (1927)
Beuick, Marshall D. "The Limited Social Effect of Radio Broadcasting." *The American Journal of Sociology* 32 (1927): 615–622.
Blazek, Ron. "The Library, the Chautauqua, and the Railroads in DeFuniak Springs, Florida." *Journal of Library History* 22 (1986): 377–396.
Boer, B.C. "Keep Unpopular Music Off Popular Programs." *The Lyceum Magazine*, 1914.
Bonin, Jean M. "Music from 'The Splendidest Sight': The American Circus Songster." *Notes* 45 (1989): 699–713.
Bray, Frank. "Social and Ethical Ideas in Summer Assemblies." *The Chautauquan: A Weekly Newsmagazine* 47 (1907): 171–78.
———. "The Educational Value of Chautauquas." *Talent*, 1906.
Bridges, Russell. "The Relation Between Lyceum and Vaudeville." *The Lyceumite and Talent*, 1912.
Brooks, Tim. "'Might Take One Disc of This Trash as a Novelty': Early Recordings by the Fisk Jubilee Singers and the Popularization of 'Negro Folk Music.'" *American Music* 18 (2000): 278–316.
Browner, Tara. "'Breathing the Indian Spirit': Thoughts on Musical Borrowing and the 'Indianist' Movement in American Music." *American Music* 15 (1997): 265–284.

Burdette, Robert. "Worth Trying." *The Lyceumite*, 1903.
Cadman, Charles. "The American Indian's Music Idealized." *Etude* 38 (1920): 659–660.
Canning, Charlotte. "The Platform Versus the Stage: Circuit Chautauqua's Antitheatrical Theatre." *Theatre Journal* 50 (1998): 303–318.
Coursey, O.W. "Chautauqua Vs. Street Carnival." *The Lyceum Magazine*, 1916.
Crane, Frederick. "A.F. Thaviu Redux." *Journal of Band Research* 36 (2000): 1–25.
———. "The Music of Chautauqua and Lyceum." *Black Music Research Journal* 10 (1990): 103–106.
Culbertson, Evelyn. "Arthur Farwell's Early Efforts on Behalf of American Music, 1889–1921." *American Music* 5 (1987): 156–175.
Current Opinion 59 (1915): 1. "Current Tendencies in the Development of the Chautauqua Movement."
Curtis, A.L. "The Fisk Jubilee Singers." *Talent* 16 (1906): 1–4.
Curtis, Anna. "A Quartet with a History." *Talent* (1903.
Dalgety, George S. Northwestern University. "Chautauqua's Contribution to American Life." *Current History, New York* 34 (1931): 39.
Denton (MD) Journal, July 3, 1915. "Chautauqua Movement and Culture."
Des Moines Register and Leader, 1911. "Iowa City Friends of Miss Rachel Lasheck."
Dixon, Charles. "Can Music Win on Its Merit?" *The Lyceumite and Talent*, 1923.
Eaklor, Vicki L. "Roots of an Ambivalent Culture: Music, Education, and Music Education in Antebellum America." *Journal of Research in Music Education* 33 (1985): 87.
Edstrom, David. "Medicine Shows of the '80s." *Reader's Digest*, 1938.
Ehrlich, George. "Chautauqua, 1880–1900: Education in Art History and Appreciation." *Art Bulletin* 38 (1956): 175–184.
Emmettsburg (IA) Palo Alto Reporter, 1919. "The Chautauqua Closes."
Erb, J. Lawrence. "Music in the Education of the Common Man." *Musical Quarterly* 5 (1919): 308–315.
Family Lyceum 1 (1833): 1. "Pleasure Derived from Fine Music."
Farnsworth, Charles H. "Education Through

Music." *Elementary School Teacher* 4 (1904): 623–628.

Farwell, Arthur. "Aspects of Indian Music." *Southern Workman* 31 (1902): 211–217.

———. Introduction. *Wa Wan Press* 2 (1903): 64.

Fletcher, Brooks. "Bury Your Hammer and Buy a Horn." *The Lyceum Magazine*, 1916.

Freeman, Frank N. "Requirements of Education with Reference to Motion Pictures." *School Review* 31 (1923): 340–350.

Garrett, Charles Hiroshi. "Chinatown: Whose Chinatown? Defining America's Borders with Musical Orientalism." *Journal of the American Musicological Society* 57 (2004): 119–173.

Gatewood, Esther L. "The Business of Teaching Music." *Music Supervisors' Journal* 11 (1925): 46–48.

Gibbs, Philip. "The Adventures of a Lecture Tour." *Harper's* 145 (1922): 724.

Glenn, Mabelle. "Our Children's Concert Activities." *Music Supervisors' Journal* 16 (1929): 39–43.

Green, Rayna. "The Tribe Called Wannabee: Playing Indian in America and Europe." *Folklore* 99 (1988): 30–55.

Haskin, Frederic. "Our Intellectual Circus." *Portsmouth (OH) Daily Times*, 1921.

———. "The Chautauqua Movement." *Salt Lake City (UT) Salt Lake Tribune*, July 17, 1907, 8.

Hibschman, Harry. "Chautauqua Pro and Contra." *North American Review* (1928): 597–605.

Horowitz, Joseph. "'Sermons in Tones': Sacralization as a Theme in American Classical Music." *American Music* 16 (1998): 311–340.

Howe, Sondra Wieland. "The NBC Music Appreciation Hour: Radio Broadcasts of Walter Damrosch, 1928–1942." *Journal of Research in Music Education* 51 (2003): 64–77.

Howell, Daniel. "Assembly Ideals and Practice." *Chautauquan*, 1908.

Johnson, Russell. "'Dancing Mothers': The Chautauqua Movement in Twentieth-Century American Popular Culture." *American Studies International* 39 (2001): 53–70.

Judd, Charles H. "Education and the Movies." *School Review* 31 (1923): 173–178.

Kaplan, Max. "Music and Mass Culture." *Music Journal* 18 (1960): 20.

Keller, Luella. "Good Music Winning the Masses." *The Lyceum Magazine*, 1914.

Koon, John. "Indian Musicians in the Modern World." *Etude* 38 (1920): 665–666.

Libraries and Culture 41 (2006): 169–188. "'One Cathedral More' or 'Mere Lounging Places for Bummers'? The Cultural Politics of Leisure and the Public Library in Gilded Age America."

Lindeman, Eduard. "After Lyceums and Chautauquas, What?" *Bookman: A Review of Books and Life* 65 (1927): 246–250.

Locke, Ralph P. "Music Lovers, Patrons, and the 'Sacralization' of Culture in America." *19th-Century Music* 17 (1993): 149–173.

The Lyceum Magazine, February 1917. "The Plymouth Singing Party."

The Lyceum Magazine, June 1919. "Magic Educational."

The Lyceum Magazine, June 1921. "Stick to English Language and American Compositions."

The Lyceum Magazine, 1915. "The Lyceum Arts Conservatory."

The Lyceum Magazine, 1914. "The Lyceum 'Purpose Companies.'"

The Lyceum Magazine, 1916. "Boston Lyceum School."

The Lyceum Magazine, 1913. "From Our Viewpoint."

The Lyceum Magazine 26 (1916): 1. "A Lyceum and Chautauqua Platform."

The Lyceumite 4 (1906): 274–275. "The Lyceumiteman Talks."

The Lyceumite and Talent, 1916. "Art and the Musician."

Mansfield (OH) News, 1915, 5. "Community Improves as People Improve."

Mazzola, Sandy R. "Bands and Orchestras at the World's Columbian Exposition." *American Music* 4 (1986): 407–424.

McClure, W. Frank. "Circuit or System Chautauquas." *Chautauquan* 72 (1914): 2.

McLeansboro (IL) Times, 1924. "Klantauqua Goes Over Despite Bad Weather."

McNamara, Brooks. "The Indian Medicine Show." *Educational Theatre Journal* 23 (1971): 431–445.

———. "The Medicine Show Log: Reconstructing a Traditional American Entertainment." *Drama Review (TDR)* 28 (1984): 74–97.

McNutt, James. "John Comfort Fillmore: A Student of Indian Music Reconsidered." *American Music* 2 (1984): 61–70.

Mead, David. "1914: The Chautauqua and

American Innocence." *Journal of Popular Culture* 1 (1968): 339–56.
Merriam, Alan P. "Music in American Culture." *American Anthropologist* 57 (1955): 1173.
Mintz, Lawrence. "Humor and Ethnic Stereotypes in Vaudeville and Burlesque." *Melus* 21 (1996): 19–28.
Mooney, Matthew. "An 'Invasion of Vulgarity': American Popular Music and Modernity in Print Media Discourse, 1900–1925." *Americana: Journal of American Popular Culture* 3, 2004): 1–19.
Morgan, Frank. "An Explanation." *The Lyceumite*, 1905.
Musical Courier, 1913. "Alice Nielsen, Prima Donna Soprano."
Nashua (NH) Telegraph, December 9, 1904, evening edition. "Star Course."
New York Herald, 1893. "Real Value of Negro Melodies."
Nidiffer, Jana. "Poor Historiography: The 'Poorest' in American Higher Education." *History of Education Quarterly* 39 (1999): 321–336.
North American Review 199 (1914): 321. "Mr. Bryan Rides Behind."
Orchard, Hugh A. "The Lyceum Course Versus the Cheap Show." *The Lyceumite and Talent*, 1912.
Ott, Edward. "Some Practical Needs of the Lyceum." *The Lyceumite*, 1906.
Otto, John S., and Augustus M. Burns. "Black and White Cultural Interaction in the Early Twentieth Century South: Race and Hillbilly Music." *Phylon* 35 (1974): 407–417.
Parlette, Ralph Albert. "Musical Program Patriotism." *The Lyceum Magazine*, April 1917.
Pearson, Paul M. "The Chautauqua Movement." *Annals of the American Academy of Political and Social Science* 40 (1912): 211–216.
Petteys, Leslie. "Theodore Thomas's 'March to the Sea.'" *American Music* 10 (1992): 170–182.
Pisani, Michael. "From Hiawatha to Wa-Wan: Musical Boston and the Uses of Native American Lore." *American Music* 19 (2001): 39–50.
Pringle, Henry. "Chautauqua in the Jazz Age." *American Mercury* 16 (1929): 85–93.
Quayle, Nolbert. "The Cornet's Sole Survivor." *Music Journal* 19 (1961): 44, 97.
Rao, Nancy Yunhwa. "Songs of the Exclusion Era: New York Chinatown's Opera Theaters in the 1920s." *American Music* 20 (2002): 399–444.
Roanoke World News, June 30, 1927. "Band That Can't Hear Itself Play Here on Monday."
Rosenberg, Neil. "An Icy Mountain Brook': Revival, Aesthetics, and the 'Coal Creek March.'" *Journal of Folklore Research* 28 (1991): 23.
Schafer, William, and Johannes Riedel. "Indian Intermezzi: 'Play It One More Time, Chief!'" *Journal of American Folklore* 86 (1973): 382–387.
Schultz, John Richie. "Chautauqua Talk." *American Speech* 7 (1932): 405–411.
Scott, Donald. "The Popular Lecture and the Creation of a Public in Mid-Nineteenth-Century America." *Journal of American History* 66 (1980): 791–809.
Scott, John. "The Chautauqua Movement: Revolution in Popular Higher Education." *Journal of Higher Education* 70 (1999): 389–412.
Seeger, Charles. "Music and Class Structure in the United States." *American Quarterly* 9, no. 3 (Autumn 1957): 281–294.
Sibley, S.W. "Makes Critical Estimate of the Wesleyan Singers." *Coshocton (OH) Weekly Times*, 1906.
Singer, Stan. "Vaudeville in Los Angeles, 1910–1926: Theaters, Management and the Orpheum." *Pacific Historical Review* 61 (1992): 103–113.
Spalding, Walter. "The War in Its Relation to American Music." *Musical Quarterly* 4 (1918): 1–11.
Squire, Belle. "The Unpopularity of a Popular Instrument." *The Lyceumite*, 1904.
Tapia, John. "Circuit Chautauqua Program Brochures: A Study in Social and Intellectual History." *Quarterly Journal of Speech* 67 (1981): 167–77.
Terril (IA) Record, 1930. "More Lowdown on Chautauqua."
Thomson (IL) Review, 1925. "Why Boston Signs a Guarantee."
Thomson (IL) Review, 1926. "Chautauqua Revue Easy to Listen To."
Thornburg, A.A. "What the Lyceum May Learn from Vaudeville." *The Lyceumite and Talent*, 1912.
Thornton, Harrison. "The Roosevelts at Chautauqua." *New York History* 28 (1947): 33.
Tigert, J.J. "Radio in the American School

System." *Annals of the American Academy of Political and Social Science* 142 (1929): 71–77.

Tischler, Barbara. "One Hundred Percent Americanism and Music in Boston During World War I." *American Music* 4 (1986): 164–176.

Tozier, R.B. "A Short Life-History of the Chautauqua." *American Journal of Sociology* 40 (1934): 69–73.

Trennert, Robert. "Selling Indian Education at World's Fairs and Expositions, 1893–1904." *American Indian Quarterly* 11 (1987): 203–220.

Tsou, Judy. "Gendering Race: Stereotypes of Chinese Americans in Popular Sheet Music." *Repercussions* 6 (1997): 25–62.

Vincent, George. "How to Make an Assembly Truly Educational." *The Lyceumite and Talent*, 1908.

Wagner, Vern. "The Lecture Lyceum and the Problem of Controversy." *Journal of the History of Ideas* 15, no. 1 (January 1, 1954): 119–135.

Waterloo (IA) Daily Times Tribune, 1906, 5. "Opened with Large Crowd."

Whitesitt, Linda. "The Role of Women Impresarios in American Concert Life, 1871–1933." *American Music* 7 (1989): 159–180.

Woodman, Ned. "The Home Town Spirit." *The Lyceum Magazine*, August 1918.

Index

ability of musicians 177, 183
Acme Chautauquas 110
"Acres of Diamonds" 144
Adriatic Tamburica Orchestra 34
advertising 14, 30, 67, 82, 88, 96, 124–125, 181, 189–190
African American music 148–155
Alden, Iowa 62
All College Glee Club 151
"America" 145–146
American Federation of Musicians 160
American Girls 143
Ames, Iowa 16
Ames Band 16
Associated Chautauqua 24
Ata, Te 161, 168
Auburns 20
Austin, Marguerite 184
Automobile 180, 182, 189–191, 193

Balmer, Jason (John) 132
Balmer's Kaffir Boy Choir of Africa 132
barn dances 185
Barnhart, Harry 136
Black-Face Minstrels 151–152
blackface minstrelsy 150–154, 184, 188–189
Blackstone, Tsianina Redfeather 159, 162–164, 170
Bland, Harry 44–45, 89
Bland's Wesleyan Quartet 45
Blue Danube Light Opera Company 103–104
Boer, B.C. 85
Boston Lyceum Bureau 12
Boston Lyceum School 27–28
Boston Lyrics 180
The Brightville Indoor Chautauqua 187–189
Brockway, Howard 129
Browne, Van 110–111

Brown's Jubilee Singers 23
Buck, Dudley 43, 78
"By the Waters of Minnetonka" 167–168

Cadman, Charles 156, 161, 163–166, 170
Cadmean bureau 139
The Captain of Plymouth 114
Cardin, Fred 160–161, 165, 168
Cardin, Wanita 161, 168
Carey, Sansa 161
Carlisle Indian Band 159–160
Carmen 28, 103, 186
Castle Square Entertainers 86
Cathedral Choir 119, 121
Central Iowa Chautauqua 176–177
Century Opera Company of New York 85
Channing, William Ellory 135–136
Charles City, Iowa 192
Chautauqua Assembly 13, 60–61
Chautauqua Hymnal and Liturgy 72
"Chautauqua Lake Waltz" 77
Chautauqua Literary and Scientific Circle 69–70, 95, 193
Chautauqua Opera 62, 193
Chautauqua Symphony Orchestra 62, 193
The Chautauquan 69–70
Chicago Bureau Agency of Music 28
Chicago Symphonic Orchestra 134
Chicago Symphony Orchestra 41–42
Chimes of Normandy Company 32
The Chocolate Soldier 28
Choral Union of One Hundred Voices 15
Cimera, Jaroslav 37, 54–55
Clark, Elsie 132
Claussen, Julia 33, 56–58
Cleveland Ladies Orchestra 15
Coit-Alber Chautauqua Bureau 29, 37, 40, 77, 147
"The Coit-Alber Chautauqua March Two-Step" 77

Index

college 107, 112, 126
College Girls 31, 46, 48–49, 74, 112, 129–130
College Singing Girls 31
comic opera 29, 103
Community Chautauquas 142
community support 5, 7, 38, 59, 67, 90, 123–125, 138–140, 175, 178
Concert Spirituel 117
conservatism 143, 174–175
contracts 31, 33, 37–39, 56
Conwell, Russell 144
Coonville Jubilee Singers 187–189
Cord-Rummell Recital Company 32
Cossack Chorus 99, 106
critical response to chautauqua music 87–91
Crotty, L.B. 54

Dancing Mothers 23
Day, Elias 27, 109
Dearborn Concert Party 109
Decatur, Illinois 64
Deep River Plantation Singers 184
Denton Grand Opera Company 103
"Dixie" 128, 153
Dixie Broadcasters 184
Dixie Chorus 31, 37, 149–151
Dixon, Charles 136
drama 11, 24, 27, 99, 102
dress code 34–35
Dunbar, Harry 28
Dunbar, Ralph 84, 104, 137, 150, 182
Dunbar American School of Opera 29
Dunbar Chautauqua Bureau 28
The Dunbars 15
Dunbar's Black Hussars 30
Dunbar's Tennessee Ten 31
Dunbar's White Hussars 30, 182
Dvořák, Antonín 107, 148

Eau Claire, Wisconsin 67
Eccles, Walter 49, 112
1812 Overture 117
El Dorado Grand Opera 116
Eldridge Entertainment House 187–188
Elliott, Alonzo 142
Ellison, Roy 19
Ellison-White Chautauquas 28, 55, 72–74, 94, 97, 132, 183, 190
Ellison-White Community Song Sheet 73
Elman, Misha 76
Elson, Louis 63
Epic of the Negro 150
Ernest Gamble Concert Party 15
escapism 130, 132–133

Ethiopian Serenaders 152
Eureka Jubilee Singers 27, 177
exoticism 6, 99, 106–107, 129–131, 133, 140; in popular music 79; presentation of Native Americans 155, 159, 167; versus isolationism 170–171
expansion 177–178, 185

Farwell, Arthur 156, 166, 169, 172
Fighting Yanks Quartet 147–148
Filipino Collegians 118–119
Fisk Jubilee Singers 66, 149–151
Fisk Quartet 149–150
Florentine Musicians 37, 71
Flotow, Friedrich 67, 68, 103, 117
Franklin, C. Benjamin 24, 139

Gale, Albert 128, 169
Gale, Martha 128, 169
Garretson, George 20
German language 148
German music 145, 148, 155–156, 161, 169–172
Gershwin, George 62, 194
Goforth, George 16
Going Up 104
The Gondoliers 108
"Goodbye Shanghai" 79–81
Government Official World's Fair Indian Band 158–160
Grand Ole Opry 185
Great Depression 22
Grilley, Charles 133
guarantee 21, 88, 102, 123–124, 139, 178, 180

Hanson, Howard 42, 74
Harder, Edwin 35–37, 44
Harrison, Harry 21, 23–24, 33–34, 38–42, 54–57, 97, 102, 106, 114, 144, 149, 189
Hathaway, George 12
Heink, Felix 127
Hensel & Jones Agency 39–40
Herbert, Victor 30, 56, 62, 104
Hiawatha 156–157
Hibschman, Harry 136
high culture 66, 127, 133, 135, 140, 174–175
Hill, David 157
Hoffman, Katherine 114
Holbrook, Josiah 9–11
L'Hombre 67
Horner, Charles 24, 26–28, 41–42, 75, 107, 135, 143–144, 178, 185
Horner Institute Conservatory of Music 27, 66
Horner Institute of Fine Arts 26–28

hymns 1, 13, 20, 60–61, 72–73, 78, 101, 116–117, 184

Ideal Quartet 45–46
In Romany 104
Independence, Kansas 117
Independence Concert Band 117
Indian Art and Musical Company 161–162, 165
Indian Rhapsody 161
International Lyceum Association 126

Jackson Concert Artists 119
Jacksonville Boys Brass Band 180
Japan 81, 128
jazz 130, 143, 174–175, 181–183
Jess Pugh Concert Company 184
jubilee acts 23, 27, 29, 31, 61, 107, 149–152
junior chautauqua 96, 128, 143
junior girl 96

Keith Vaudeville Circuit 164
Kellog-Haines Singing Party 137
Kellor, Luella 85
Kickapoo Medicine Show 166
Kimball, Nebraska 141
Krantz Family Concert Company 119
Kryl, Bohumir 35–37, 50–57, 103, 117, 181, 189, 191
Kryl, Frank 37
Kryl's Saxophone Sextette 54
Kryl's Spanish Orchestra 53
Ku Klux Klan 16

La Sheck, Katharine 31, 45–49, 73
lecture-recitals 64, 120, 127–129, 150, 157, 169, 182
Leftwich, D.L. 153
Lewis, Sinclair 174, 186, 187
Liefeld, Alfred 145–146
Lieurance, Thurlow 143, 144, 156, 161, 164–165, 167–169
Lincoln Chautauqua System 70
Loar, James 177
lodging 33, 36, 37, 149
Lonesome Tunes: Kentucky Mountain Balladry 129
Lucia di Lammermoor 28, 50, 87, 101
Lucille Elmore Revue 104
Lyceum Arts Conservatory 27–28
Lyceum Grand Concert Company 65
Lyndon-Gordon Company 32

MacCorry, Fr. P.J. 64
MacLaren, Gay 30, 103, 105
Madden, George 74

Main Street 174, 186, 187
Manhattan Opera Company 134
Mankato, Minnesota 54
Manning Glee Club 153–154
Marigolds 47–49, 74
Marshalltown, Iowa 40, 176
Martha 103, 117
Maupin's Band 183
McGuffey Readers 134
Mediapolis, Iowa 24, 177
medicine shows 67, 102, 123, 166–167, 169
Melodivov, Alex 160
Metropolitan Opera 32, 38, 66, 150, 163
Meyer, Joseph 80
Midland Chautauquas 14, 94, 116–117, 142–143
The Mikado 28, 100, 103, 109, 186
Military Girls 143
Miller, Lewis 13
"Minstrel Reminiscences" 153
minstrelsy *see* blackface minstrelsy
Mormon Tabernacle Choir 184
motion pictures 157, 175, 177, 180, 185–186
Mozart, Wolfgang Amadeus 66, 69, 134–135
Mozart Symphony Club of New York 66
Music and the Spoken Word 184
Music Box Girls 89
The Music Shop 104
musical comedy 103–104
Musical Maids 165

National American Lyceum 9
National Barn Dance 185
Nelson, N.S. 158
New Haven scholars 136
New Piasa Chautauqua 70
New York City Marine Band 97
newspaper coverage 38, 66–67, 88, 90–91
Nicolar, Lucy *see* Watahwaso, Princess
Nielsen, Alice 32, 55–58
Nielsen, Thomas 56–57
A Night in Arabia 104
North English, Iowa 94, 116
Norwegian Choral Union of Story County 15
novelty 6, 20, 45, 52, 59, 65, 106, 107, 109, 110, 130–132; embrace of 180–181; instruments 180; in Native American music 165

Old Home Singers 107, 143–144
"On Old Chautauqua Lake" 75–76
"On the Chautauqua Lake" 77
Onondaga Indian Concert Band 156–158
opera 102–104

Index

Palin, William 160
Parnell, Emory 16
Patriotic Songs of America and the Allies 73
patriotism 73, 90, 141–148, 171–172, 184
Patterson, Idelle 32
Pearsall, Clarence 74
Pearson, Paul 149, 176, 178
Peffer, Crawford 24, 53–54, 94, 102
Philippine Bolero Overture 119
Phillips Sisters Orchestra 44–45
phonograph 175, 186
Pittsburgh Ladies Orchestra 145–146
platform superintendent 34–35, 38, 83, 85
Plotts, Harold 44, 89
Pond, J.B. 12
Ponselle, Rosa 32
Poolaw, Bruce 164
popular music 20, 49, 58–66, 77, 79, 81, 84–89, 91, 98, 107–112, 122, 126, 130–131, 140, 143, 186, 193
Powers-Thomas, Caroline 32
prelude 97, 102, 105, 108
purpose groups 143

The Quaker Girl 144
quartets 42–49
Quintano's Italian Band 136

racism 149–150, 152
Radanovitz, Sandor 103
Radcliffe Chautauquas 94–95, 101–102, 180, 184
radio 5, 6, 16, 23, 58, 83, 175, 177, 183–185, 187
ragtime 144, 166, 183
Rahm Family Concert Orchestra 119
Raweis 99–101
Read, Opie 42
Reddie, William 160–161, 168
Redpath, James 12, 67
Redpath-Chicago 21, 23, 35, 36, 56
Redpath-Columbus 21
Redpath-Horner 21, 22, 26, 107, 144, 178
Redpath Lyceum Bureau 12, 17, 19, 21, 24, 46, 105, 110, 112, 183
Redpath–New York–New England 17, 21, 24, 53, 94
Redpath-Vawter 21, 38, 73–74, 103, 116, 126, 151, 189–190
Robin Hood 28, 154
Rocky Mountain Warblers 23
Roney, Henry 84–85
Roney's Boys 85
Rosenberg, Earl 26
Royal Gypsy Orchestra 32
Royal Handbell Ringers and Glee Men 61

Royal Hungarian Orchestra 15
Russian Balalaika Orchestra 111

St. Cecilia Society 85
Schildkretz Orchestra 137
Schoenberg, Arnold 62
Schubert, Franz 66, 134
Schubert Quartette 61
Schumann-Heink, Ernestine 2, 38–41, 56, 58, 66, 114–115
Schumann Quintet 112
Seeger, Charles 187
Shanewis 163
Shannon Quartet 183
Shumate Brothers 182
"Silver Threads Among The Gold" 62, 87
Smith, Clay 38, 61–62, 76, 87
Snyder, Ted 79
Sousa, John Philip 41–42, 50, 183
spirituals 61, 148–149, 166, 184
Stabat Mater (Rossini) 117
Standard Chautauqua Bureau of Chicago 19
star course 12–13, 18
"The Star Spangled Banner" 99, 145, 153, 158
Steckel, Edward 127–128
"The Story Beautiful" 64
Sunday, Billy 183
Sunday programming 49, 72–73, 96, 103, 115–118
The Sunny South 153
Suttel, Sara 114
Swarthmore Chautauquas 21, 149, 176–180, 184
Sweethearts 30, 104

technology 15, 171, 173, 183, 186, 189
Temple Male Quartette 20
Thaviu, A.F. 33–34, 50–52, 103, 191
Thaviu's Oriental Band 50, 52
"There's a Long, Long Trail" 82, 142
Tooley Comic Opera Quintette 103
travel 36–37
Turney, Ruthyn 160–161
Tuskegee Singers 149
Two Rivers, Wisconsin 68
Tyler, Moses Coit 11

Uncle Eli and His Down Home Entertainers 84
union affiliation 31–34
United States Marine Band 145
university *see* college
urban culture 131, 134–135, 186

Index

vaudeville 5, 7, 29–31, 54, 56, 65, 67, 123, 135–137, 174, 182, 184, 186
vespers 72–74, 116
Victor Herbert Orchestra 62
Vierra, Albert 30
Vierra, George 30
Vincent, George 126
Vincent, Harry 63
Vincent, John Heyl 13–14, 69, 126

Watahwaso, Princess 163–164, 167
Waterloo, IA 14
Weatherwax Brothers 43–44, 192
Weber, Henriette 128
Wesleyan Singers 89
West Virginia Institute Program and Song Book 73
Wheelock, J. Riley 159, 165
White, Edna 108, 119, 120
White, J. Shannon 128
White and Myers Chautauquas 128, 135
Wild West shows 166, 169
Williams, Esther 27
Wilson, Edna 135
Wilson, Woodrow 141, 171
Witmark and Sons 82, 142
Woodman, Ned 125
Wooley, Edna (Nah Mee) 167–168
World War I 40, 43, 52, 106, 141–142, 145, 147–148, 156, 163, 169–172
Wyman, Lorraine 129

"Yankee Doodle" 128
"You Gave Me Your Heart" 79
Young, Eliza 12

www.ingramcontent.com/pod-product-compliance
Lightning Source LLC
Chambersburg PA
CBHW032049300426
44116CB00007B/666